The Jokowi-Prabowo Elections 2.0

The ISEAS – Yusof Ishak Institute (formerly Institute of Southeast Asian Studies) is an autonomous organization established in 1968. It is a regional centre dedicated to the study of socio-political, security, and economic trends and developments in Southeast Asia and its wider geostrategic and economic environment. The Institute's research programmes are grouped under Regional Economic Studies (RES), Regional Strategic and Political Studies (RSPS), and Regional Social and Cultural Studies (RSCS). The Institute is also home to the ASEAN Studies Centre (ASC), the Singapore APEC Study Centre, and the Temasek History Research Centre (THRC).

ISEAS Publishing, an established academic press, has issued more than 2,000 books and journals. It is the largest scholarly publisher of research about Southeast Asia from within the region. ISEAS Publishing works with many other academic and trade publishers and distributors to disseminate important research and analyses from and about Southeast Asia to the rest of the world.

The Jokowi-Prabowo Elections 2.0

Presidential and Parliamentary Elections in Indonesia in 2019

EDITED BY

MADE SUPRIATMA

HUI YEW-FOONG

First published in Singapore in 2022 by
ISEAS Publishing
30 Heng Mui Keng Terrace
Singapore 119614

E-mail: publish@iseas.edu.sg
Website: <http://bookshop.iseas.edu.sg>

All rights reserved. No part of this publication may be reproduced, stored in a retrieval system, or transmitted in any form or by any means, electronic, mechanical, photocopying, recording or otherwise, without the prior permission of the ISEAS – Yusof Ishak Institute.

© 2022 ISEAS – Yusof Ishak Institute, Singapore

The responsibility for facts and opinions in this publication rests exclusively with the authors and their interpretations do not necessarily reflect the views or the policy of the publisher or its supporters.

This publication is made possible with the support of Konrad-Adenauer-Stiftung.

ISEAS Library Cataloguing-in-Publication Data

Name(s): Supriatma, A. Made Tony, 1966-, editor. | Hui, Yew-Foong, editor.
Title: The Jokowi-Prabowo Elections 2.0: Presidential and Parliamentary Elections in Indonesia in 2019 / edited by Made Supriatma and Hui Yew-Foong.
Description: Singapore : ISEAS-Yusof Ishak Institute, 2022. | Includes index.
Identifiers: ISBN 978-981-5011-36-4 (soft cover) | ISBN 978-981-5011-37-1 (pdf)
Subjects: LCSH: Elections—Indonesia. | Indonesia—Politics and government.
Classification: LCC JQ778 J742

Cover illustration by Agus Goh
Cover design by Lee Meng Hui
Index compiled by DiacriTech Technologies Pte Ltd
Typesetting by International Typesetters Pte Ltd
Printed in Singapore by Mainland Press Pte Ltd

CONTENTS

Acknowledgements		*vii*
2019 Indonesian Elections Timeline		*viii*
About the Contributors		*xiv*
1.	The 2019 Indonesian Elections: A Political Déjà vu? *Made Supriatma and Hui Yew-Foong*	1

PART I: DEMOCRACY, CYBER-POLITICS AND DISINFORMATION

2.	The 2019 Election as a Reflection of the Stagnation of Indonesian Democracy? *Firman Noor*	21
3.	Understanding Indonesia's Democracy: Class, Cliques and Politics After the 2019 Elections *Max Lane*	46
4.	Politics of New Tools in Post-truth Indonesia: Big Data, AI and Micro-targeting *Okamoto Masaaki and Kameda Akihiro*	67
5.	Disinformation, Post-election Violence and the Evolution of Anti-Chinese Sentiment *Quinton Temby*	90

PART II: CONSTITUENCIES

6. The Political Economy of Polarization: Militias, Street Authority and the 2019 Elections
   Ian Wilson — 109

7. Unions and Elections: The Case of the Metal Workers Union in Elections in Bekasi, West Java
   Amalinda Savirani — 127

8. The Power of *Emak-Emak*: Women and the Political Agenda of Islamic Conservatives in Indonesia's 2019 Election
   Dyah Ayu Kartika — 145

9. Chinese Political Participation Since Independence: Between National Identity and Ethnic Identity
   Leo Suryadinata — 165

PART III: REGIONAL DYNAMICS

10. "Awakening the Sleeping Bull": Central Java in the 2019 Indonesian Elections
    Budi Irawanto — 199

11. Lessons from Madura: Nahdlatul Ulama, Conservatism and the Presidential Election
    Ahmad Najib Burhani — 220

12. Religious Binarism and "Geopolitical" Cleavage: North Sumatra in the 2019 Presidential Election
    Deasy Simandjuntak — 238

13. Money or Identity? Election Insights from South Sumatra and Lampung Provinces
    Made Supriatma — 266

Index — 283

ACKNOWLEDGEMENTS

This book evolved out of a symposium held in the aftermath of the 2019 Indonesian elections. The Symposium on "The Future of Indonesian Politics: Analyzing the Outcomes and Implications of the 2019 Elections" was held on 11–12 July 2019 at the ISEAS – Yusof Ishak Institute (ISEAS) in Singapore. It was a collaboration between the Indonesia Studies Programme, ISEAS and the Centre for Strategic and International Studies (Indonesia). Both the symposium and this volume are co-funded by the Konrad-Adenauer-Stiftung.

The cover illustration is done by Agus Goh, who has generously shared his artwork with us.

2019 INDONESIAN ELECTIONS TIMELINE

(prepared by Aninda Dewayanti)

11 October 2017
The Indonesian Democratic Party of Struggle (PDI-P) registers its candidacy to run for the 2019 Elections at the General Elections Commission (KPU), Jakarta. 11 October is claimed to be a good day in Javanese horoscope.

13 October 2017
Different from other parties who came to KPU with rallies, Gerindra politicians visit KPU to give the necessary documents needed for the 2019 elections registration.

16 October 2017
The National Awakening Party (PKB) is the last party to register its participation in the elections at KPU. The members are bringing Garuda pledge as a symbol of promoting democracy and people's sovereignty.

17 February 2018
KPU announces 16 national parties to run in the 2019 General Elections:
1. National Awakening Party (PKB)
2. Great Indonesia Movement Party (Gerindra)
3. Indonesian Democratic Party of Struggle (PDI-P)
4. Golkar Party
5. National Democratic Party (Nasdem)
6. Indonesian Transformation Movement Party (Partai Garuda)
7. Berkarya Party

8. Prosperous Justice Party (PKS)
9. Indonesian Unity Party (Perindo)
10. United Development Party (PPP)
11. Indonesian Solidarity Party (PSI)
12. National Mandate Party (PAN)
13. People's Conscience Party (Hanura)
14. Democratic Party (Partai Demokrat)
15. Crescent Star Party (PBB)
16. Indonesian Justice and Unity Party (PKPI)

27 June 2018
Simultaneous local elections (*Pilkada Serentak*) are held in 171 regions in Indonesia, including in 17 provinces, 39 cities, and 115 regencies.

9 August 2018
The incumbent President Joko Widodo (Jokowi) announces that he has chosen Ma'ruf Amin, chairman of the Indonesian Council of Ulama (MUI), as his running mate for the 2019 Presidential Election.

10 August 2018
In the morning, Jokowi officially registers himself and Ma'ruf Amin to KPU as the President and Vice-presidential candidate for the 2019 presidential election. Starting the rally from Gedoeng Joeang '45, both candidates are accompanied by the leaders from the party coalition, including PDI-P chairwoman Megawati Sukarnoputri and PKB chairman Muhaimin Iskandar.

Later in the afternoon, Prabowo and Sandiaga also publicly register themselves to run against Jokowi-Ma'ruf. Together with the candidates, also in attendance were the Jakarta Governor Anies Baswedan, Chairman of PAN Zulkifli Hasan, and some leaders of PKS. Additionally, Berkarya politician Titik Soeharto, and both of Yudhoyono's sons from the Democrat Party, Agus Harimurti and Edhie Baskoro are attending this monumental event.

20 September 2018
KPU announces that both registered candidates, Jokowi–Ma'ruf and Prabowo–Sandi, are to officially run for the presidential election.

23 September 2018
The campaign period is officially started.

19 October 2018
Prabowo meets a community of young mothers in West Java called *"Barisan Emak-Emak Milenial"* (United Millennial Moms).

23 October 2018
Prabowo invites young bloggers, vloggers or YouTubers and media influencers to his house in Jakarta. As the mainstream media tends to favour the incumbent, this meeting is important for Prabowo as a member of the opposition to capitalize on social media as a new platform.

7 December 2018
A group of Chinese businessmen invites Prabowo to give a talk as the Guest of Honour at a gala dinner in Sun City Jakarta. The group is soliciting donations for Prabowo's presidential campaign fund.

2 January 2019
Fake news has been circulated in social media about the arrival of seven containers of pre-marked ballots imported from China in Tanjung Priok Port, Jakarta.

17 January 2019
First presidential election TV debate on law, human rights, corruption, and terrorism.

17 February 2019
Second presidential election TV debate on energy and food, natural resources and the environment, and infrastructure.

17 March 2019
Third presidential election TV debate on education, healthcare, employment, social and cultural development.

30 March 2019
Fourth presidential election TV debate on ideology, governance, defence and security, and international relation.

7 April 2019
Prabowo–Sandi's final election campaign in Gelora Bung Karno, Jakarta.

13 April 2019
During the day, Jokowi–Ma'ruf hosts their final election campaign, "Putih Bersatu", at Gelora Bung Karno, Jakarta.

Later in the evening, they are on TV for the final presidential election debate on economy and social welfare, finance and investment, and trade industry.

14–16 April 2019
Quiet period. No campaigning allowed.

17 April 2019
National election day. 192 million eligible voters in 800,000 polling stations to vote for their president and vice president, members of national parliament, and local representatives in their respective regencies/cities and province.

18 April–22 May 2019
Vote counting period by KPU.

18 April 2019
Prabowo declares his 62 per cent lead over Jokowi based on their campaign team's internal quick count.

19 April 2019
Prabowo declares his victory and begins a prostration of gratitude (*sujud syukur*) with 212 Movement Alumni Association.

14 May 2019
Health Minister Nina F. Moeloek delivers a press conference on the death of 485 elections staff following the country's 17 April vote. 51 per cent of them died due to cardiovascular problems, including heart failure. Meanwhile, around 10,997 people have fallen sick.

21 May 2019
KPU officially announces Jokowi–Ma'ruf as the elected Indonesian president and vice-president. Jokowi–Ma'ruf won in 21 provinces, while Prabowo–Sandiaga emerged victorious in 13 provinces. KPU also announces the nine parties to be seated in the parliament: PDIP, Gerindra, Golkar, PKB, Nasdem, PKS, Demokrat, PAN, PPP.

21–22 May 2019
In Jakarta, people are protesting to demand the result of the election across the city. Nine people (who are suspected as *"perusuh"* by the police) died during the riot. Retired General Kivlan Zen was suspected to be the architect of this riot, as he was sued of illegally owning 4 guns and 117 bullets.

24 May 2019
Prabowo–Sandi team, represented by Bambang Widjajanto, presents "51 evidences" to the Indonesian Constitutional Court. The team claims that they have gathered evidence to prove that Jokowi–Ma'ruf had structurally, systematically, and massively been cheating the people during the presidential election.

27 June 2019
The Constitutional Court rejects the entire petition of Prabowo–Sandi campaign team due to groundless reasons according to law.

13 July 2019
Jokowi meets Prabowo for the first time since presidential election at the newly-launched Jakarta MRT station.

31 August 2019
KPU announces the nine political parties to officially hold seats in the national parliament, including PKB, Gerindra, PDIP, Golkar, Nasdem, PKS, PPP, PAN and Demokrat. The other four parties are not eligible due to the inability to achieve 4 per cent of minimum votes: Garuda Party, Berkarya Party, Perindo, PSI, PBB, Hanura and PKPI.

17 September 2019
The DPR passed the KPK Bill into national law.

24–30 September 2019
Simultaneous mass protests in many urban areas in the country. Using #ReformasiDikorupsi as a hashtag, the protests vocalize disappointment to the government, triggered in particular by moves to weaken the anti-corruption body. The police arrests 1,489 people, 380 of whom are suspected of organizing the protests. Two students die.

1 October 2019
Puan Maharani, the daughter of former President Megawati Sukarnoputri, is officially inaugurated as the first woman Speaker of the Indonesian House Representatives.

20 October 2019
Presidential and vice-presidential inauguration. During his inauguration speech, Jokowi mentioned that the issue of economy, bureaucracy, and human capital would be the priorities of his second term.

21 October 2019
Prabowo and Edhy Prabowo are invited to the Palace to meet the President. Jokowi appointed Prabowo to be the country's Defense Minister.

23 October 2019
Edhy Prabowo is formally introduced as the Fisheries Minister, replacing his predecessor Susi Pudjiastuti.

1 November 2019
Idham Aziz is promoted to the rank of National Police Chief, replacing Tito Karnavian who is appointed as the Home Affairs Minister.

21 November 2019
Jokowi appoints seven executive staff from the millennial generation. He instructs them to create innovations in different subjects and deliver solutions to national issues.

ABOUT THE CONTRIBUTORS

Kameda Akihiro is Research Assistant Professor, National Museum of Japanese History.

Ahmad Najib Burhani is Chairman, Institute of Social Sciences and Humanities, National Research and Innovation Agency, Indonesia.

Hui Yew-Foong is Associate Professor, Department of Sociology, Hong Kong Shue Yan University; Visiting Senior Fellow, ISEAS – Yusof Ishak Institute.

Budi Irawanto is Associate Professor, Department of Communications, Faculty of Social and Political Sciences, Universitas Gadjah Mada.

Dyah Ayu Kartika (Kathy) is a Research Analyst at the Institute for Policy Analysis of Conflict, Jakarta.

Max Lane is Visiting Senior Fellow, ISEAS – Yusof Ishak Institute.

Okamoto Masaaki is Professor, Center for Southeast Asian Studies, Kyoto University.

Firman Noor is Senior Researcher, Research Center for Politics, National Research and Innovation Agency, Indonesia.

Amalinda Savirani is Associate Professor, Department of Politics and Government, Universitas Gadjah Mada.

About the Contributors

Deasy Simandjuntak is International Visiting Fellow, Taiwan Foundation for Democracy; Adjunct Associate Professor, National Chengchi University; Associate Fellow, ISEAS – Yusof Ishak Institute.

Made Supriatma is Visiting Fellow, ISEAS – Yusof Ishak Institute.

Leo Suryadinata is Visiting Senior Fellow, ISEAS – Yusof Ishak Institute; Adjunct Professor, S. Rajaratnam School of International Studies, Nanyang Technological University.

Quinton Temby is Assistant Professor in Public Policy, Monash University, Indonesia.

Ian Douglas Wilson is Senior Lecturer and Academic Chair, Global Security Programme, Murdoch University.

1

THE 2019 INDONESIAN ELECTIONS: A POLITICAL DÉJÀ VU?

Made Supriatma and Hui Yew-Foong

On 17 April 2019, Indonesians marched to the polls to elect their president and vice president directly for the fourth time since direct election of the highest offices of Indonesia was introduced in 2004. And for the first time, concurrently, Indonesians had to elect 575 members of the national parliament (Dewan Perwakilan Rakyat, DPR), 136 members of the Regional Representative Council (Dewan Perwakilan Daerah, DPD), and 19,722 members of the regional legislatures (2,207 members of the provincial legislature and 17,515 members of the district/municipal legislatures) (BPS 2019, p. 26). While this combination of elections was a major historical undertaking, attention was more focused on the presidential election, not just because the presidential office holds significant executive powers, but also because the key contenders were the same as those for the last presidential election.

The incumbent, President Joko Widodo (popularly known as Jokowi), had to face off against the same rival, former army general and founder of the Great Indonesia Movement Party (Partai Gerakan Indonesia

Raya or Gerindra), Prabowo Subianto. Although the vice-presidential candidates were different—Jokowi picked Muslim cleric Ma'ruf Amin while Prabowo settled on the successful self-made businessman Sandiaga Uno—the political support bases did not differ significantly from the last contest five years before. In fact, we could make the case, based on the electoral outcome, that the polarization between the two camps of supporters—loosely framed as Islamic moderates-pluralists and Islamic conservatives—had intensified. No doubt, this is in large part due to the curious fact that the key players and dynamics of Indonesia's political major league had remained largely unchanged, such that the same pair of frontrunners had emerged again. It is in this vein that we may consider the 2019 elections as the Jokowi–Prabowo elections 2.0, and it is the objective of this volume to unravel the dynamics of the elections.

The aforementioned polarization, or the emergence of an ideological divide among voters, was already apparent during the first Jokowi–Prabowo presidential race in 2014. Jokowi had more sway among moderate Muslims and ethnic and religious minorities, who preferred a more pluralist Indonesia. In contrast, Prabowo garnered more votes from conservative Muslims, who desired a more extensive role for Islam in Indonesia's social and political life. This remains a working characterization for now, as the boundary between moderate and conservative Muslims is not easy to clearly define. While in the economy of political signs, Jokowi had come to be associated with Islamic moderates and pluralists and Prabowo with Islamic conservatives, how these signs structured the Indonesian body politic continued to be fluid, and part of the political contest was to navigate this fluidity successfully.

Maneuvers along these lines that could be considered the first salvo for the second Jokowi–Prabowo contest took place during the campaign for the governorship of Jakarta in 2016. The incumbent Chinese Christian governor, Basuki Tjahaja Purnama (popularly known as Ahok), was accused of blasphemy against Islam due to his comments over a Quranic verse in September 2016. This led to mass demonstrations against Ahok, the most prominent of which was the protest at Merdeka Square in Jakarta on 2 December 2016. In the run-off election held on 19 April 2017, Ahok lost to former education and culture minister

Anies Baswedan. A *kafir* commenting on the holy Quran was an act that crossed the line and made it necessary for Islam to be defended. On 9 May 2017, Ahok was found guilty of blasphemy against Islam and sentenced to two years in jail. Seen as an ally of Jokowi, Ahok's defeat and incarceration were considered political setbacks for what Jokowi stood for, and signs that conservative Islam could not be ignored as a political force.

Jokowi's association with Ahok, his alleged liaisons with communist (read atheist) China, and the banning of the Hizbut Tahrir Indonesia in July 2017 fed rumours and assertions that Jokowi was anti-Islam. Thus, declaring Ma'ruf Amin, chairman of the Indonesian Council of Ulama (MUI) and one of the leaders of the 2 December 2016 mass protest, as his vice-presidential running mate in August 2018, though not an original choice, was nevertheless a convenient choice that boosted Jokowi's Islamic credentials. Prabowo, on the other hand, could shun the clerics and adopt a businessman, not least because the conservative Prosperous Justice Party (Partai Keadilan Sejahtera, PKS) and Islamic Defenders Front (Front Pembela Islam, FPI) were already on his side.

Official campaigning started on 23 September 2018 and both sides went all out to reach the 192.8 million eligible voters. Needless to say, political rallies and social media were some of the main channels for reaching the electorate of the vast archipelagic nation, but the five televised debates between the candidates from January to April 2019 also garnered significant attention as the campaigns gained momentum (see "2019 Indonesian Elections Timeline", this volume).

Opinion polls conducted in March 2019 showed that the Jokowi–Ma'ruf Amin pair had a lead of 18–20 per cent over their opponents (Hui et al. 2019). On polling day, the elections went smoothly and no serious incidents were reported. Eventually, the General Elections Commission declared Jokowi–Ma'ruf Amin the winners on 21 May 2019 with 55.5 per cent of the votes. Compared to 2014, Jokowi had extended his lead over Prabowo to 11 per cent, an increase of 2.35 per cent. Moreover, if we apply broad strokes of interpretation, and consider Central Java, East Java, Kalimantan (except South Kalimantan) and eastern Indonesia as signifying support for moderate Islam-pluralism, and Sumatra, West Java, Banten, and parts of Sulawesi as signifying conservative Islam, then we see that the ideological divide first seen in 2014 has intensified in 2019 (see Figure 1.1).

FIGURE 1.1
Support for Jokowi and Prabowo across provinces in 2014 and 2019

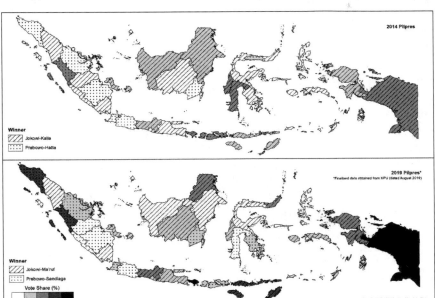

After the General Elections Commission announced the results of the presidential election, Prabowo's supporters led protests that ended up with riots in downtown Jakarta lasting two days (Supriatma 2019). As was the case in 2014, Prabowo challenged the results via the Constitutional Court, but once again, lost the court battle.

Where the parliamentary elections were concerned, the biggest winners were the Indonesian Democratic Party of Struggle (Partai Demokrasi Indonesia Perjuangan, PDIP) with 19.33 per cent, Gerindra with 12.57 per cent and the Party of Functional Groups (Partai Golongan Karya, Golkar) with 12.31 per cent. These parties, together with six other parties that passed the threshold of four per cent to obtain seats in the national parliament, will continue to serve as gatekeepers of the

Indonesian political scene, since legislative powers and the power to nominate future presidential candidates remain in their hands.

While Indonesian politics is not only about the presidential election, the presidential election and its outcome do have significant ramifications for Indonesian politics. This volume seeks to unravel the multidimensional aspects of the 2019 elections. Although the spotlight may be given to the rematch between Jokowi and Prabowo, the volume will also reflect on the larger political ecology and latest developments in Indonesia's electoral politics. Part I of the volume will examine some of the larger themes that pervade the elections, such as the state of Indonesian democracy, the role of elite clique rule, the influence of data analytics and cyber-tactics in electoral strategies, and the impact of disinformation. Part II will highlight the roles of particular constituencies in the campaigns, including social or mass organizations (*ormas*), unions, women, and the ethnic Chinese minority. Part III will showcase regional dynamics, especially in Java, Madura and Sumatra. In the tradition of area studies, this volume harnesses insights from different disciplines to enrich our understanding of Indonesia's 2019 elections.

COMPARING 2014 AND 2019: ELITES, STAGNATION AND CYBER-POLITICS

There are several immediate observations we can make concerning the 2019 elections in comparison with the 2014 elections. Although we have suggested that the 2019 elections could be considered an extension of the 2014 elections, it would be more accurate to think of 2014 as a reference point for understanding 2019, so that we remain sensitive to the changes and not simply read 2019 as a replay of 2014. One main difference is that by 2019, Jokowi was running as the incumbent and part of the Indonesian political establishment, rather than as a new actor and rising star of Indonesia's political scene.[1]

In 2014, Jokowi was seen as a fresh face in Indonesian politics. He represented an alternative to the Jakarta establishment and the possibility for change. As an SME businessman without political lineage, Jokowi benefitted from the post-*Reformasi*[2] decentralization of Indonesia and became the first directly elected mayor of Solo (Surakarta) by defeating the incumbent at the polls. His success at running the Solo municipality increased his national visibility and he was nominated to contest the Jakarta gubernatorial election in 2012, which he won, and again, by defeating the incumbent.[3] Jokowi's meteoric rise from outside the political establishment led to him being seen as a prospective reformer. He attracted activists who had longed for changes, changes that were yet to be fulfilled through the *Reformasi*.[4]

As an outsider to the Jakarta ruling clique, Jokowi did not pursue his presidential bid as a key leader of a political party.[5] He joined PDIP in 2004, a year before he ran for mayor in his hometown Surakarta. He campaigned through volunteer teams and did not rely too much on support from political parties and their campaign machinery. Even though he is formally a member of the PDIP, Jokowi is not seen as a representative of the party.[6]

Although Jokowi made a successful bid for the presidency through the popular vote in 2014, his political honeymoon was short-lived, and he had to face significant challenges. Among them was the coagulation of conservative Islamic elements, which led to the ousting of Ahok (mentioned earlier) and thereby the loss of influence from a close ally in the nation's capital. Conservative Islam became a position from which opposition to Jokowi was staged, eventually leading to support for Prabowo's second joust with Jokowi for the presidency in 2019.

While Prabowo was a frontrunner in consolidating his position with the support of Islamic hardliners and some retired generals, there were other challengers as well, such as then military chief-of-staff General Gatot Nurmantyo, who was baring his political ambitions even while he was still active in the military. Jokowi countered Gatot's political maneuvers[7] by aligning himself with the police.[8] As a result, Jokowi was criticized for using police powers to suppress opposition, and such use of police powers was seen as excessive and a violation of democratic norms.

The use of the instruments of government to crush political opposition and activists have generated criticism from pundits and scholars who argued that Indonesian democracy under Jokowi was undergoing a setback (Warburton and Aspinall 2019; Power and Warburton 2020; Aspinall et al. 2019), with some describing it as democratic stagnation or even regression (Diamond and Plattner 2015; Diamond 2020).[9] Noor (Chapter 2) highlights this concern with "democratic stagnation" in the context of the elections, especially in terms of the roles played by political parties, state agencies responsible for elections, political education and civil society.

Yet, it is also true that such institutional regression, as observed by these analysts, has developed in tandem with the increasing division of society along religious and primordial lines, which in turn has hampered the ability of civil society to engage through more democratic norms (Mietzner 2020). Given the circumstances, it is fortunate that no institution or individual has been strong enough to capture the state, or for that matter, put post-1998 electoral reforms on a regressive path and bring back New Order electoral practices.

To put the regression thesis in context, we do have to recognize that Jokowi shot onto the political scene as an outlier that directly challenged the post-*Reformasi* oligarchic elite, which had been forced to work together in spite of how fractious Indonesian politics was in order to maximize their shared interests (Winters 2012; Robison and Hadiz 2004; Ford and Pepinsky 2014). Max Lane (Chapter 3) argues that Indonesian elites (which he calls *cliques*) have created unwritten "rules of the game", whereby they hold power collectively and rule over the masses. In the larger picture of this power matrix, Jokowi had been co-opted due to his ability to mobilize voters independently, although he did face opposition from certain sectors of the oligarchic elite. Ahok's defeat, through the mobilization of conservative Islamic forces by a faction of this elite, may be seen as the outcome of this opposition. Jokowi responded by using the police to weaken the opposition and silence critics, and forming his own clique within elite circles. Eventually, in his bid for re-election, Jokowi was no longer touted as a reformer that challenged elite politics, but became part of the establishment with the majority of political parties firmly behind him.

For 2019, the "rules of the game" had also changed with the advent and use of new technologies, such that Okamoto and Kameda (Chapter 4) argue that the 2019 presidential election was Indonesia's first "full-fledged cyber election". In a post-truth Indonesia, it is not only that disinformation abounds in the online election campaigns and campaign teams have to discern the real facts and voices of voters amidst the cyber noise, but new tools employing Artificial Intelligence (AI) to sift through big data and execute micro-targeting have become part of the political arsenal.

Indeed, much of politics now takes place online, but with offline implications. Temby (Chapter 5) examines how, in the aftermath of the elections, disinformation related to the outcome ("stolen election") and drawing on anti-Chinese and religious sentiments fuelled protests and riots on 21–23 May 2019. It seems then, that cyber-politics has taken on a life of its own, and will remain a tactical playing field for the future of Indonesian politics.

POLITICAL PARTIES AND BEYOND: *ORMAS*, UNIONS, WOMEN AND THE CHINESE

What is connecting the elites who want to be elected to public office and the masses who will elect them? This question brings to the fore one of the most important institutions linking the elite and masses, namely, political parties. As chapters in this volume will reveal, the salience of political parties varies across campaigns. The Jokowi camp, for example, used less party machineries than Prabowo, as Jokowi relied more on volunteers to gear up his campaign (Lay 2018; Suaedy 2014; Mietzner 2014). But even Prabowo's campaign was not fully engaging with parties within his coalition, except for Gerindra, the party he established and chaired.[10]

In the contest for legislative seats, candidates have to form their own campaign teams to reach out to voters. In most cases, legislative candidates fund their own campaigns. The 2019 legislative election was different from previous elections. Candidates had to compete, not only against candidates from other parties, but also from their own party.[11] Intra- and inter-party competition had made it more difficult to be elected, and hindered candidates from the same party from working together. As a consequence, legislative candidates had also become less reliant on party support and what mattered more was material resources for running campaigns.

A party stalwart may not get a nomination if she/he has no resources for campaigning, and it is common for parties to nominate outsiders as candidates for elections.[12] Such candidates usually join parties nearer to the nomination date.[13] While ideal candidates are usually those with high electability, such as public figures and celebrities, there are many cases where candidates with deep pockets can gain the party ticket. Thus, elections often involve financial transactions, where vote buying or trading votes for material benefits is common in Indonesia (Muhtadi 2019). Political parties have come to be seen not so much as institutions based on ideology where cadres are educated and offered a path to political office, but more as organizations for extending the reach of the elite from the national to the local level (Aspinall and Berenschot 2019; Mietzner 2013).

Aside from political parties, there are also organizations known as *ormas* (*organisasi kemasyarakatan* or mass/social organizations). Some *ormas* are affiliated with political parties but many are not, and just like political parties, they vary ideologically.[14] Although most *ormas* are officially non-political, they are nevertheless politically significant and politicians tend to solicit their support. One example is the women's organization affiliated with Nahdlatul Ulama (NU) known as Fatayat,[15] which was partly responsible for Jokowi's landslide victories in Central and East Java (see Budi Irawanto, Chapter 12).

Ian Wilson (Chapter 6) offers a glimpse into how *ormas* as a constituency are playing a strategic political role at street level in Jakarta by trading influence for the benefit of the organization and their leaders. Wilson studies the case of Pemuda Pancasila (PP) and Forum Betawi Rempug (FBR), which endorsed Prabowo in 2014 but shifted their support to Jokowi in 2019. This was due to the threat posed by their rival FPI, which had gained a leading position within the hardline Islamic community and among Prabowo's supporters. By aligning themselves with Jokowi, PP and FBR were seeking to strengthen their position as *ormas* and regain their spots in the political limelight.

Unions are another constituency that has been asserting its influence on electoral politics. After being suppressed during the New Order, union politics have been revived in recent years. Amalinda Savirani (Chapter 7) relates how union members were mobilized and tried to capture power at the local level in Bekasi, West Java. Although this was an industrial region where union influence was more pronounced, union nominees had limited success in both the elections for local executive leaders and legislatures. Part of the constraint comes from the challenge of articulating interests beyond unions to win voters in the same geographical region with different socio-economic and political concerns. Moreover, as nominees need to run on a party ticket to enter the electoral race, they also need to contend with the tension between party interests and union interests. In short, where political representation is organized geographically, unions, in representing the interests of a cross-section of the population, will continue to find difficulty in securing their political footing.

Another cross-section of the electorate that has often been left out of the dialogue on Indonesian politics is women. Dyah Ayu Kartika (Chapter 8) fills this gap by discussing how women's groups across the political spectrum were negotiating the moderate-conservative Islam divide discussed earlier in this chapter. In particular, Kartika delves into social media and *majlis taklim* (Islamic study groups) as critical arenas for such negotiations, focusing on women-centred moral issues, and reflects on the prospects for Islamic feminism in Indonesia.

Leo Suryadinata (Chapter 9) considers the role of Chinese Indonesians in Indonesian politics. With the democratization of the political arena in post-*Reformasi* Indonesia, Chinese Indonesians have been participating much more actively in politics, both formally as electoral candidates, and informally through civil society. While Chinese Indonesians have had some success in getting elected, they find that, as with the union representatives, they had to embrace much broader interests than that of a particular cross-section of the Indonesian population in order to remain relevant to their supporters.

REGIONAL DYNAMICS

As a vast archipelagic nation that had introduced extensive regional autonomy policies since 1999, such that regional politics can differ significantly, studies into electoral politics in Indonesia that consider only the aggregate without examining the fine grain of regional dynamics will miss the complex cultural political character of Indonesia. Indeed, candidates have to juggle this cultural political complexity with finesse in order to gain success at the polls. As the 2019 elections include not only the presidential election, but the election of legislative representatives at the national, provincial and district levels as well, we have to ask if these elections at different levels have an influence on each other? In particular, does the presidential election, which attracts the most attention and is the most divisive, have an effect on the other elections?

Four chapters in this volume give us the fine-grained picture from the regions. Irawanto (Chapter 10) introduces us to the battleground of Central Java, the most homogenous province in Indonesia with 97.72 per cent Javanese (Arifin et al. 2015). Stakes were high as Prabowo established his campaign headquarters in Solo, Jokowi's home ground and PDIP's electoral stronghold. This blatant challenge, as Irawanto suggests, "awakened the sleeping bull" and galvanized the PDIP and Jokowi's supporters to campaign with gusto. These efforts, together with the support of NU, Indonesia's largest Muslim organization, and Ganjar Pranowo, Central Java's governor and Jokowi's ally, eventually gave Jokowi a landslide victory of 77.7 per cent of the votes in the province, an 11.02 per cent increase compared to 2014. At the same time, while the symbiotic relationship between Jokowi and the PDIP in Central Java had led to big wins for PDIP parliamentary candidates, other parties in Jokowi's coalition were not able to benefit as much from the so-called coat-tail effects as the province remains very much the electoral base of the PDIP.

The picture is significantly different in Madura, an island off the coast of East Java. Although the Madurese are known for being staunch supporters of the NU, which in turn was firmly behind Jokowi's candidature since one of its key leaders Ma'ruf Amin had been selected as Jokowi's vice-presidential candidate, Jokowi was still unable to bag the majority of votes in Madura. Ahmad Najib Burhani (Chapter 11) explains that this was due to the overwhelming influence of local leaders and *kiai* (religious teachers), such that the political stance of NU at the national level bore little relevance for the Madurese voters. Other factors that weighed in was the rising influence of the FPI in Madura, the growth of conservatism, and the sway held by big *pesantren* (Islamic schools). The Madura case demonstrates how local dynamics can run counter to and challenge national directives, and the deeply steeped role of religious patrons in influencing political behaviour.

Beyond Java, Sumatra offers glimpses into how the electoral contest unfolded in other key battlegrounds. North Sumatra, which has the highest concentration of Christians (31 per cent) among the ten provinces of Sumatra, set the stage for what Deasy Simandjuntak (Chapter 12) calls "religious binarism", resulting in Muslim districts on the east coast voting overwhelmingly for Prabowo, while the Christian districts on the west coast supported Jokowi. This "religious binarism" in turn plays out the moderate Islam-pluralist and conservative Islam dichotomy pervading the national electoral scene that we have highlighted earlier in this chapter. Eventually, Jokowi won a majority in the province with 52.32 per cent of the votes, but this was lower than the 55.24 per cent share that he achieved in 2014. Where parliamentary elections were concerned, the debates were focused more on money politics issues. Nevertheless, Simandjuntak suggests that the mobilization of religious sentiments will continue to feature heavily in elections involving religiously heterogenous regions in Indonesia.

Made Supriatma's (Chapter 13) findings in South Sumatra and Lampung were similar. While identity politics and ideology were decisive factors for the presidential election, what mattered for the legislative elections were candidates' personal appeal and the material benefits they could share with voters. In other words, while the presidential election operates on a more abstract level for most voters, parliamentary elections signify more immediate material concerns and voters' approach tend to be more pragmatic.

AFTERWORD

This volume highlights both the broad strokes of prevailing themes in the 2019 Indonesian elections as well as portraits of how local electoral scenes unfold, sometimes in tandem with and sometimes counter to the prevailing narratives. This complexity, embedded in the cultural politics of Indonesia, gives us insights into the parameters that define Indonesian politics, and why it developed the way it did.

After the dust had settled where the elections were concerned, Jokowi invited Prabowo to join his cabinet in the heavyweight post of Defence Minister. Subsequently, Jokowi also invited Sandiaga Uno to assume the position of Minister of Tourism and Creative Economy. Both had obliged, and we have the unique picture, in Indonesia, of erstwhile political opponents serving in the same cabinet. It seems that the political bifurcation that had polarized Indonesia had merely served the positioning of candidates in the economy of signs. Or, conversely, the current rapprochement is merely a veneer stretched over deep cracks that will surface again in future political jousts.

One is tempted to see Indonesian politics as a perennial shadow play repeating scripted themes that the audience does not tire of. Jokowi, who had shot onto the political scene out of left field, is now part of the political establishment and few would still see him as a reformer. In fact, with his son and son-in-law contesting and winning the seats of mayor in Solo and Medan respectively in the December 2020 regional elections, he is seen to have joined the elites in the practice of safeguarding their political legacies through dynastic politics (Wilson and Hui 2020).

However, such developments should not deter us from seeing what is possibly new in Indonesian politics. For one, post-*Reformasi* political decentralization and democratization had made it possible for someone without political lineage like Jokowi to challenge the elites and win the highest office in Indonesia, which would have been quite unthinkable previously. Moreover, as demonstrated in this volume, the online world and social media have disrupted political engagement to the extent that shadow play has to assume an online mode and be executed with greater sophistry in today's political contests. Finally, the Covid-19 pandemic has disrupted business and politics as usual, and the new political normal that will shape the 2024 elections, where a new generation of politicians will be vying for Indonesia's top offices, is still evolving.

Indonesian democracy is treading its own path, sometimes in ways similar to other democracies, and sometimes with its own unique character. Like some other democracies, democratic dynasties (Chandra 2016), such as those in India, whereby political parties are dominated by dynasts or clans, are being perpetuated in Indonesia. At the same time, we see polarization and elite unity coexisting in Indonesian politics—the elite polarizing the masses but at the same time working together to advance their interests. Thus, paradoxically, while polarization could potentially destabilize Indonesian politics, elites compromising among themselves and bringing about stability will continue to be a feature of the political scene.

NOTES

1. When running for president in 2014, Jokowi was supported by a minority of parties in the parliament. The so-called *Koalisi Indonesia Hebat*, supported by five political parties (PDIP, PKB, Nasdem, Hanura and PKPI), controlled 208 seats (37.1 per cent) in parliament. Meanwhile his opponent, Prabowo Subianto, brought together *Koalisi Merah Putih*, which consisted of six parties (Gerindra, Golkar, PPP, PAN, PKS, PBB) that controlled 353 seats

(62.9 per cent) in parliament. In 2019, however, President Jokowi built a huge coalition known as *Indonesia Maju*, which consisted of the majority of parties in parliament (PDIP, Golkar, PKB, Nasdem, PPP, PKPI, PBB, PSI, Perindo). Together, these parties controlled 338 parliamentary seats (60.3 per cent). Meanwhile, Prabowo was supported by the *Indonesia Adil Makmur* coalition, comprising of five political parties (Gerindra, Democrat, PAN, PKS, and Berkarya), which controlled 222 (39.7 per cent) seats in parliament.

2. The *Reformasi*, or Reform Movement, took place with the fall of Suharto in 1998, leading to the democratization of Indonesian politics and the implementation of policies related to regional autonomy.
3. On Jokowi's political career, see Bland (2020).
4. Many activists were attracted to Jokowi because he promoted a clean and efficient government. He also promised to solve major cases of human rights violations such as finding activists who had disappeared during 1996–97 before the fall of Suharto. However, this hope was dashed because, after coming to power, Jokowi inducted people suspected of being perpetrators of gross human rights violations, such as General Wiranto, into his administration.
5. Right after this election in 2014, groups of volunteers urged him to establish a political party, but he refused.
6. After being elected president in 2014, Megawati Sukarnoputri, PDIP chairwoman, called Jokowi a "party officer". However, Jokowi showed his independence from the PDIP when he governed, and it was clear that the influence of the party was secondary.
7. Gatot Nurmantyo had openly used his post to pursue his political ambitions. He built his political capital through speaking circuits to students in major universities in Indonesia. He specifically spoke about the "proxy wars" that were carried out by the world's great powers against Indonesia. The proxy war theory, which was more like a conspiracy theory, had raised Nurmantyo's political prospects. On Nurmantyo's political ambitions, see Wangge (2018).
8. Under Jokowi, the Indonesian police had received special privileges, which were not given by previous administrations. Their budget had burgeoned, and their generals were appointed to several strategic positions that in the past were usually filled by army generals. Their role in Indonesia's body politic had expanded through laws involving defamation and insults to the head of state, as well as the Law on Internet and Electronic Transactions (UU ITE). See Supriatma (2020).
9. In fact, Aspinall, Mietzner and Tomsa (2015) had observed that Indonesia was already experiencing democratic stagnation under President Susilo Bambang Yudhoyono, Jokowi's immediate predecessor.

10. See Supriatma (Chapter 13).
11. Mietzner (2020, p. 191) argues that the use of an open proportional system increases the personalization of elections. In the absence of robust financing for political parties, which is deliberately conditioned by party elites, candidates have to bear the campaign costs themselves. It is not unusual for candidates to get their election funds from oligarchs or from corrupt practices. Thus, the role of political parties becomes weak. As Aspinall and Berenschot (2019, p. 7) note, the role of parties is often reduced to just a "toll keeper", selling nominations to candidates but not helping them much in campaigning or controlling their behaviour when elected and serving their term. What matters most is not political parties but patronage networks that connect the elites and the constituents.
12. The practice is not limited to legislative elections. Even in regional leader elections, the selection of a candidate involved outsiders who are willing to pay a "dowry" (*mahar*) to political parties. A candidate also has to pay *mahar* to each party in his coalition.
13. For example, Jokowi only became a member of PDIP less than a year before the Surakarta mayoral election in 2005.
14. See for example Ryter (2001) on Pemuda Pancasila; Wilson (2006) on Front Pembela Islam; Kingsley (2012) on Amphibi religious *ormas* in Lombok; and also Wilson (2015) on varieties of civilian organized violent organizations.
15. On Fatayat, see Arnez (2010).

REFERENCES

Arifin, Evi Nurvidya, Aris Ananta, Dwi Retno Wilujeng Wahyu Utami, Nur Budi Handayani and Agus Pramono. 2015. "Quantifying Indonesia's Ethnic Diversity". *Asian Population Studies* 11, no. 3: 233–56. https://doi.org/10.1080/17441730.2015.1090692.

Arnez, Monika. 2010. "Empowering Women Through Islam: Fatayat NU Between Tradition and Change". *Journal of Islamic Studies* 21, no. 1: 59–88. https://doi.org/10.1093/jis/etp025.

Aspinall, Edward, Diego Fossati, Burhanuddin Muhtadi, and Eve Warburton. 2019. "Elites, Masses, and Democratic Decline in Indonesia". *Democratization* 27: 1–22. https://doi.org/10.1080/13510347.2019.1680971.

Aspinall, Edward, Marcus Mietzner, and Dirk Tomsa. 2015. The *Yudhoyono Presidency: Indonesia's Decade of Stability and Stagnation*. Singapore: Institute of Southeast Asian Studies

Aspinall, Edward and Ward Berenschot. 2019. *Democracy for Sale: Elections, Clientilism, and The State in Indonesia*. Ithaca, NY: Cornell University Press.

Biro Pusat Statistik. 2019. *Statistik Politik 2019*. Jakarta: BPS.

Bland, Ben. 2020. *Man of Contradictions: Joko Widodo and the Struggle to Remake Indonesia*. Sidney, Australia: Lowy Institute.

Chandra, Kanchan. 2016. *Democratic Dynasties: State, Party, and Family in Contemporary Indian Politics*. London: Cambridge University Press.

Cribb, Robert and Audrey Kahin. 2004. *Historical Dictionary of Indonesia*, 2nd ed. Lanham, Maryland: The Scarecrow Press, pp. 491–93.

Diamond, Lary and Marc F. Plattner. 2015. *Democracy in Decline?* Baltimore: John Hopkins University Press.

———. 2020. "Democratic Regression in Comparative Perspective: Scope, Methods, and Causes". *Democratization* 27: 1–21. https://doi.org/10.1080/13510347.2020.1807517.

Ford, Michelle and Thomas B. Pepinsky, eds. 2014. *Beyond Oligarchy: Wealth, Power, and Contemporary Indonesian Politics*. Cornell Modern Indonesia Project. NY: Cornell University Press.

Hui Yew-Foong, Made Supriatma, Aninda Dewayanti and Benjamin Hu. 2019. "Preview of the 2019 Indonesian Elections". *ISEAS Perspective*, no. 2019/24, 9 April 2019.

Kingsley, Jeremy. 2012. "Peacemakers or Peace-breakers? Provincial Elections and Religious Leadership in Lombok, Indonesia". *Indonesia* 93: 53–82.

Lay, Cornelis. 2018. "Hometown Volunteers: A Case Study of Volunteer Organizations in Surakarta Supporting Joko Widodo's Presidential Campaign". *The Copenhagen Journal of Asian Studies* 36, no. 1: 79–105. https://doi.org/10.22439/cjas.v36i1.5513.

Mietzner, Marcus. 2013. *Money, Power, and Ideology: Political Parties in Post-Authoritarian Indonesia*. Singapore: NUS Press.

———. 2014. "How Jokowi Won and Democracy Survived". *Journal of Democracy* 25, no. 4: 111–25. https://doi.org/10.1353/jod.2014.0073.

———. 2020. "Indonesian Parties Revisited: Systemic Exclusivism, Electoral Personalisation and Declining Intraparty Democracy". In *Democracy in Indonesia: From Stagnation to Regression?*, edited by Thomas Power and Eve Warburton. Singapore: ISEAS – Yusof Ishak Institute, pp. 191–209.

Muhtadi, Burhannudin. 2019. *Vote Buying in Indonesia: The Mechanics of Electoral Bribery*. Singapore: Palgrave Macmillan. https://doi.org/10.1007/978-981-13-6779-3.

Power, Thomas and Eve Warburton. 2020. *Democracy in Indonesia: From Stagnation to Regression?* Singapore: ISEAS – Yusof Ishak Institute.

Robison, Richard and Vedi R. Hadiz. 2004. *Reorganising Power in Indonesia: The Politics of Oligarchy in an Age of Markets*. London: Routledge.

Ryter, Loren. 2001. "Pemuda Pancasila: The Last Loyalist Free Men of Suharto's Order". In *Violence and the State in Suharto's Indonesia*, edited by B.enedict Anderson (ed.), . New York: Cornell Southeast Asia Program, pp. 124–55.

Suaedy, Ahmad. 2014. "The Role of Volunteers and Political Participation in the 2012 Jakarta Gubernatorial Election". *Journal of Current Southeast Asian Affairs* 33, no. 1: 111–38.

Supriatma, Made. 2019. "Tensions Among Indonesia's Security Forces Underlying the May 2019 Riots in Jakarta". *ISEAS Perspective*, no. 2019/61, 13 August 2019.

──────. 2020. "The Indonesian Police's Dual Function under Jokowi". *East Asia Forum*, 6 October 2020.

Wangge, Hipolitus Yolisandry Ringgi. 2018. "An Indonesian General's Political Aspirations". *The Diplomat*, 9 January 2018.

Warburton, Eve and Edward Aspinall. 2019. "Explaining Indonesia's Democratic Regression: Structure, Agency and Popular Opinion". *Contemporary Southeast Asia* 41: 255–85.

Wilson, Ian D. 2006. "Continuity and Change: The Changing Contours of Organized Violence in post-New Order Indonesia". *Critical Asian Studies* 38: 265–97.

──────. 2015. *The Politics of Protection Rackets in Post-New Order Indonesia: Coercive Capital, Authority and Street Politics*. New York: Routledge.

Wilson, Ian D. and Hui Yew-Foong. 2020. "Signs of Democratic Contraction and Recentralisation of Power in Indonesia's 2020 Regional Elections". *ISEAS Perspective*, no. 2020/140, 7 December 2020.

Winters, Jeffrey A. 2012. *Oligarchy*. London: Cambridge University Press.

PART I:

Democracy, Cyber-politics and Disinformation

2

THE 2019 ELECTION AS A REFLECTION OF THE STAGNATION OF INDONESIAN DEMOCRACY?

Firman Noor

INTRODUCTION

The challenges posed by the 2019 election were not only important in terms of implementing a new election mechanism, namely concurrent elections, but also in supporting the establishment of better democracy. Democracy itself has today created opportunities for people, political parties and non-governmental organizations to play greater roles in the decision-making process. It also has given the people greater freedom of expression, including the freedom to oppose the government. People in general have more political options as no party has absolute power any longer. Democracy has also allowed for regular, peaceful change of leadership for more than twenty years now.

On the other hand, democracy in Indonesia is not advanced yet. Some observers view Indonesian politics as still being under the control of oligarchs (Robison and Hadiz 2004; Winters 2014). The rule of law in general is still weak as is genuine participation, creating an artificial form of political representation. Corruption and money politics, mainly related to electoral contestation, still occur at both national and local levels (Aspinall and Berenschot 2019; Muhtadi 2019; Aspinall and Sukmajati 2015; Amrullah 2009; Choi 2007) and detract from the fairness and equality that the election system is supposed to deliver. There is a tendency to create cartels rather than government with accountability (Ambardi 2009). In recent years, the authorities have shown a streak of authoritarianism by arbitrarily arresting anyone who opposed or criticized the government (Power 2018). Moreover, Indonesian political contestation is coloured by primordial issues, identity politics and populism, rather than policy programmes. Those conditions indicate that the flaws of Indonesia democracy—the tendency towards oligarchism—still hold, as pointed out by several scholars (Slater 2004; Davidson 2009; Slater and Simmons 2012; Bunte and Ufen 2009; Aspinall and Mietzner 2010; Ford and Pepinsky 2014). Indonesian democracy has been rated mediocre or even low by various national and domestic observers, including Asian Democracy Index (4.9/10), Economist Intelligence Unit (6.39/10) and Freedom House (Partly Free).

This chapter will discuss the quality of the 2019 election and its relation to Indonesian democracy, which is believed to be experiencing potential stagnation. Specifically, the chapter will explore questions such as: how the quality of Indonesia's political conditions is connected to the quality of elections, what the causes of democratic stagnation are, and what should be done to overcome stagnation. What is meant by democratic stagnation here is the continuing prevalence of conditions that contributed to the low quality of democracy and elections in 2014, such as strong oligarchic tendencies, weak political parties, money politics, a politicized bureaucracy, weak civil society and biased media. These conditions impede democratic progress.

THE CONDUCT OF THE ELECTIONS

The election allowed incumbent President Joko Widodo (Jokowi) a second term. Jokowi and his vice-presidential candidate, Ma'ruf Amin, obtained 55.5 per cent of the votes, beating their opponents, Prabowo Subianto and Sandiaga Uno, by approximately 16.96 million votes (nearly 11 per cent). Jokowi won in twenty-three provinces while Prabowo won in eleven provinces.

TABLE 2.1
Results of the 2019 Presidential Election

Candidates	Votes	(%)
Joko Widodo–Ma'ruf Amin	85,607,362	55.5
Prabowo Subianto–Sandiaga Uno	68,650,239	44.5

Source: General Elections Commission.

Meanwhile, the legislative elections led to the majority of seats in the Dewan Perwakilan Rakyat (parliament or DPR, for short) being controlled by parties supporting Jokowi. Notably, the Partai Demokrasi Indonesia Perjuangan (PDI-P) was returned as the party with the most votes. Of the nine parties eligible to take seats in parliament, only NasDem and the Partai Keadilan Sejahtera (Prosperous Justice Party or PKS, for short) were able to increase their vote shares by more than one per cent while four parties—Golkar, Partai Demokrat, Partai Amanat Nasional (National Mandate Party or PAN, for short) and Partai Persatuan Pembangunan (United Development Party or PPP, for short)—saw their vote shares decline.

The rest of the parties, such as Hanura, Partai Bulan Bintang (PBB), Partai Keadilan dan Persatuan Indonesia (PKPI), Perindo, Partai Solidaritas Indonesia (PSI) and Garuda, could not pass the parliamentary threshold (at least four per cent of total votes) to gain seats. The situation for new parties was equally bad as none of them managed to get even a single seat in parliament. Some new parties, however, were able to place their candidates in local parliaments.

Although some of the parties initially rejected the election results owing to what they believed were irregularities that had occurred before and during the election, in particular problems related to money politics, they eventually accepted them. However, the results of the presidential election were legally challenged by the Prabowo–Sandiaga team, who felt that the election had not been run fairly. Prabowo accused the incumbent of having committed structured, systematic

TABLE 2.2
Political Parties that Passed the Parliamentary Threshold

No	Parties	2014 (Votes)	2014 (%)	2019 (Votes)	2019 (%)	+/−
1	PDI-P	23,681,471	18.95	27,053,961	19.33	+ 0.38
2	Gerindra	14,760,371	11.81	17,594,839	12.57	+ 0.76
3	Golkar	18,432,312	14.75	17,229,789	12.31	− 2.44
4	PKB	11,298,957	9.04	13,570,097	9.69	+ 0.65
5	NasDem	8,402,812	6.72	12,661,792	9.05	+ 2.35
6	PKS	8,480,204	6.79	11,493,663	8.21	+ 1.42
7	Demokrat	12,728,913	10.19	10,876,507	7.77	− 2.42
8	PAN	9,481,621	7.59	9,572,623	6.84	− 0.75
9	PPP	8,157,488	6.53	6,323,147	4.52	− 2.01
10	Others	9,548,342	7.63	13,594,842	9.71	+ 2.08

Source: General Elections Commission.

and massive fraud (*Republika.id* 2019; *Tribunnews* 2019a). However, the Constitutional Court eventually ruled that the election results announced by the General Elections Commission (KPU) were valid.

The turnout for the 2019 legislative election was nearly 82 per cent, almost similar to the turnout for the presidential election, both percentages marking the highest turnout seen in the past ten years. In the 2009 election the turnout was 70.9 per cent for the legislative election and 71.7 per cent for the presidential election, while in the 2014 election the corresponding percentages were 75.11 per cent and 69.58 per cent. The increased turnout in 2019 was mainly driven by the public's eagerness to participate in the presidential election. High public participation was not only seen in the number of voters but also in the number of volunteer networks supporting the two candidates and the number of members in their respective campaign committees. Volunteers and supporters of the respective candidates not only tried to make the election safe and smooth but also sought to get more voters to participate, fearing that a low voter turnout would negatively affect the winning chances of their respective presidential candidates. They seemed to believe that the election was particularly important because the two popular candidates seemed to have almost diametrically opposite tendencies and agendas. In other words, two popular figures with different personalities and policies become the main reasons for the exceptionally high voter turnout.

Apart from increased participation, another feature of the 2019 elections was the major problems that arose. The first problem revolved around the validity of the Eligible Voter List (DPT). This is a classic problem that from time to time stokes controversy over the way elections are implemented, and some DPR members have protested against the KPU for allowing the DPT problem (*Rmol.id*. 2014). The main cause of the problem is that population records are scattered across the country. Many residents are not registered or have multiple identity cards (KTPs). The KPU has continued to use these questionable identity records as a main reference to set up the DPT. In addition, according to the Election Supervisory Agency or Bawaslu, foreigners holding electronic KTPs also were included in the DPT (*Tirto.id*. 2019). In the implementation of elections, the DPT problem allows for the manipulation of voting through vote mark-ups (*penggelembungan suara*). This problem led to protests, not only in the context of the 2019 presidential election but also the legislative elections. Some parties, including PKS, PKB and Hanura (Andriansyah 2019; *Faktual News* 2019; *Kompas.com* 2019b), protested. The DPT problem clearly goes against the fundamental principle of elections, especially the notions of fairness, honesty, justice and the right to vote.

Another problem that became a public concern was the number of casualties arising from the polling and vote-counting process and the demonstration on 22 May, after the KPU had announced the election results. The demonstration was held by Prabowo's supporters protesting against alleged election fraud. It involved thousands of people, mainly in Jakarta (*Kompas.com* 2019g). As for casualties during polling and vote-counting, the government reported that 554 people died, of whom 440 were polling officers, while the rest were from Bawaslu and the police. These deaths occurred mainly because of pre-existing diseases and fatigue. In addition, 11,239 officials reportedly became victim to various illnesses during the polling and vote-counting process (*Kompas.com* 2019f).

Many later related the high number of casualties during polling and vote-counting to the implementation of simultaneous elections, which forced the officials concerned to work extra hours to complete all stages of the polling. Some advocated a review of simultaneous elections, calling for separate elections. Some even suggested electronic voting and counting. Above all, the number of casualties clearly indicated lack of readiness on the part of the KPU, especially its failure to anticipate the varies problems related to the implementation of elections. In regard to the casualties incurred during the demonstration, many felt the police should be responsible for reporting what had actually happened during the event.[1]

SIGNS OF DEMOCRATIC STAGNATION

Elections are ideally the means to actualize people's interests and aspirations. Elections allow the people to determine which party is worthy of occupying political office. Hence, the holding of elections is one of the indicators of the presence of democracy (Mayo 1991; Schumpeter 1975; Przeworski 1991). But this does not mean that the holding of elections by itself indicates the success of democracy. In authoritarian countries, elections are held regularly, as had happened in Indonesia during the New Order era. Therefore, the quality of democracy is not necessarily dependent merely on the holding of elections. Elections must be properly implemented, among other things.

Some of the indications of successful democratic elections are: equal rights for all citizens, equal opportunity to access information on all the candidates and their programmes, regularity, rule of law, equal opportunities for contestation, free and fair competition, an impartial press, neutrality of the bureaucracy and state apparatus, transparency of the election process but confidentiality of one's vote, the existence of a mechanism for resolving electoral disputes, and the presence of an independent election body (Ranney 1992; IDEA 2002).

In addition, the quality of an election cannot be judged by evaluating the processes on polling day alone. This is because what happens before and after the casting of votes also determines the quality of the election. In the New Order era, people cast their votes quite peacefully on polling day. But one could never consider the implementation of elections in that era as democratic since there was systematic manipulation (Irwan and Edriana 1995).

Indeed, the election of 2019 also saw cheating, fraud and other serious irregularities. Some of these irregularities had occurred in recent elections as well. These problems were mainly related to the system of counting and errors in inputting data from the poll count. According to Bawaslu, the KPU had committed a violation related to the counting system. Also, it claimed, many polling officers made mistakes during the data input process.[2] Other irregularities included the disappearance or moving of some polling stations (TPS) on election day, which made people confused and discouraged them from voting. Some TPS also were burnt by a number of individuals owing to the disappointment arising from losing the election (CNN Indonesia 2019b; *Kompas.com* 2019a). In addition, Bawaslu noted that hundreds of members from the vote organizing committees (KPPS) in the 2019 election lacked impartiality.[3]

One other important feature of the 2019 election was media bias or partiality. Some of the mainstream media did try to maintain their objectivity, but most others were far from independent in their coverage, choosing to cover one or the other presidential candidate but not both. Almost all the television networks, including Metro TV and Berita Satu, sided with the incumbent, effectively becoming government spokesmen. They tended to play down the opposition or ignore important moments initiated by the opposition. In one case, this unbalanced stance caused the Prabowo team to boycott Metro TV.

Only TV One dared on various occasions to broadcast activities involving the opposition or groups critical of the incumbent. TV One was indeed unique because its owner, Aburizal Bakrie, was actually supportive of Jokowi, making the television station's stance look far more objective than that of the other stations, such as TVRI, a state television, Metro TV (owned by Surya Paloh, chairman of NasDem), or television stations under the multinational group (owned by Hary Tanoesoedibjo, chairman of Perindo).

A similar lack of objectivity was evident in the print media and some online media. In fact, *Republika*, which is popularly known as the Muslim community's newspaper, tended to support Jokowi. This was due to the position of its owner, Erick Thohir, the leader of the Mahaka Media group, who in the 2019 election headed the Jokowi–Ma'ruf campaign team.

The main reason for the biased coverage was that the owners of the various media groups had a political interest in bolstering the standing of the incumbent. Their stances then meant that Indonesia lacked the critical role that a free press could play in upholding democracy (VOA Indonesia 2019).

Another feature that marred the workings of democracy during the 2019 election was the continued prevalence of *politik uang* (money politics). The practice of money politics was varied in nature, including giving money to campaign attendees or providing social/humanitarian assistance with persuasive messages calling on the recipients to elect the candidate in question. In the days prior to the campaign period, campaign teams spread out to establish networks in the community and communicate with the people. In doing so sometimes they gave money or assistance to the people or built public facilities to appeal to them. Not surprisingly, the candidates' campaign expenses reached their peak as election day approached. The most recent example of money politics was the discovery in May 2019 by the Corruption Eradication Commission (KPK) of a total of Rp8.45 billion (approximately US$605,595) inside hundreds of thousands of envelopes, which were expected to be distributed to the people (*Kompas.com* 2019h; *Tempo.co* 2019a).

Rural areas became the preferred place to conduct money politics; money politics was less prevalent in the urban areas, particularly in areas where the well-educated reside. During the campaign period, particularly just prior to the D Day of elections, a series of what is known as *serangan fajar* (dawn attack) took place in the rural areas because poverty in these areas makes the people easy targets for money politics. Also, people in the rural areas have little awareness of the need to report such activities or of the avenues for reporting them. In fact, many have no idea how they should react.

Money politics in its various forms clearly has the impact of reducing fairness in elections and manipulating the people's aspirations. In the 2019 election, it contributed to the high cost of elections: to successfully contest at the national level, a candidate would have had to secure between Rp1–2 billion; at the province level, this would amount to about Rp500 million–Rp1 billion; and at the district level about Rp250–300 million (Rosandya 2018). The high cost of fighting elections was not a new development in 2019; it was already in evidence at the beginning of the reform era (Aspinall and Sukmajati 2015). Recent studies on clientelism, money politics and the role of oligarchs (Aspinall and Berenschot 2019; Rahmawati 2018) clearly indicates that money does indeed talk in current Indonesian politics.

In addition, a recurrent problem in elections in Indonesia re-appeared in the 2019 election—the use of the state apparatus in campaigning. Although bureaucrats were ordered by the government to maintain neutrality, in reality this order cannot make them completely free from political activity (Moksen, Dwiputratni, Muhammad 2018), which violates the spirit of neutrality (Utomo and Untung 2019). At the practical level, government bureaucrats are often used as tools to serve political interests, especially by incumbents.[4] In the presidential election, several heads of local government clearly expressed their support for one or the other of the candidates, Jowoki or Prabowo. This happened not only at the provincial level but also at the district/city level (*Liputan 6* 2019).

Where the bureaucracy is not truly professional but has a strong culture of *ewuh pakewuh* (being obsequious, in other words, being yes-men), the personal support that a regional leader shows for one or the other candidate becomes a kind of clue to the political direction that must be taken by his or her subordinates. The political preferences of the heads of local government became tantamount to unwritten instructions to their subordinates, who feared that their positions might be jeopardized if they dared argue with their superiors.

Several bureaucrats and even the police thus proved to be partisan in their approach (Nurita 2019; *Tempo.co* 2019b; Hasanudin 2019). It was also no wonder then that government facilities such as vehicles, communication equipment and meeting rooms were provided to assist the candidates supported by the respective regional leaders during the campaign. In some areas, the heads of local government made it a point to emphasize to their subordinates that the president played an important role in helping them with many programmes and policies and also in giving out government aid. Meanwhile, the police in some regions supervised and even limited the campaign activities of certain candidates. And in fact, they were also involved in the vote-counting process (CNN Indonesia 2018). As a result, fair competition as an indicator of democracy was absent.

Moreover, in the 2019 election, the visions or programmes of the candidates were not readily available for public scrutiny. This was especially the case for legislative candidates—and, in particular, those standing for election to the Dewan Perwakilan Daerah (Senate or DPD, for short). Many DPD candidates were unknowns who were not well exposed during the campaign. Public attention was generally focused on the presidential election rather than the legislative elections, which obscured the programmes of candidates for legislative positions. The election campaign period, in fact, lost its purpose and serious discussion or debate was absent. As a result, many people did not know what the programmes put forth by the various candidates were or even whom to vote for on election day. In short, the notion of political representation has lost its meaning.

Above all, people were highly vulnerable to the influence of fake news and hoaxes and the politicization of identity. Fake news was perpetrated by supporters of all the contestants and was aimed primarily at improving the image of their preferred candidates and character assassination of the opponent. Identity was also politicized and served as a political tool among certain groups to strengthen the legitimacy of their preferred candidate while at the same time attacking that of their opponent. As a result, the quality of the elections and democracy as a whole suffered and the result was that divisions in society were merely accentuated.

Prior to the announcement of the election results by the KPU, another problem arose, namely, the establishment of the "Legal Assistance Team" by Wiranto, Coordinating Minister for Politics, Law and Security (Menkopolhukam). The main aim of this team was to ensure law and order and to determine whether a person or group should be regarded as an enemy of the state. As armed forces commander in the Suharto era, Wiranto was criticized by many as being seized with paranoia and tending to be excessive in his approach to anything out of the ordinary (*Viva.co.id* 2019). Many regarded his team as irrelevant because existing institutions of state had been handling the function of maintaining security and law and order enforcement (*Kompas. com* 2019d, 2019e; *Merdeka.com* 2019). Unfortunately, President Jokowi remained silent on his minister's initiative.

IMPLICATIONS FOR DEMOCRACY

The above political shortcomings will continue if there are no significant efforts to address them. One of the most worrying aspects is the persistence of money politics, which has come to be accepted by politicians and the people in general as a normal facet of politicking. The absence of punitive measures that could act as a deterrent seems to be contributing to the persistence of money politics. Until today, Bawaslu, for instance, is powerless to act against perpetrators of money politics, which allows them to continue the practice with impunity.

Equally disconcerting is the fact that reforms to transform the bureaucracy into a more modern and professional one have yet to be undertaken, resulting in the prevalence of the culture of *ewuh pakewuh*. In the context of political contestation, the bureaucracy lacks impartiality. Without significant improvement, there will always be opportunities to manipulate bureaucratic institutions and turn them into part of a political candidate's electoral machinery.

If such conditions persist, the potential for a weakening of trust in democratic institutions will be higher in the future. Public trust in political parties and the DPR has already receded (LIPI 2012). According to a survey by Litbang Kompas done in September 2019, about 66.2 per cent of the respondents felt their aspirations were not being properly channelled by the political parties or parliamentarians (*Kompas.com* 2019j). This finding relates not only to the fact that the positions of party members and parliamentarians were often seen to be at variance with the aspirations and interests of society in general, but also to people having witnessed behaviour on the part of political parties and their cadres that is not in accordance with ideal politics. It was on this account that the KPK even labelled the party as being at the *epicentrum* or core of political problems, including the rise of corruption and money politics (Suparman 2021). In addition to political parties and the DPR, the KPU and Bawaslu too could potentially find themselves losing some public trust. This is mainly due to their lack of professionalism and weak performance from time to time, including the lack of independence. This situation will worsen if there is no commitment to improve the performance and professionalism of these institutions.

Campaigning could also potentially continue to be plagued by various issues. Political campaigns thus far have still not focused on discussions of programmes nor have they featured profound and meaningful debates; instead, they are characterized by identity politics, personal attacks and even black campaigns and hoaxes. Unfortunately, many contestants for political office and political parties still use and manipulate identity-based narratives to attract attention and political support, which only serves to entrench primordial tensions. Substantive issues seem to be increasingly marginalized by the strengthening of post-truth and populist discourse. In short, campaign tactics carry a high potential for creating division in society, which is counter-productive to strengthening substantial democracy and maintaining national unity.

FACTORS BEHIND THE STAGNATION OF ELECTIONS AND DEMOCRACY

There are several factors contributing to democratic stagnation in Indonesia, as reflected in the 2019 election. The first is the failure of democratic institutions, especially political parties, to perform optimally. Political parties have not been able to live up to their expected roles as bearers of the people's aspirations (Irsyam and Romli 2003; Tan 2006; Noor 2012). There is a high aspiration gap between political parties, including their cadres in parliament, and the aspirations of most people. The gap consists in the following aspects of party behaviour: failing to implement internal democracy, still living under the shadow of the founders of the party or prominent party leaders, frequently violating their own internal party rules, not planning well for party regeneration, and failing to implement their stated ideologies. Such behaviour causes parties to be trapped in their elite interests, becoming nests of oligarchy, prone to corruption, and standing against people's aspirations. Political parties today are among the less trusted democratic institutions in the country.

In the context of elections, members of political parties or candidates supported by the parties are often inclined towards engaging in money politics and violations of various election norms. Most of those who are caught by the KPK on corruption charges have political backgrounds or are politicians. Furthermore, the placement of candidates in electoral districts is often determined not on merit but on pragmatic grounds and often through horse-trading. Party central figures have played key roles in determining the candidate selection process for elections since the first decades of the *Reformasi* era (Haris 2004). As for the KPU and the Bawaslu, although some believe that these two institutions have worked well, others assess that the KPU is not yet truly professional and independent. In the 2019 election, the sudden announcement of election results and the many errors in inputting data are some examples of lack of professionalism, which caused the quality of the elections to be frequently questioned.

The second factor is weak party ideology. Pragmatism rather than ideology dominates the orientation, attitudes and programmes of almost all the parties (Mietzner 2013). The complexity of thought that once influenced the nation's political life has increasingly been abandoned as it is considered not practicable. Ideological debates between or within parties are rare. The main reason is that the public today is not ideologically oriented or easily mobilized by ideas. In such circumstances, people and society in general have become easy targets for money politics. This is reflected in some surveys, which indicate that the number of people who regard money politics as something common or acceptable during the election process is quite high or has increased (*Kompas.com* 2018; Kurniawan and Hermawan 2019, pp. 33–35). However, parties themselves are in fact still not rising above crass methods of approaching the public and actually seem to be taking advantage of the situation.

Pragmatism to some extent overcomes the gridlock that often arises from a rigid and idealistic adherence to ideology. But, on the other hand, it is often tantamount to expediency driven by self-interest and results in a lack of integrity. One of the worst effects of pragmatism is trapping people in identity politics. It also is conducive to "post-truth", where emotional rather than rational/objective narratives are used to win political support. In the context of elections, the cynical attitude to political idealism contributes to the development of unethical and corrupt electoral practices. Maintaining power by all means trumps idealism and the spirit of democracy. In general, the principle of the end justifying the means has become a fact of political life in Indonesia today.

The third factor contributing to stagnation is the high economic disparity in Indonesia. Jeffrey Winters (2014) notes that economic disparity is so acute that only 0.0000002 per cent of the total population controls 10 per cent of the country's gross domestic product. Indonesia's unequal economic-political structure is a legacy of the New Order. Inequality has created two groups in Indonesian society, namely, those who have excessive economic power and those who lack economic independence, resulting in their political dependence. The existence of this dependency relationship has allowed the widespread and open practice of political manipulation. This happens not only at the national level but also at the local level (Kartika 2016; Sutisna 2017). Most importantly, economic inequality has allowed the oligarchs to survive in Indonesia till today. Oligarchs currently control democratic institutions, including political parties, both in the context of management and direction of their interests.

In addition, oligarchs can influence the course of democratic processes from campaigns to voting. Thus, the voting behaviour of the Indonesian people cannot be completely disentangled from the political machinations of the oligarchs. Political candidates often allow themselves to be controlled by the oligarchs so that they can win political contests. These candidates sometimes work in the interests of the oligarchs both before and during campaigns and are able to indulge in money politics through the largesse of the oligarchs. On election day, some of their supporters are even able to engineer the election results to their advantage. This they do by securing roles in the voting committees (KPPS) that conduct the elections and count the votes at each polling station.

The fourth factor is the silence of civil society. This is reflected in the absence of any rigorous efforts to safeguard the quality of elections amid rampant violations. Civil society groups have not been assiduous in complaining about various violations occurring in the conduct of elections. These include violations such as pressure being applied to influence the way people cast their votes, especially when people were inclined to vote for the opposition. Civil society groups also seemed to be oblivious of or indifferent to developments such as Wiranto's establishment of the Legal Assistance Team or the deaths during the riot that occurred after the KPU had announced the results of the presidential election. Government pressure on opposition groups or anti-establishment groups has served to deter civil society groups that could have monitored the elections. On the other hand, many civil society elements have been co-opted into politics, which makes it difficult for them to be neutral, objective and critical of government.

Moreover, the 2019 election also was the most brutal election where the dissemination of fake news and the use of identity politics were concerned. Allegations that one group or the other were "supporters of the caliphate", "radical Muslims" or "anti-Pancasila", on the one hand, or, on the other hand, "Chinese accomplices", "communist minions", "anti-Islam or *kafir*s (infidel)" were widely disseminated during the campaign period.

WHAT MUST BE DONE

Considering that the quality of democracy in general and elections in particular is closely related to the quality of democratic institutions, reforming these institutions is a must. In this case, the institutionalization of political parties (Randal and Svasand 2002; Ufen 2007; Tomsa 2008) becomes especially urgent. In particular, political parties must be encouraged to reform themselves so that they are not merely vehicles for political ambition and advancing the business interests of the oligarchs who dominate those parties from within or outside. Notably, parties should establish disciplined, hierarchically organized structures with clear mechanisms for leadership selection, decision-making and conflict resolution as well as inculcate shared values among their cadres based on their party ideology or principles. In short, they should set in place systems that allow for party regeneration or what among Indonesian scholars is known as "cadrerization" (*kaderisasi*). In addition to having strong financial oversight procedures, parties also must be able to raise funds without becoming beholden to big benefactors. The laws on political parties and elections must be improved to force parties to reform themselves in these aspects (Junaidi et al. 2011; Suprianto and Wulandari 2012; Noor 2018). Both institutionalization and stringent financial management are important in creating party cadres who have integrity and are not easily trapped in oligarchic structures. Although people like Michels (1966) believe that oligarchy is inevitable, it should be reduced to a level where it does not dominate the decision-making process.

The regulations currently in place have not made parties free from the grip of oligarchs—the types who have an interest in establishing close ties to the party or government elites with a view to influencing the policy-making process and expanding their business empires or political interests. These oligarchs could be members of the party or have access to control or influence the party from outside in order to maintain their exclusive benefits. They play a salient role in the electoral process since the existing election regulations allow for "sponsors", both individuals and institutions, who can almost wholly finance a party's activities for national or local elections (Hafidz and Sadikin 2017; Mietzner 2014). Under such conditions, the party's "biggest share" is ultimately owned by a handful of people. Consequently, party cadres, the people who should have ultimate authority on many aspects of party policy, especially strategic policy, become marginalized.

The multiparty system is another aspect that must be reviewed. A simple multiparty system should comprise six to eight parties, with rigid requirements governing the establishment of new parties and their eligibility to participate in elections. The parliamentary threshold could be increased to five per cent from the current four per cent. This change would be part and parcel of efforts to transform parties into more modern and professional entities, which is crucial for democracy. The existence of numerous parties does not guarantee that democracy will be better. Merkl (2005, p. 14) suggests that in an extreme multiparty system with a multitude of parties the linkage function of parties—i.e., the ability of parties to function as the channel through which citizens interact with government and the policy-making process—sometimes becomes difficult to uphold.

Two other institutions that need to be reformed are those responsible for overseeing and implementing elections, namely, KPU and Bawaslu. A more rigorous selection mechanism needs to be established for selecting election commissioners so that more professionals rather than politicians are picked. This would allow for these institutions to be more independent, authoritative and effective in carrying out their duties. The main lesson learnt from elections in the past is that without committed institutions for overseeing and implementing elections, the country will face insurmountable problems (Zein et al. 2015; Firmantoro 2017; Perdana et al. 2018). In addition, some new regulations and approaches are needed to enhance the capacity of these institutions to solve problems related to election rule violations (Siboy 2018).

Apart from reforms to institutions, there is a need to develop political education for the people in order to build a strong democratic mindset (Noor 2018; Habobudin 2016). Political education will help to ensure that democratic values such as equality, participation, freedom and respect for the rule of law can steadily grow and positively influence Indonesia's political processes, including elections. Instilled with such values, the people will have greater awareness of how to carry out political activities in accordance with the constitution and rule of law. With good political education, the public can be more rational in their responses and less susceptible to demagoguery, which eventually could encourage political parties to be more modern and professional in their approaches, including by campaigning on policy platforms rather than by stoking primordial sentiments.

A public that is fairly well educated on democratic politics can also help limit the influence of the oligarchy, which will otherwise continue to grow. Government and the people could support each other to develop political education. In addition, economic development efforts must be geared towards creating prosperity and improving the people's livelihoods so that there is greater political independence (Noor 2018). Ignoring this condition will only bring about a pseudo political participation model, which effectively keeps the people away from having a decisive role in electing their representatives and instead allows the elites and oligarchs to continue to dominate the election and decision-making process.

Strengthening the civil society is also a necessary part of efforts to strengthen democracy and maintain the quality of elections. Many believe that there is a clear correlation between the existence of civil society and the proper functioning of democracy. Civil society helps to ensure that the distributive role of politics—determining who gets what, when and how—works in a proportional manner (Cohen and Arato 1992), that is, it can be expected to be a watchdog to ensure that political institutions function within the boundaries of democracy. A strong civil society (e.g., religious groups, the middle class, labour unions, the mass media, the youth and social activists) also could serve as an effective counterweight to political parties. The various problems that occurred in the 2019 election, including violations of election rules and money politics, attest to the absence of a strong civil society. In addition, a weak and co-opted civil society will allow the government to embark on controversial policies, including limiting the freedom of expression, unchallenged. Thus, in many ways it is clear that the development of a strong civil society is necessary for strengthening democracy.

CONCLUSION

This chapter showed that the 2019 election experienced a number of problems owing to the slow pace of democratic reform. Although public participation in the election was higher than before, several irregularities and setbacks occurred, including money politics, a partisan bureaucracy, lack of media objectivity, identity politics, post-truth manoeuvres, and the influence of the oligarchy. The discussion highlighted the factors behind this situation, namely, the low quality of democratic institutions, the tendency to accord priority to pragmatism over ideology, economic disparity and the weakness of civil society. Comprehensive efforts are needed to improve the quality of democracy, including improving the quality of democratic institutions, strengthening civil society and developing political education for the public. These efforts clearly require strong cooperation from all sectors of the nation; they cannot be solely resolved by the government.

NOTES

1. See *Kompas.com* (2019i). Some others even asked the head of Indonesia Police to resign for this matter. See *Rmol.id* (2019).
2. CNN Indonesia (2019c); Yugo Trianto (2019); *Rmol.id* (2019); *Era Muslim* (2019); Gelora Media (2019). Invitation letters for the voters were also not properly distributed. See *Kumparan* (2019).
3. CNN Indonesia (2019a); *Kompas.com* (2019c); *Tribunnews* (2019b). According to Bawaslu, there were also serious problems related to the Permanent Voter List (DPT) that the KPU could not satisfactorily resolve. See *Tirto.id* (2019). KPU also allowed the police to have copies of C1 vote tabulation forms, which according to Bawaslu is forbidden. See Ansyari and Sadat (2019); *Investor.id* (2019).
4. Interview with Dede Yusuf, Member of Parliament, 26 June 2019, in Jakarta; interview with Nurul Arifin, Member of Parliament, 20 June 2019, in Jakarta; interview with a civil servant, 12 May 2018, in Padang.

REFERENCES

Ambardi, Kuskridho. 2009. *Mengungkap Politik Kartel: Studi tentang Sistem Kepartaian di Indonesia Era Reformasi*. Jakarta: Kepustaan Populer Gramedia.

Amrullah, A. 2009. "Corruption, Politics and *Pilkada* in the Perspective of Corruption Eradication in Indonesia". *Syiar Hukum* 11, no. 3: 271–84.
Aspinall, Edward and Mada Sukmajati. 2015. *Politik Uang di Indonesia, Patronase dan Klientelisme pada Pemilu Legislatif 2014*. Yogyakarta: Polgov.
Aspinall, Edward and Marcus Mietzner. 2010. *Problems of Democratization in Indonesia*. Singapore: Institute of Southeast Asian Studies.
Aspinall, Edward and Ward Berenschot. 2019. *Democracy for Sale, Election, Clientism and the State in Indonesia*. Ithaca: Cornell University Press.
Bunte, Marco and Andreas Ufen. 2009. "The New Order and Its Legacy: Reflections on Democratization in Indonesia". In *Democratization on Post-Suharto Indonesia*, edited by Marco Bunte and Andreas Ufen. London: Routledge.
Choi, Nankyung. 2007. "Local Elections and Democracy in Indonesia". *Contemporary Asia* 37, no. 3: 326–45.
Cohen, Jean and Andrew Arato. 1992. *Civil Society and Political Theory*. Massachusetts: MIT Press.
Davidson, Jamie S. 2009. "Dilemmas of Democratic Consolidation in Indonesia". *The Pacific Review* 22, no. 3: 293–310.
Firmantoro, Zuhad Aji. 2017. *Dilema Penanganan Pelanggaran Pemilu Legislatif*. Yogyakarta: The Phinisi Press.
Ford, Michele and Thomas B. Pepinsky, eds. 2014. *Beyond Oligarchy: Wealth, Power and Contemporary Indonesian Politics*. Ithaca, NY: Cornell Southeast Asia Program Publications, Cornell University Press.
Habobudin, M. 2016. *Pemilu dan Partai Politik di Indonesia*. Malang: UB Press.
Hafidz, Masykurudin and Usep Hasan Sadikin. 2017. *Penyelenggaraan Pilkada Serentak 2015 dan 2017*. Jakarta: Komisi Pemilihan Umum.
Haris, Syamsuddin, ed. 2004. *Pemilu Langsung di Tengah Oligarki Partai: Proses Nominasi dan Seleksi Calon Legislatif Pemilu 2004*. Jakarta: Gramedia, LIPI and IMD.
IDEA. 2002. *Standar-Standar Internasional untuk Pemilihan Umum-Pedoman Peninjauan Kembali Kerangka Hukum Pemilu*. Halmstead: Bulls Trykeri.
Irsyam, Mahrus and Lili Romli, eds. 2003. *Menggugat Partai Politik*. Depok: Laboratorium Ilmu Politik FISIP UI.
Irwan, Alexander and Edriana. 1995. *Pemilu: Pelanggaran Asas Luber. Hegemoni Tak Sampai*. Jakarta: Pustaka Sinar Harapan.
Junaidi, Veri, et al. 2011. *Anomali Keuangan Partai Politik: Pengaturan dan Praktek*. Jakarta: Kemitraan bagi Pembangunan Tata Pemerintahan di Indonesia.
Kartika, Titiek. 2016. *Penyelenggaraan Pilkada Gubernur Bengkulu 2015: Suatu Catatan Pengetahuan tentang Demokrasi di Daerah*. Jakarta: Yayasan Pustaka Obor Indonesia.

Kurniawan, Robi Cahyadi and Dedy Hermawan. 2019. "Strategi Sosial Pencegahan Politik Uang di Indonesia". *Jurnal Antikorupsi Integritas* 1 (June): 29–41.
Mayo, Henry. 1991. *An Introduction to Democratic Theory*. Cambridge: Polity Press.
Merkl, Peter. 2005. "Linkage or What Else? The Place of Linkage Theory in the Study of Political Parties". In *Political Parties and Political Systems: The Concept of Linkage Revisited*, by A.ndrea Röommele, David M. Farrell, and Piero Ignazi. Westport: Praeger.
Michels, Robert. 1966. *Political Parties: A Sociological Study of the Oligarchical Tendencies of Modern Democracy*. New York: The Free Press.
Mietzner, Marcus. 2013. *Money, Power, and Ideology: Political Parties in Post-Authoritarian Indonesia*. Singapore: ASAA Southeast Asia Publication Series, Asian Studies Association of Australia in association with NUS Press and NIAS Press.
―――. 2014. "Oligarchs, Politicians, and Activists: Contesting Party Politics in Post-Soeharto Indonesia". In *Beyond Oligarchy. Wealth, Power and Contemporary Indonesian Politics*, edited by Michele Ford and Thomas B. Pepinsky. Ithaca: Cornell Southeast Asia Program Publications, Cornell University Press.
Mokhsen, Nuraida, Septiana Dwiputranti, and Syaugi Muhammad. 2018. *Pengawasan Netralitas Aparatur Sipil Negara*. Jakarta: Komisi Aparatur Sipil Negara.
Muhtadi, Burhanuddin. 2019. *Vote Buying in Indonesia: The Mechanics of Electoral Bribery*. Singapore: Springer.
Noor, Firman. 2012. "Evaluasi Kondisi Kepartaian 14 Tahun Reformasi dalam Perspektif Pelembagaan sistem Kepartaian". *Masyarakat Indonesia* 38, no. 2 (December): 221–50.
―――. 2017. "The Phenomenon of Post-Democracy Party". *Jurnal Penelitian Politik* 14, no. 2.
―――. 2018. *Partai Politik Sebagai Problem Demokrasi*. Jakarta: LIPI Press.
Perdana, Aditya, Hurriyah, Amri Yusra, Donni Edwin, Panji Anugrah Permana, Syaiful Bahri, and Ikhsan Darmawan. 2018. *DKPP dan Etika Kemandirian dalam Penyelenggaraan Pemilu*. Jakarta: Rajawali Press.
Power, Thomas P. 2018. "Jokowi's Authoritarian Turn and Indonesia's Democratic Decline". *Bulletin of Indonesian Economic Studies* 54, no. 3: 307–38.
Przeworski, Adam. 1991. *Democracy and the Market: Political and Economic Reforms in Eastern Europe and Latin America*. Cambridge: Cambridge University Press.
Pusat Penelitian Politik-LIPI. 2012. *Survei Nasional 25 Juni–10 Juli 2012*. Jakarta: Pusat Penelitian Politik-LIPI.

Rahmawati, Desi. 2018. *Demokrasi dalam Genggaman Para Pemburu Rente*. Yogyakarta: Departemen Politik dan Pemerintahan, UGM.
Randall, Vicky and Lars Svasand. 2002. "Party Institutionalization in New Democracies". *Party Politics* 8, no. 1 (January): 5–29.
Ranney, Austin. 1992. *Governing: An Introduction to Political Science*. New Jersey: Prentice-Hall.
Robison, Richard and Vedi R. Hadiz. 2004. *Reorganising Power in Indonesia: The Politics of Oligarchy in an Age of Markets*. London: RoutledgeCurzon.
Schumpeter, Joseph. 1975. *Capitalism, Socialism and Democracy*. New York: Harper and Row.
Siboy, Ahmad. 2018. *Konstruksi Hukum Pilkada, Jalan Tengah Keadilan Prosedural dan Substansial dalam Penyelesaian Perselisihan Hasil Pilkada Serentak*. Depok: Rajawali Pers.
Slater, Dan. 2004. "Indonesia's Accountability Trap: Party Cartels and Presidential Power after Democratic Transition". *Indonesia* 78: 61–92.
Slater, Dan and Erica Simmons. 2012. "Coping by Colluding: Political Uncertainty and Promiscus Powersharing in Indonesia and Bolivia". *Comparative Political Studies* 46, no. 11: 1366–93.
Supriyanto, Didik and Lia Wulandari. 2012. *Bantuan Keuangan Partai Politik*. Jakarta: Yayasan Perludem.
Sutisna, Agus. 2017. *Memilih Gubernur, Bukan Bandit, Demokrasi Elektoral Pilgub 2017 di Tanah Jawa*. Yogayakarta: Deepublish.
Tan, Paige J. 2006. "Indonesia Seven Years after Soeharto: Party System Institutionalization in a New Democracy". *Contemporary Southeast Asia* 28, no. 1: 88–114.
Tomsa, Dirk. 2008. *Party Politics and Democratization in Indonesia: Golkar in the Post Soeharto Era*. New York: Routledge.
Ufen, Andreas. 2007. "Political Party and Party System Institutionalization in South East Asia: A Comparison of Indonesia, The Philippines and Thailand". *GIGA Working Papers* 44 (March).
Utomo, Sad Dian and Bejo Untung. 2019. *Laporan Hasil Pemantauan Pelanggaran Netralitas ASN dalam Pemilu 2019*. Jakarta: PATTIRO, KASN, KPPOD.
Winters, Jeffrey A. 2004. *Oligarchy*. New York: Cambridge University Press.
_____. 2014. "Oligarchy and Democracy in Indonesia". In *Beyond Oligarchy: Wealth, Power and Contemporary Indonesian Politics*, edited by Michele Ford and Thomas B. Pepinsky. Ithaca: Cornell Southeast Asia Program Publications, Cornell University Press.
Zein, Kurniawan, Alamsyah M. Nur, T. Wratama Rahadi, and Prihatono Hari. 2015. *Asesmen Partisipatif Pemilu 2014: Pemilihan Model Evaluasi Pemilu di Indonesia*. Jakarta: LP3ES.

Other Sources:

Amindoni, Ayomi. 2019. "Puluhan Kepala daerah di Jawa Tengah Langgar Netralitas Pemilu, Apa konsekuensinya?" BBC, 25 February 2019. https://www.bbc.com/indonesia/indonesia-47348188.

Andriansyah, Moch. 2019. "PKB Tuding PDIP Gelembungkan Suara Pileg 2019 Di Surabaya". *Merdeka.com*, 20 April 2019. https://www.merdeka.com/politik/pkb-tuding-pdip-gelembungkan-suara-pileg-2019-di-surabaya.html.

Ansyari, Syahrul and Anwar Sadat. 2019. "KPU Sebut Polisi Boleh Minta Salinan Formulir C1". *Viva.co.id*, 19 April 2019. https://m.viva.co.id/amp/pemilu/berita-pemilu/1141349.

CNN Indonesia. 2018. "SBY Ungkap Oknum BIN Polri Dan TNI Tak Netral Di Pilkada", 23 June 2018. https://www.cnnindonesia.com/nasional/20180623154852-32-308381/sby-ungkap-oknum-bin-polri-dan-tni-tak-netral-di-pilkada.

———. 2019a. "Bawaslu Sebut Ribuan KPPS di Pemilu 2019 Tidak Netral", 17 April 2019. https://www.cnnindonesia.com/nasional/20190417204008-32-387416/bawaslu-sebut-ribuan-kpps-di-pemilu-2019-tidak-netral.

———. 2019b. "Caleg PDIP Jadi Tersangka Pembakaran Kotak Suara Di Jambi", 22 April 2019. https://www.cnnindonesia.com/nasional/20190422113655-12-388416/caleg-pdip-jadi-tersangka-pembakaran-kotak-suara-di-jambi.

———. 2019c. "Salah Input Situng KPU Jokowi Ma'ruf 72, Ditulis 723 Suara", 30 April 2019. https://www.cnnindonesia.com/nasional/20190430095702-32-390738/salah-input-situng-kpu-jokowi-maruf-72-ditulis-723-suara.

Era Muslim. 2019. "Edan! Suara Jokowi Ditambah 500 Prabowo Dikurangi 100 di TPS 18 Malakasari", 22 April 2019. https://www.eramuslim.com/berita/nasional/edan-suara-jokowi-ditambah-500-prabowo-dikurangi-100-di-tps-18-malakasari.htm.

Faktual News. 2019. "Proses Rekapitulasi di Jember Selesai, Hanura Tidak Tanda Tangan", 3 May 2019. http://share.babe.news/s/QNYycmb.

Gelora Media. 2019. "Soroti Kinerja KPU, Mahfud MD: Masak Salah Input Data Sampai di 9 Daerah?", 21 April 2019. https://www.gelora.co/2019/04/soroti-kinerja-kpu-mahfud-md-masak.html.

Hasanudin, Ujang. 2019. "Pilkada Bantul: Ingatkan Soal Netralitas Bawaslu Datangi OPD". *Harian Jogja*, 12 November 2019. https://jogjapolitan.harianjogja.com/read/2019/11/12/511/1024519/.

Investor.id. 2019. "Bawaslu: Polisi Tidak Boleh Pegang Salinan Formulir C1", 23 April 2019. https://investor.id/national/bawaslu-polisi-tidak-boleh-pegang-salinan-formulir-c1.

Kompas.com. 2018. "Survei SSC: 99 Persen Pemilih Pilkada Jatim Akan Terima 'Serangan Fajar'", 22 June 2018. https://regional.kompas.com/

read/2018/06/22/19293321/survei-ssc-99-persen-pemilih-pilkada-jatim-akan-terima-serangan-fajar.

———. 2019a. "Caleg PDIP Tersangka Pembakaran Kotak Suara Ditangkap Saat Bersembunyi", 22 April 2019. https://regional.kompas.com/read/2019/04/22/15071451/caleg-pdi-p-tersangka-pembakaran-kotak-suara-ditangkap-saat-bersembunyi.

———. 2019b. "Datangi KPU, Pimpinan Parpol Di Surabaya Bawa Bukti Praktik Penggelembungan", 22 April 2019. https://regional.kompas.com/read/2019/04/22/17374351/datangi-kpu-pimpinan-parpol-di-surabaya-bawa-bukti-praktik-penggelembungan.

———. 2019c. "Viral Video Petugas KPPS di Boyolali Cobloskan Surat Suara Warga, Bawaslu: Kita Surati KPU untuk PSU", 25 April 2019. https://regional.kompas.com/read/2019/04/25/13065031/viral-video-petugas-kpps-di-boyolali-cobloskan-surat-suara-warga-bawaslu.

———. 2019d. "Amnesty Internasional Nilai Tim Hukum Nasional Rawan Disalahgunakan", 10 May 2019. https://nasional.kompas.com/read/2019/05/10/10161001/amnesty-internasional-nilai-tim-hukum-nasional-rawan-disalahgunakan?page=all.

———. 2019e. "Adian Napitupulu Nilai Tim Hukum Bentukan Wiranto Tidak Diperlukan", 12 May 2019. https://nasional.kompas.com/read/2019/05/12/22042491/adian-napitupulu-nilai-tim-hukum-bentukan-wiranto-tidak-diperlukan.

———. 2019f. "Data Kemenkes: 527 Petugas KPPS Meninggal, 11.239 Orang Sakit", 16 May 2019. https://nasional.kompas.com/read/2019/05/16/17073701/data-kemenkes-527-petugas-kpps-meninggal-11239-orang-sakit?page=all.

———. 2019g. "Demo Penolakan Hasil Pilpres Berujung Rusuh, Ini Komentar BPN Prabowo", 22 May 2019. https://nasional.kompas.com/read/2019/05/22/14095491/demo-penolakan-hasil-pilpres-berujung-rusuh-ini-komentar-bpn-prabowo.

———. 2019h. "KPK Selesai Hitung 400.000 Amplop Bowo Sidik, Ditemukan Total Rp. 8,45 Miliar", 23 May 2019. https://nasional.kompas.com/read/2019/05/23/18580291/kpk-selesai-hitung-400000-amplop-bowo-sidik-ditemukan-total-rp-845-miliar.https

———. 2019i. "Misteri Tewasnya Harun Al Rasyid di Kerusuhan 22 Mei Mulai Terkuak", 6 July 2019. https://nasional.kompas.com/read/2019/07/06/08294541/misteri-tewasnya-harun-al-rasyid-di-kerusuhan-22-mei-mulai-terkuak?page=all.

———. 2019j. "Litbang Kompas: 66,2 persen responden merasa aspirasiny tidak terwakili DPR", 23 September 2019. https://nasional.kompas.com/read/2019/09/23/08370591/litbang-kompas-662-persen-responden-merasa-aspirasinya-tak-terwakili-dpr?page=all.

Kumparan. 2019. "Bawaslu Bali Temukan Ratusan Ribu Undangan Memilih Belum dikirim", 16 April 2019. https://kumparan.com/kumparannews/bawaslu-bali-temukan-ratusan-ribu-undangan-memilih-belum-dikirim-1qtp7cPyUjg.

Liputan 6. 2019. "Bawaslu dan Mendagri Diminta Tindak ASN dan Kepala Daerah Tak Netral di Pemilu", 27 February 2019. https://www.liputan6.com/pilpres/read/3904851/bawaslu-dan-mendagri-diminta-tindak-asn-dan-kepala-daerah-tak-netral-di-pemilu.

Merdeka.com. 2019. "Komnas HAM Sebut Tim Hukum Nasional Bentukan Wiranto Mirip Pangkopkamtib Era Soeharto", 11 May 2019. https://www.merdeka.com/peristiwa/komnas-ham-sebut-tim-hukum-nasional-bentukan-wiranto-mirip-pangkopkamtib-era-soeharto.html.

Nurita, Dewi. 2019. "Soal Ribuan Pelanggaran Netralitas ASN Begini Tindaklanjut KASN". *Temp.co*, 10 June 2019. https://pemilu.tempo.co/read/1213263/soal-ribuan-pelanggaran-netralitas-asn-begini-tindaklanjut-kasn.

Republika.id. 2019. "BPN Resmi Laporkan 1200 Dugaan Kecurangan Pilpres 2019", 20 April 2019. https://www.republika.co.id/berita/pq9ja7430/bpn-resmi-laporkan-1200-dugaan-kecurangan-pilpres-2019.

Rmol.id. 2014. "Arif Wibowo: PDIP Akan Menempuh Jalur Hukum Gugat DPT", 2 January 2014. https://rmol.id/read/2014/01/02/138485/arif-wibowo-pdip-akan-menempuh-jalur-hukum-gugat-dpt.

_____. 2019. "6,7 Juta Pemilih Tidak Dapat C6, Benteng Prabowo Minta KPU Diadili", 22 April 2019. https://politik.rmol.id/read/2019/04/22/387119/6-7-juta-pemilih-tidak-dapat-c-6-benteng-prabowo-minta-kpu-diadili.

_____. 2019. "PB HMI Minta Kapolri Mundur Karena Pengamanan Aksi 22 Mei Langgar HAM", 26 May 2019. https://politik.rmol.id/read/2019/05/26/391111/PB-HMI-Minta-Kapolri-Tito-Mundur-Karena-Pengamanan-Aksi-22-Mei-Langgar-HAM-.

Rosandya, Rindy. 2018. "Duh, Mahalnya Ongkos Pileg 2019". *Harian Ekonomi Neraca*, 15 September 2018. https://www.neraca.co.id/article/106157/duh-mahalnya-ongkos-pileg-2019.

Suparman, Fana F. 2021. "KPK Sebut Sistem Politik dan Parpol Episentrum Persoalan Korupsi di Indonesia". *BeritaSatu*, 29 January 2021. .https://www.beritasatu.com/nasional/725369/kpk-sebut-sistem-politik-dan-parpol-episentrum-persoalan-korupsi-di-indonesia.

Tempo.co. 2019a. "Bowo Sidik Mengaku Mendapatkan Rp. 2 M Dari Menteri Enggartiasto", 22 April 2019. https://nasional.tempo.co/read/1197734/bowo-sidik-mengaku-mendapatkan-rp-2-m-dari-menteri-enggartiasto.

_____. 2019b. "Bawaslu Temukan 1.096 Pelanggaran Netralitas", 7 June 2019. https://pemilu.tempo.co/read/1212776/bawaslu-temukan-1-096-pelanggaran-netralitas.

Tirto.id. 2019. "Banyak Masalah Soal DPT, Bawaslu Kritik Coklit KPU Tak Maksimal", 19 March 2019. https://tirto.id/banyak-masalah-soal-dpt-bawaslu-kritik-coklit-kpu-tak-maksimal-djQb.

Tribunnews. 2019a. "Temukan 1.200 Dugaan Kecurangan Pilpres 2019 BPN Prabowo Sandiaga Sudah Lapor ke Bawaslu", 20 April 2019. https://www.tribunnews.com/pilpres-2019/2019/04/20/temukan-1200-dugaan-kecurangan-pilpres-2019-bpn-prabowo-sandiaga-sudah-lapor-ke-bawaslu.

──────. 2019b. "Soal Dugaan Kecurangan Pemilu, Effendi Simbolon Ungkap Ada Calo di Tingkat Kecamatan", 27 April 2019. http://share.babe.news/s/dRcsdcS.

Viva.co.id. 2019. "Wiranto: Penangkapan Tokoh-Tokoh akan Terus Dilakukan", 21 May 2019. https://www.viva.co.id/berita/nasional/1151016-wiranto-penangkapan-tokoh-tokoh-akan-terus-dilakukan.

VOA Indonesia. 2019. "Peringkat Kebebasan Pers Indonesia Stagnan, Peringkat AS Merosot", 3 May 2019. https://www.voaindonesia.com/a/peringkat-kebebasan-pers-indonesia-stagnan-peringkat-as-merosot/4901413.html.

Yugo Trianto, Ismail. 2019. "Selisih Suara Puluhan Ribu, Saksi Gerindra Minta Hentikan Pleno". *Sindonews.com*, 24 April 2019. https://daerah.sindonews.com/berita/1398609/174/selisih-suara-puluhan-ribu-saksi-gerindra-minta-hentikan-pleno.

Interviews:

Interview with Nurul Arifin, Member of Parliament, Jakarta, 20 June 2019
Interview with Dede Yusuf, Member of Parliament, Jakarta, 26 June 2019
Interview with Bureaucrat (ASN), Padang, 12 May 2018

3

UNDERSTANDING INDONESIA'S DEMOCRACY: CLASS, CLIQUES AND POLITICS AFTER THE 2019 ELECTIONS

Max Lane

By the end of 2020, Indonesia's post-1998 form of rule in its more perfect form had been trialled for over a year. In this chapter, I argue that the form of rule changed after 1998 from that of *clique rule* under a *class absolutist* form of state to that of *collective clique rule* under a slightly weakened form of class absolutism. During the years 1998 to 2019, collective clique rule was marred by divisions created by rivalries between cliques, which, in the 2013–19 period, also saw several infringements of the rules of the game that had been accepted by all the participating cliques. In late 2019, however, President Joko Widodo (Jokowi), together with his trusted cabinet minister Luhut Pandjaitan, established the broadest ever collectivity of cliques as the basis for a coalition government. Its establishment guaranteed a greater deal of stability to Indonesian political life—at least for the last twelve months—than any previous ruling configuration had. But how long will such stability last?

There can be no doubt that a major change in the form of governance has taken place in Indonesia since May 1998. The resignation of President Suharto in the face of escalating mass opposition, under the banner of *Reformasi*, ended an extended era of authoritarian government that had lasted thirty-two years.[1] In order to understand the precise nature of this change, we need also to be precise about the character of the authoritarian rule that collapsed, especially in relation to which of its elements did and did not survive its collapse.

THE NEW ORDER: CLASS ABSOLUTISM AND CLIQUE RULE

The New Order emerged through the process of Sukarno's overthrow and the physical and institutional elimination of all those forces supporting the Sukarno–Left alliance that had grown in popularity between 1957 and 1965 but had not achieved government. This meant the destruction, in particular, of the Indonesian Communist Party (PKI) and the majority left wing of the Indonesian National Party (PNI) and the various mass organizations connected to those two parties (as well as some smaller parties). Furthermore, as was specifically articulated in New Order political publications, and as is still contained in school textbooks today, this suppression included the suppression of that specific mode of politics that was based on the competitive and open mobilization of grassroots support behind different ideological perspectives. This policy of suppression was known as the *floating mass* policy.

Central to the *floating mass* policy was a ban on membership of political parties at the village and small-town levels and the "simplification" of the numerous political parties, from more than ten to only three, all of which were also subject to direct government intervention in their internal affairs. By that time the PKI and other left-wing parties had already been banned and annihilated. Additionally, all mass organizations—such as trade unions and peasant organizations—were "simplified", in the sense that only one of each kind of mass organization was allowed, and these were effectively placed under direct government control. A formal ban was also imposed on the "spreading of Marxism-Leninism". The concrete manifestation of this was the ban on all left-wing publishing and the withdrawal from circulation of many writings, including the speeches from after 1945 of Sukarno, the country's founding president (Lane 2008).

The state policies described above continued without serious interruption for thirty-two years. Furthermore, this thirty-two-year stretch of anti-mobilization authoritarianism began only fifteen years after the colonial power had left Indonesia (in 1949–50). During the period 1950–65, while there was generally extensive open, competitive political mobilization, this was not a part of any consolidated system of governance but a period of deepening contestation about what kind of governance would be eventually consolidated. The system of governance that began in 1965 and lasted thirty-two years was the first-ever consolidated system of governance in Indonesia, which, having been consolidated so soon after independence, has also served to form and *define* contemporary Indonesia.

These general conditions—centrally embodied in the floating mass policy and ideology and the physical suppression of popular mobilization as a mode of politics—established what can be called *class absolutism*. Non-elite popular classes *were entirely eliminated as participating subjects* in all formal political life, even as opposition or marginal actors. Ideologies—both moderate (social democracy) and radical (socialist-communist)—that have been historically reproduced through the participation in politics of non-elite forces in capitalist societies,[2] including Indonesia since colonial times, also disappeared from political life. It should be emphasized here that the influence of non-elite classes did not simply decrease, but rather *entirely disappeared* as any kind of political actor in national politics. The elite class ruled absolutely.

In most industrialized societies, including Japan, the evolution of a clear bi-class political economy gave rise to large trade union movements, with social democratic parties based upon or at least linked to those trade unions. This also gave rise to electoral systems that had two major, seemingly opposing parties at their core, with smaller parties positioned in relation to those two core parties.[3] In non-industrialized developing countries, including most of Asia, the extent to which non-elite political forces have been effective as subjects in the political processes *has been dependent not on the labour movement but the political and ideological legacies of anti-colonial movements*. Such legacies have less of a consolidated base and a weakened reason to exist in the post-independence political economies and have therefore been more easily suppressed, co-opted or demobilized. In Indonesia's case, after 1965, that legacy was totally destroyed. Being the only form of consolidated governance the country has ever experienced, the thirty-two-year period of class absolutism has left a fundamental and foundational legacy for everything that has come after it. Indeed, even twenty years after the fall of Suharto, the key socio-political foundations of absolutist class rule remain in place.

If the overall national mode of governance, and of political life, was class absolutism, the specific form of rule was *clique rule*. This concept needs elaboration as Indonesia's clique rule was specific to its own historical development.

CLIQUE RULE

The political suppression which was the foundation of the New Order was aimed at those organizations that had been mobilizing class forces at the grassroots level on mass scales: the PKI and the left wing of the PNI. The new regime, under Major General Suharto, did inherit a legacy of suppression of other forces, namely elements from the leaderships of three political blocs that had actually also been opposed to the PKI and PNI (Left). The Masyumi Party, the Indonesian Socialist Party (PSI) and the Murba Party had been banned by the Sukarno government. The Suharto regime did not lift the bans on these blocs but rather entered into negotiation with them. The latter eventually accepted a subdued role under the new regime, whose power was centred in the hands of Suharto and his clique of generals. The Masyumi Party was allowed to restart under a new name (Parmusi) but without any of its pre-1965 leaders allowed to hold positions. The PSI remained banned as did Murba, although a Murba figure, Adam Malik, was appointed foreign minister under Suharto for a while (and later became vice-president) and PSI-connected academics also became cabinet ministers.

In late 1965, there were no social forces, including within the political and business elite, that could offer any serious political challenge to the concentration of power in Suharto's clique of generals.[4] Even the non-left political parties could be subdued easily, having been saved from oblivion by Suharto's suppression of the Left. The biggest players in the business elite were military officers running state-owned companies arising from the nationalization of Dutch and other foreign companies.

These companies, in fact, comprised almost the whole of the modern sector of the economy in the late 1950s. As this was during a period of martial law, military officers could manage the companies without having to account to any higher authority.

The resolution of an elite-mass conflict in a situation where the elite was tiny, and where the civilian elements of the elite (Masyumi, the PSI and the PNI right wing) were weak, delivered power into the hands not of the elite as a whole but into the best-armed section of the elite, the army officers around the head of the Army Strategic Command (KOSTRAD), Major General Suharto.

The thirty-year period between 1968, by which time the suppression of the PKI and PNI (Left) was more or less completed, and 1998 saw the character of this clique rule evolve through various phases. The most important aspect of the evolution was its transformation from being a clique almost solely based on military power to one based on combined military and conglomerate capital power. The clique also had to deal with the growth and increased complexity of the political and business elite, both at national and local levels, in which its status as a single, hegemonic entity was becoming more complicated. By the 1990s, before the clique could work out a formula to deal with its place in a much bigger ruling layer than that which had existed in the 1970s, it also faced increasing resistance from a wave of youth-led rebellion from outside the elite, that is, from below.

As resistance from below escalated after 1989 (Lane 2008), and in the crisis period of 1997–98, but before any new formula for a broader elite regime could be established, Suharto had no choice but to appoint the most clique-rule-based cabinet of his whole time in power, appointing even his daughter, Tutut Suharto, and his close business crony, Bob Hasan, as ministers. The New Order's discussions of proposals for the decentralization of governance were not able to come to fruition before the collapse of this clique rule.[5]

THE END OF AUTHORITARIANISM: TWO AXES OF CHANGE

President Suharto's resignation resulted in two major overall changes. The first was a decisive end to clique rule and its replacement by an electoral system which has facilitated various power-sharing arrangements between the numerous factions (cliques) of the broader political and business elite. The form of governance shifted from single-clique rule to rule by a shifting coalition of cliques, or, more precisely, *rule by a shifting coalition of elite factions*. The second change was the weakening of, though not a decisive end to, *absolutist class rule*. This involved the relaxation of restrictions on "grassroots" organizing and of ideological indoctrination. It is these two changes that have been the basis for the "democratization"—*i.e., expansion of democratic space*—that has occurred since 1998. The fundamental factor here is expansion of *space* (reduction of repression) rather than expansion or broadening of participation in decision-making.

The Weakening of Absolutist Class Rule and its Contradictions

The major restriction on class-struggle-based ideology—the ban on the spread of Marxism–Leninism—has remained in place. Signalling that this ban could be relaxed was one of the factors in President Abdurrahman Wahid's loss of support within the political elite in 2001. Since then, the consensus among the political and business elite has been to support and retain this restriction. At the same time, during the Habibie presidency, the restrictions on the formation of trade unions were significantly eased, resulting in the rapid mushrooming of thousands of new or reconstituted enterprise unions and the emergence of new unions and confederations of unions (Lane 2019).

Equally important, in the immediate aftermath of May 1998, the army had to accept its withdrawal from direct political activity, namely repressive activity (except in Papua, and for a few years in Aceh[6]). This also increased the space for more grassroots-based political activism.

Despite these changes, however, no national-scale labour- or peasant-based political movements have emerged in Indonesia since 1998. Between 2010 and 2013 there was an escalation of trade union activity around socio-economic issues. Before this could create a sustained level of activity on a national scale, the leading unions retreated into electoral activity, ultimately dividing into two main camps. One grouping aligned with the Jokowi government, while the other with the Gerindra "opposition", led by Prabowo Subianto. A spectrum of smaller unions supported neither camp and have not entered electoral politics; their leaderships usually contain elements that can be traced back to the grassroots and student movement of the 1990s that opposed

Suharto.[7] Having subordinated themselves to the parties of the elite factions, the larger trade unions thus have not developed as a challenge to the absolutist nature of elite rule. Labour has no serious bargaining power in national politics.[8] This lack of power is also reflected in its failure to mount any effective resistance to a new regulation in 2017 ending annual negotiations over minimum wage levels or the widespread practice of outsourcing, let alone campaign for a broader range of policy changes. The unions have also been unable to prevent the passing of a new law in 2020 that severely restricts their political and economic rights (Lane 2020b).

This marginalization of the labour movement in national politics is not a product of current suppression but of several generations of almost totalitarian suppression between 1965 and 1998. Apart from having to re-organize out of formerly state-controlled unions, the labour movement lacks both ideological and experiential continuity. In addition, only a tiny percentage of the workforce is employed on a permanent or semi-permanent basis in medium or large workplaces, which are the only ones sufficiently modern in industrial terms for mobilization into unions.

The rural population is even less organized, except for sporadic local campaigns that have not generated any movement at the national level. There are large religious organizations with bases in rural society, but their political orientations are towards one or other of the existing political parties.[9]

There has, however, been a real expansion of the democratic space for grassroots organizing and ideological discussion compared to the period before 1998. While there are regulations that make some policy demands harder to achieve, and also harassment by local authorities during specific disputes, there has been no systematic regime suppression of unions or other sectoral organizations. Although there have been small waves of local authorities harassing bookshops selling left-wing books, there is no systematic regime suppression of any activity espousing alternative ideologies. There are more radical and leftist publications, websites and public forums today than in any period of post-Suharto Indonesia.

During Megawati Sukarnoputri's presidency, political activists who attacked her regime were arrested and tried on charges of insulting the head of state. More than forty activists were sentenced to over two years in jail (Human Rights Watch 2003). This kind of national-scale political imprisonment did not occur under Susilo Bambang Yudhoyono, nor has it occurred under Jokowi. Local authorities have charged and sentenced environmental and farmer activists, and there have been many documented cases of deaths in land conflict cases. But such acts are the result of local authorities being allowed to act with little oversight rather than the initiation of a systematic policy of suppression. Campaigns for agrarian- and other land-related causes have been allowed to continue.

During the Yudhoyono period, right-wing militia groups were able to harass the more radical activist political groups, such as Papernas, to the point of threatening their development and even survival (*Detik.com* 2007). However, there was no state repression of such groups. Their collapse has more to do with broader objective conditions flowing from the ideological and cultural legacies of the 1965–98 period, similar to how the growth of trade unions has been constrained by general objective conditions.

It should be pointed out here also that there has been no retreat by civil society opposition groups—unions, other sectoral organizations, human rights organizations, etc.—in their criticism of government policy or figures. Between October 2019 and October 2020, the issues of corruption, violence in Papua and labour and environmental abuses aroused substantial protest movements. That these protests occurred in spite of arrests and even several trials and prison sentences suggests they are likely to continue (Lane 2019b, 2020b).

The level of open hostility in the media, not to mention in the social media, that is expressed towards government policy and officials, including the president (and even towards the elite among the opposition) is far greater than in many liberal democracies of the West.[10] While there has been no systematic regime suppression of any of this dissent, the fact that regime power is now based on a coalition of competing elite factions and cliques has strained the codes of conduct among these competing elements since some of them have missed out on securing a place in the coalition. A culture of reporting each other under the Undang-undang Informasi dan Transaksi Elektronik (Law on Information and Electronic Transactions or UU ITE, for short) for criminal libel has resulted in people from a wide spectrum being charged, put on trial and even jailed. This culture of mutual reporting among the elite has legitimized the practice in general.[11] In August 2019, Jakarta-based activists supporting self-determination for Papua were arrested as a result of an individual reporting their activities. They were later sentenced to nine months in prison and released in May 2020. This is a by-product of the mutually predatory and self-interested nature of all the elite factions.

Grassroots and progressive political activity has not yet grown to a level where it can assert a presence in mainstream national political life. This is a result of the difficulties these embryonic movements face in overcoming the weaknesses inherited as a result of the legacies of 1965–98, as well as the exhaustion that results from facing ongoing harassment by local state apparatus. However, the regime has not initiated *systematic* repression of political activities by non-elite activist groups.

THE END OF CLIQUE RULE, ELECTORAL DEMOCRACY AND ITS CONTRADICTIONS

Despite the sustained opening up of democratic space, even if imperfectly protected, especially since the end of the Megawati presidency, some observers of Indonesian politics note that there has been a significant regression of democratic political life "under Widodo's watch" (Power and Warburton 2020). Notable among these observers are those who had uncritically supported Jokowi in 2013/14. What lies behind these concerns? There are two aspects in the answers to this question. One concerns the serious flaws of analysis and perspective by some of the uncritical supporters of Jokowi in 2013/14 and the contortions of analysis that flow from that today. This is the less important or significant aspect. The second, and more important aspect, relates to the problems faced by electoral democracy as a mechanism for managing power-sharing among a large number of elite factions/cliques following the end of *single-clique rule* and erosion of class absolutism.

A major theoretical problem in much analysis of post-authoritarian Indonesia relates to the idea of a "transition to democracy" that is assumed to be taking place since 1998. A transition is certainly taking place and that transition has brought with it more democratic space, that is to say, less repression and even a total end to systematic regime repression of political activity. However, the particular usage of the term "democracy" by many commentators confuses the situation. This is because their understanding of the term draws from their romanticized notion of liberal democracy in the "West".

Hadiz and Robison (2004), in their first book after the fall of Suharto, argue that there is no transition under way at all since 1998. For them, the "democracy" that has evolved since 1998 is "illiberal democracy", which, as such, will not "transition" to a more perfect goal, presumably a more perfect liberal democracy. For them, the cry that democracy may even be regressing in Indonesia at this point may very well seem logical and unsurprising.

I wish to argue, however, that the point is not to debate the extent to which Indonesia is transitioning towards a model liberal democracy. For the notion of a model liberal democracy is highly romanticized: money politics is not uncommon in the Netherlands or Australia or the United States. The more useful approach is to try to explain what is happening in Indonesia in its own terms rather than in relation to a "transition" towards some idealized end goal.

The period from 1998 until now can be best understood as a transition from class absolutist clique rule to a weakened class absolutist clique regime in which power is shared by competing cliques.

The political life of the non-elite (grassroots) sector has experienced greatly expanded democratic space, despite occasional harassment by local state apparatus. On the other hand, the political life of the broad political and business elite has experienced a massive expansion in the "democratic space" in which it operates. The most obvious manifestation of this is that different factions and cliques within this elite now have the right and capacity to pursue their individual ambitions through their own political parties, media and other institutions. There were twenty political parties that had sufficient financial backing from within the elite to be considered eligible to participate in the 2019 elections. Unlike the three parties that were allowed to exist during the New Order, these parties all operate free from state intervention in their internal affairs. No holds have been barred in terms of what they can say, and what they have said, about each other. There has been an almost free-for-all atmosphere in terms of what members of the public can say about one another, with no formal restrictions prohibiting such speech. Many activists were sent to jail in 2003 for two years for "insulting the head of state", but open attacks and insults on a president by hostile factions from within the elite incurred no punishment. The exception is when different elite elements are happy to report each other to the police and see rivals go to jail.

While legal restrictions on such freedoms of speech have been absent, or weak, practical considerations have constrained elite cliques. These relate to the *primary function* of the post-1998 electoral system, namely, to order the sharing of power between the factions. The primary form of this power-sharing involves coalitions, both to govern and to struggle to gain government. There is no one faction of the elite that can win anywhere near majority public support in an election. The need to be open to coalitions *with anybody and in any combination* has meant that there is also a need for a certain level of civility, the need for accepted "rules of the game" for electoral competition. It has been this acceptance of more or less civil rules of the game during the period from Megawati's presidency until around 2017/18 that has allowed the electoral system to operate as a power-sharing mechanism with minimum resort to repressive actions against other elite elements. Those who most frequently break these rules, such as reporting rivals to the police, are the ones who find themselves excluded from the major coalitions.

The consensus among a very fractured political and business elite that electoral politics should be constrained within a civil power-sharing arrangement, avoiding even the term "opposition" wherever possible, flows from the post-Suharto political economy. The capitalist class is fractured because it is at the district and provincial levels that the majority of businesses are concentrated. (This is a reflection of the extreme under-industrialization of the country.) Political parties tend to have their main bases in particular geographic areas, tied to local business and bureaucratic elites. Bigger capital—conglomerates and larger companies serving the national market—are not aligned to specific political groups, except in opportunistic ways. There are no serious objections among any significant sector of large-scale national business to the way foreign capital is being enticed into the country. Anti-foreign capital agitation occurs mainly at the demagogic level, hoping to attract the support of dissatisfied sectors of the population open to xenophobic politics. Left-wing criticism of foreign capital exists but is so far confined to groups as yet unable to assert a presence in national politics.

There is one cleavage that can perhaps be identified which has played a role in recent national-level politics. Those capitalists with the longest and deepest history of connection with the crony capitalism of the Suharto era, such as the Suharto family members themselves, were also concentrated within the coalition supporting the candidacy of the Prabowo–Sandiaga Uno team in the 2019 presidential election. It was clear throughout the lead-up to the campaign and during the campaign that Prabowo's approach to coalition building was different from that of Jokowi's. Jokowi's approach was to build a coalition of a majority of the elite factions/parties through making concessions. Prabowo's approach eschewed making concessions, more or less demanding hegemony within such a coalition. This seems to reflect a hankering for a return to the Suharto-era style of clique rule. Jokowi's win in 2019 defeated the approach, resulting in a rapprochement (Lane 2020a) between Jokowi and Prabowo and a disappearance of this cleavage from mainstream politics.

Since 2017 (perhaps it could even be argued since 2013/14), some of the unspoken rules of the game have been violated. Even though there were sharp tensions between Yudhoyono and Megawati in 2004, and again in 2009, certain "rules" were adhered to. Probably the two most important of these rules were: (1) there should be no serious black propaganda against each other; and (2) there is to be no mass mobilization on the basis of religious identity or other use of religious identity for electoral purposes. There was also a general consensus that there should be no political initiatives outside the electoral arena: that extra-parliamentary activity and manoeuvres be avoided. It should be noted that in 2004, when Prabowo was chosen as Megawati's vice-presidential candidate, these norms were also adhered to.

During Yudhoyono's presidency, when he brought the Islamist Partai Keadilan Sejahtera (Prosperous Justice Party or PKS, for short) into his government and also made concessions to conservative political Islam in strengthening and using the blasphemy law, there was still no major use of religious identity as an electoral weapon against an opponent.

In 2013 and 2014, this consensus started to break down. The process of breakdown accelerated in 2016–17 in the campaign to unseat Jakarta Governor Basuki Tjahaja Purnama (Ahok), who had replaced Jokowi after the latter's election as president. The first and most overt sign of the erosion of this consensus was the escalation of black propaganda against Jokowi, with claims that he was a member of the PKI and was not a genuine Muslim. Rumours also circulated on social media that he was actually of Chinese descent. Campaigning of this sort and level of escalation was a new phenomenon and attracted a lot of comments. The black propaganda against Jokowi, which was also carried in a hard copy newspaper, was not a part of any official campaign by Prabowo, who never made any such accusations. However, the campaign was undertaken by other elements as part of their efforts to weaken Jokowi's position vis-à-vis that of Prabowo.

While the issue of religion was not the primary issue in these first attacks against Jokowi, it was certainly already present. Furthermore, key propagandists for such claims were often figures associated with conservative Muslim organizations. The use of black propaganda, subsequently labelled as "hoaks", escalated in 2017, when the campaign began against Governor Purnama, demanding that he be arrested for blasphemy after he had made statements regarding what Islamic scripture taught about choosing non-Muslim leaders (Setijadi 2017). This was the first nationally significant political campaign using mass mobilization as a method since the fall of President Wahid. It used direct appeals to religious identity. It merged with electoral politics when Prabowo appeared to give it support by attending events organized by what has come to be called the 212 Movement, a hardline Islamist movement in which Habib Rizieq Shihab, also holding the position of grand imam of the Front Pembela Islam (Islamic Defenders Front or FPI, for short), played a central role.[12]

Prabowo's alignment with the 212 Movement challenged the hitherto accepted rules of the game for electoral contestation. His move constituted alignment with forces using religious identity for mobilization. These forces were also part of the elements resorting to the anti-Jokowi black propaganda campaign in general. Prabowo's association with the 212 Movement and the FPI leadership drew into the fray organized political forces that had not been "legalized" through the political party verification process. Again, Prabowo's own statements remained essentially "secular" and he himself never resorted to black propaganda campaigning. However, he had aligned himself with the momentum that had come out of the anti-Purnama movement. He had also attended assemblies of Islamic teachers and preachers that were associated with the 212 Movement.

This rupture with the post-Wahid rules of the game had still another manifestation. Again, this was not the result, it would seem, of moves by forces directly led by Prabowo, but by elements supporting him. In early December 2016, a grouping of mostly late-

New Order politicians and prominent figures met to discuss what I would consider the unrealistic prospect of mobilizing people to occupy parliamentary buildings as part of a process to force a change of government (*Tempo.co* 2016). As far as the evidence to date shows, this was something that never went beyond their own speculation as to that possibility. The police arrested some of these figures and charged them with attempted *makar* (a coup d'etat), although no further action seems to have been taken since then and none are in jail. But neither have the charges been withdrawn, it appears. One of those charged, Rachmawati Sukarnoputri, later became part of the Prabowo campaign team structure.

Until shortly after the 2019 election campaign, what had been a relatively civil process for managing power-sharing among the elite as a whole had become a less civil process. The state apparatus, whether with or without central direction, took repressive actions, for example, banning mobilizations such as the Ganti President (Change the President) rallies, organized by non-party supporters of Prabowo (Harmawan 2018). Pro-government individuals and groups started to replicate what the 212 campaign had started: reporting individuals to the police for blasphemy or other forms of hate speech. Rizieq, who had supported charging Purnama with blasphemy, was himself reported for *penistaan* (sacrilege) against the Pancasila. Tit-for-tat reporting to police escalated.[13] Some pro-Prabowo figures, such as the famous pop singer Ahmad Dhani, have ended up in jail, as well as the Jokowi-aligned Purnama, who served his full sentence of two years.

As the Islamist aspect of the anti-Jokowi campaigning escalated, the government eventually moved to issue a decree to ban the Hizbut Tahir Indonesia (HTI) on the grounds that its advocacy of an Islamic caliphate for Indonesia was in opposition to the official state ideology of Pancasila (which implies there is no special status for any one religion) (Burhani 2017). The decree asserted the government had the right to ban, without resort to the courts, any organization that was in contradiction to Pancasila. To date, this regulation has not been used again.

While it is likely that a detailed study of previous incumbents might show their use of state resources for campaigning (which also happens regularly in Australia, for example), there is no doubt this kind of activity increased in 2018–19.

After the 2019 election, the rules of the game eroded further, also revealing contradictions. Team Prabowo–Sandiaga claimed that there had been massive, systematic cheating in the elections. Prabowo had even declared himself the winner and he and Sandiaga challenged the results in the Constitutional Court. The campaign to challenge the validity of the election results sharpened a contradiction among those forces supporting Prabowo, pitting those, including Prabowo and Sandiaga themselves, who wished to continue operating within electoral politics as a power-sharing mechanism, and those who rejected that framework. The contradiction became focused on the issue of whether or not anti-government mass mobilization should continue, for example outside the Constitutional Court. While Prabowo issued repeated appeals on YouTube for mass mobilization to stop, elements from those associated with the 212 Movement continued to mobilize the people.

This contradiction reached an important peak on 21–22 May, when, following earlier peaceful mobilizations in the morning of 21 May, organized groups arrived at the Constitutional Court building and faced off the police in a confrontational manner. Several people were killed or wounded in the confrontation. In the aftermath, retired military officers were arrested and charged on illegal firearms possession and some could possibly face charges of treason, *makar* or conspiracy to assassinate. Government ministers have asserted that people involved in organizing the 21–22 May actions were also plotting to assassinate government figures, hinting at the possibility of some kind of coup attempt. Again, it seems clear these too were not planned components of a Prabowo strategy but a by-product of his encouraging practices that defy the agreed rules of the game for working out power-sharing.

Towards Rapprochement

In May 2019, there was heightened campaigning and pressure for reviving the power-sharing formula. This even involved intensified discussion revolving about Prabowo's Gerindra party and Partai Amanat Nasional (National Mandate Party or PAN, for short)—a party allied with Prabowo—as well as Partai Demokrat joining the Jokowi government. In fact, there was even discussion of the PKS joining the government. The discussion around this topic was massive, obviously aimed at bringing Gerindra back into accepting the power-sharing political framework, if not actually bringing it into government. It is clear that a majority of the factions within the ruling elite prefer political stability to a situation characterized by escalating mass mobilization around religious identity and mutual black propaganda.

Prabowo declared that, although disappointed, he respected the Constitutional Court's decision against his case that there was massive cheating. This declaration elicited statements from 212 elements that Prabowo would no longer have their support. However, it appears, for now at least, that the majority of the elite that wishes to return to operating within the power-sharing framework includes Prabowo and Sandiaga, and probably also PKS and PAN, whether or not they are in or outside the government.

Jokowi himself has made calls for the two sides to come together. Other leaders from his Partai Demokrasi Indonesia Perjuangan (PDI-P) have made similar calls while also emphasizing that those outside the government need not necessarily operate as an opposition since, they note, that is a term which is not mentioned in the constitution or any laws.

ONLY A RHETORICAL POLARIZATION

This pressure towards rapprochement achieved its goals when Jokowi and Prabowo held a series of photo-opportunity meetings and Prabowo accepted the position of defence minister in the Jokowi government. Gerindra joined the governing coalition and the party was given another ministerial post.[14]

This rapprochement has opened the way for the electoral system to return more fully to its original post-1998 function of power-sharing. Even though the major cleavage represented by Prabowo's five-year hostility towards Jokowi has ended, the system will still be tested again in the next few years as individual and dynastic ambitions compete. Into the mix one must add the newly revived element of the political ambitions of the ideologically driven hardline Islamist elements, most of whom, however, do not have an electoral party properly representing them. The FPI's huge mobilizations in Jakarta in November 2020 to welcome back Rizieq from a prolonged self-exile in Saudi Arabia showed that the movement is still a force to be reckoned with.[15]

Ideological and programmatic contestation within the electoral arena has been essentially rhetorical. This has been admitted by many politicians since the 2019 elections. The rapprochement between Jokowi and Prabowo is the ultimate manifestation of this reality. Even today, in early 2021, there are no apparent major differences that would be obstacles to either Partai Demokrat or PKS joining the government. Tensions between the Demokrat Party and the government have not been around policy principles. The period of polarization is now over, many politicians declare.

However, personal and dynastic rivalries may still drive competition among key party blocs. Partai Demokrat has already started promoting Yudhoyono's son, Agus H. Yudhoyono. Megawati has been appearing at press conferences with her daughter, Puan (who has since been elected as president of the House of Representatives), and her son, Prananda, by her side. Gerindra figures claim that Prabowo may run for the presidency again in 2024, and his vice-presidential candidate, Sandiaga, also now has considerable profile. Such dynastic and individual rivalries may override the underlying ideological and programmatic compatibility when it is time to contest specific positions.

While real and substantial ideological contestation among the electoral contenders has been mostly absent, this is not to say that there is no emerging ideological contestation outside the formal electoral process. The hardline Islamist elements, to date represented most prominently by the 212 Movement and the FPI, exist outside the electoral system, as does the HTI. These forces are unlikely to fade away or give up on their political ambitions. What is unclear at the moment is the extent to which they will be able to again play a role in mainstream electoral politics, as they did in 2019, even though they were not able to have a candidate explicitly support their goals. The other related question is the extent to which the broader elite will contest the Islamist agenda directly or try to co-opt it through some form of accommodation, as they did during the election campaign. The latter option would also require greater inclusion in power-sharing arrangements of the Nahdlatul Ulama, the country's largest mainstream Islamic organization, as well as the smaller Muhammadiyah (or at least parts of it).

The 2019 election campaign also saw increased ideological contestation within civil society as advocates of electoral abstention sharpened their criticism of the Jokowi government's record on social justice, human rights, minority rights and environmental issues as well as Prabowo's past record on human rights and his alignment with the most conservative social forces. This left wing of civil society also attacked both sides for their alignment with big money (the conglomerates), especially in the resources sector. The contestation here was between these more left-inclined civil society elements and those often having similar origins in the 1990s anti-Suharto movement and who adopted more or less uncritical support for Jokowi. This contestation, carried out mainly on social media, was sharp and brutal. As it progressed, the advocates of abstention also increasingly began to discuss the need for new political vehicles to present an alternative to the political choices currently available. Taking place within a specific, relatively small, subset of political actors—the civil society milieu created by the anti-Suharto movement in the 1990s and early 2000s—these advocates of abstention did not have a big impact on voting outcome.[16] However, their activism points to the possibility of a second source of ideological politics, apart from the Islamists, developing outside of the "verified" electoral format. It was these forces that provided the spearhead and backbone for the protest movements in 2019 against violence in Papua and against the weakening of the Corruption Eradication Commission (KPK) as well as the ongoing campaigns against the 2020 Omnibus Job Creation Law, both on issues of labour rights and environmental protection (Lane 2021).

It is also possible that the left-inclined social justice currents and Islamist currents currently operating at the grassroots level may end up in direct contestation with one another as they both challenge the status quo politics of the political elite as a whole.

NOTES

1. For overall analysis of the fall of Suharto, see, for example, Lane (2008); Aspinall (2005); Eklof (2003).
2. It could be cogently argued that a similar absolutism, though of a social layer rather than a class one, also developed in the socialist-communist countries, such as the Soviet Union. In these cases, it was the state bureaucracies that enjoyed absolutist power by virtue of their ability to monopolize the coordination of all production logistics.

3. This system has been breaking down as working classes in industrial societies de-unionize under pressure from social-democratic parties accommodating to late capitalism's need to dismantle the welfare state. Electorates are becoming more fragmented.
4. The classic work on the army in politics for this period is Crouch (1988).
5. Decentralization was being discussed by the New Order government during the 1990s. See Lane (2014).
6. This was manifested in the ending of the doctrine of *dwifungsi* (dual role for the armed forces) and the dissolution of the Coordinating Agency for National Stability (Bakorstanas).
7. See Lane (2019a) for a discussion of the trade unions that traces their origins to the anti-dictatorship movement during the late New Order period.
8. There is some commentary that labour has been able to exert influence at a local level. However, what appears at the local level is the use of union bargaining positions for careerist moves by officials from unions aligned with elite factions.
9. An organization such as Nahdlatul Ulama has a significant rural base but, although remaining formally unaffiliated, mostly aligns with the Partai Kebangkitan Bangsa (PKB).
10. See, for example, this cover of *Tempo* magazine: https://en.tempo.co/read/1248604/clarification-on-tempo-magazines-jokowi-illustration-cover. This is one of many covers lampooning President Jokowi.
11. For some context to this, but with an emphasis on the role of the state, see Tapsell (2019).
12. The precise balance of forces between individuals and groups within the FPI as of 2019 is still not clear.
13. This case was eventually dropped by the police. "Jejak kasus penistaan pancasila oleh Rizieq Shihab hingga dihentikan", *Kompas.com*, 5 September 2018, https://regional.kompas.com/read/2018/05/05/12094701/jejak-kasus-penistaan-pancasila-oleh-rizieq-shihab-hingga-dihentikan.
14. In December 2020, this minister, Edhy Prabowo, lost his position after being arrested for corruption by the Corruption Eradication Commission.
15. A further unknown factor is the ambitions of retired and senior military figures who feel isolated from the party-based power-sharing formula although one such elite-based anti-government group continues to hold activities, namely Koalisi Aksi Menyelamatkan Indonesia (KAMI). See Farida (2020).
16. Some advocates of the abstention position do, however, argue that the rather high (11 per cent) informal vote (i.e., incorrectly filled or marked ballot papers) in the parliamentary elections is a reflection of increased voter alienation from the existing parties.

REFERENCES

Aspinall, Edward. 2005. *Opposing Suharto: Compromise, Resistance and Regime Change in Indonesia*. Stanford: Stanford University Press.

Burhani, Ahmad Najib. 2017. "The Banning of Hizbut Tahrir and the Consolidation of Democracy in Indonesia". *ISEAS Perspective*, no. 2017/71, 19 September 2017.

Crouch, Harold. 1988. *The Army and Politics in Indonesia*. Ithaca, New York: Cornell University Press.

Detik.com. 2007. "Papernas Minta Kasus Penyerangan oleh FPI Diusut Tuntas", 29 March 2007. https://news.detik.com/berita/d-760756/papernas-minta-kasus-penyerangan-oleh-fpi-diusut-tuntas-.

Eklof, Stefan. 2003. *Indonesian Politics in Crisis: The Long Fall of Suharto, 1996–98*. Copenhagen: Nordic Institute of Asian Studies.

Farida Al-Qodariah. 2020. "Awalnya Tak Bermaksud Deklarasikan KAMI, Gatot Nurmantyo: Saya Masih Punya Utang ke Negara". *Pikiran-rakyat.com*, 17 October 2020. https://www.pikiran-rakyat.com/nasional/pr-01840647/awalnya-tak-bermaksud-deklarasikan-kami-gatot-nurmantyo-saya-masih-punya-utang-ke-negara.

Hadiz, Vedi and Richard Robison. 2004. *Reorganising Power in Indonesia: The Politics of Oligarchy in an Age of Markets*. London: Routledge.

Harmawan, Ary. 2018. "Commentary: #2019GantiPresiden shows all that is wrong with our democracy". *The Jakarta Post*, 5 September 2018. https://www.thejakartapost.com/academia/2018/09/05/commentary-2019gantipresiden-shows-all-that-is-wrong-with-our-democracy.html.

Human Rights Watch. 2003. "Kembali Ke Orde Baru? Tahanan Politik di bawah kepemimpinan Megawati". Vol. 15, No. 4 (C) – July 2003.

Lane, Max. 2008. *Unfinished Nation: Indonesia Before and After Suharto*. London: Verso.

———. 2014. *Decentralization and Its Discontents: An Essay on Class, Political Agency and National Perspective in Indonesian Politics*. Singapore: Institute of Southeast Asian Studies.

———. 2019a. *An Introduction to the Politics of the Indonesian Union Movement*. Singapore: ISEAS – Yusof Ishak Institute.

———. 2019b. "Students Protest Against the Weakening of Corruption Eradication Commission (KPK)". *ISEAS Commentaries* 2019/79, 24 September 2019. https://www.iseas.edu.sg/media/commentaries/students-protest-against-the-weakening-of-corruption-eradication-commission-kpk-by-max-lane/.

———. 2020a. "Indonesian Politics After the Widodo–Prabowo Rapprochement". *ISEAS Perspective*, no. 2020/31, 20 April 2020.

———. 2020b. "Protests Against the Omnibus Law and the Evolution of Indonesia's Social Opposition". *ISEAS Perspective*, no. 2020/128, 9 November

2020. https://www.iseas.edu.sg/wp-content/uploads/2020/11/ISEAS_Perspective_2020_128.pdf.

───── . 2021. "Widodo's Employment Creation Law, 2020: What Its Journey Tells Us about Indonesian Politics". *Trends in Southeast Asia*, no. 13/2021. Singapore: ISEAS – Yusof Ishak Institute.

Power, Thomas and Eve Warburton. 2020. *Democracy in Indonesia: From Stagnation to Regression?* Singapore: ISEAS – Yusof Ishak Institute, 2020.

Setijadi, Charlotte. 2017. "The Jakarta Election Continues: What Next for Embattled Governor Ahok?". *ISEAS Perspective*, no. 2017/18, 21 March 2017.

Tapsell, Ross. 2019. "Indonesia's Policing of Hoax News Increasingly Politicised". *ISEAS Perspective*, no. 2019/75, 20 September 2019.

Tempo.co. 2016. "Rachmawati Ditangkap Polisi, Keluarga Sukarno Tak Peduli", 2 December 2016. https://nasional.tempo.co/read/825031/rachmawati-ditangkap-polisi-keluarga-sukarno-tak-peduli.

4

POLITICS OF NEW TOOLS IN POST-TRUTH INDONESIA:[1] BIG DATA, AI AND MICRO-TARGETING

Okamoto Masaaki and Kameda Akihiro

The Indonesian presidential election held on 18 April 2019 was markedly different from the series of elections held in Indonesia since the democratization of 1998. One of its most prominent features was the incessant and widespread use of disinformation, both online and offline. A second notable feature was the feverish online election campaigns of both the Jokowi–Ma'ruf Amin and Prabowo–Sandiaga Uno camps. Online influencers and buzzers[2] in both camps played significant roles in the election, each with distinct characteristics and patterns. The third feature of the 2019 election was the serious effort required on the part of both campaigns to discern the real facts and real voices of voters amid tremendous volumes of fake or dubious news and social media messages. Both sides used artificial intelligence (AI)[3] to analyse big data amassed from online news and social media sites as well as offline data sets. The fourth feature was the start of political micro-targeting. The Jokowi team was far more engaged with this effort; groups of information technology (IT) specialists used data analysis through AI to micro-target voters and advised the Jokowi campaign on how best to tailor local campaign activities to local needs and characteristics.

This chapter describes these new election characteristics and campaign activities, based on interviews with actors from both camps. It argues that while political campaigners are strongly motivated to disseminate disinformation to influence voters, they also must discern the "real" voices and concerns of voters, and that they do so by using big data and AI. The Jokowi camp even started political micro-targeting using AI. In this sense, Indonesian politics has finally and seriously entered the post-truth era.

ARRIVAL OF THE POST-TRUTH ERA IN INDONESIAN POLITICS

Post-truth is defined in the Oxford Dictionary as "relating to or denoting circumstances in which objective facts are less influential in shaping public opinion than appeals to emotion and personal belief". The post-truth phenomenon has become quite visible since 2016, especially in the election of Donald Trump as president of the United States and the polls for the British exit from the European Union (or Brexit). In Indonesia, it started with the Jakarta gubernatorial election of 2017, and the 2019 presidential election was the typical election of the post-truth era.

Fake or dubious news was already influential in the 2014 presidential election, in which a tabloid, *Obor Rakyat* (People's Touch) falsely reported that presidential candidate Jokowi was a communist descendant, had Chinese ancestry and was a Christian or Jewish agent. The tabloid was systematically distributed to Islamic boarding schools. However, the variety, volume and spread of fake or dubious news significantly increased during the Jakarta gubernatorial election of 2017 and the 2019 presidential election. Indonesia's Ministry of Communication and Information began tackling fake news in December 2017 with the launch of the "Automatic Identification System" or AIS, a search system that crawls the internet for fake news.[4] Figure 4.1 plots the number of fake news stories identified by AIS during the period August 2018 to April

Politics of New Tools in Post-truth Indonesia

FIGURE 4.1
Number of Politics-related Fake News Items Identified by the Ministry of Communication and Information, August 2018–April 2019

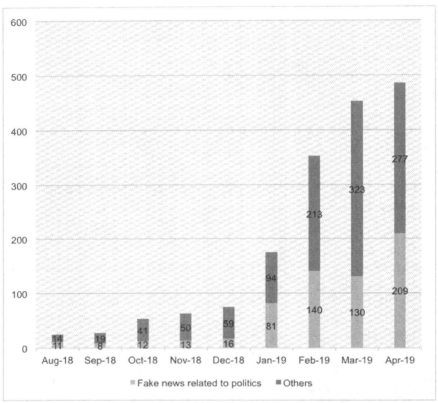

2019, illustrating an increasing volume of fake news especially related to politics as election day neared.[5]

Another conspicuous phenomenon of the 2019 election was the speed of the spread and penetration of eye-catching news in cyberspace. According to the socially led global agency We Are Social (2019), approximately 150 million people, or 56 per cent of the total population, were active social media users in Indonesia in January 2019; approximately 130 million of those used mobile devices to connect to social media. In terms of specific social media platforms, most of them used multiple platforms. According to the agency, the percentage of users by type of platform could be broken down as follows:

YouTube—88 per cent
WhatsApp—83 per cent
Facebook—81 per cent
Instagram—80 per cent
LINE—59 per cent
Twitter—52 per cent

These numbers, seen against a survey showing that 74.1 per cent of the urban population and 61.6 per cent of the rural population are internet users, suggest that not only urban dwellers but also those in rural areas are now regularly exposed to different types of dubious information online (APJII and Indonesia Polling Indonesia 2018).

Spin doctors from both political sides used false and distorted information to appeal to voters' emotions and personal beliefs. According to a survey of 1,220 persons conducted by Indikator Politik Indonesia in December 2018, 23 per cent of respondents heard the rumour that Jokowi was Chinese and 24 per cent among them (or 5.5 per cent of the total number of respondents) believed the story (Indikator Politik Indonesia 2019). That suggests that a significant number of people believed fake news that was couched in plausible terms if that was what they wanted to believe. And the echo chamber effect, in which people communicate online only with those who share similar social and political views and fail to verify information, could worsen the situation.

The question is: to what extent was the mobilization of such tactics by the two campaigns teams decisive in Indonesia's 2019 presidential election? According to a survey conducted by the Populi Center (2019), Jokowi held a 20 per cent electability advantage over Prabowo in August 2018. This margin was narrowed to about 10 per cent by election day, partly because more undecided voters chose Prabowo at the ballot box. This may imply that the Prabowo team's online strategy of discrediting Jokowi was effective in influencing some undecided voters against the president and in increasing Prabowo's own electability in the final months of the campaign. It may also imply that post-truth online campaigns might have been effective in strengthening the loyalty of voters to their respective candidates of choice.

CAMPAIGN CYBER STRATEGIES: CONCENTRATED AND RIGID VS. DISPERSED AND FLEXIBLE

Ismail Fahmi from the IT company Media Kernel Indonesia has actively publicized his analyses of online data (primarily of Twitter trends) regarding the election and other topics under the name Drone Emprit. Figure 4.2 is a social network analysis of the Twitter accounts supporting both teams from 28 January to 4 February 2019.[6] Drone Emprit searched for tweets that had the candidates' names and nicknames[7] and connected the accounts associated with them and the accounts that retweeted and spread those tweets. The connections are visualized in Figure 4.2.[8, 9] The analysis includes not only personal unique accounts, but also "bot" accounts, i.e., accounts that are programmed to do certain tasks automatically, in this case, bot accounts that automatically retweet from certain Twitter accounts. Analysing just personal unique accounts reveals the features of each "real" person's Twitter account and its network, or interrelations with the accounts of other "real" persons. Such analysis, however, does not tell us much about campaigners' online strategies to influence voters because it excludes bot accounts. Drone Emprit's analysis, which includes bot accounts, can uncover how campaign teams fight a cyberwar.[10]

Figure 4.2 graphically depicts the differences between the two teams in terms of patterns of cyber campaigning. The Jokowi side had many small, dispersed centres of Twitter activity while the Prabowo side had a few centres with strong radiating networks. The interaction rate—the frequency of retweeting and replying—was also different: the Jokowi team's rate was 3.4 while the Prabowo team's rate was 6.4, indicating that the Prabowo team had more robust communication and interaction among its supporters on Twitter. According to Ismail, the Prabowo's cyber campaign was more centralized and top-down across all social media platforms. It also was more proactive, demonstrating on many occasions that it was capable of raising a certain hashtag to the most popular trending topic in Indonesia. The Prabowo's cyber campaign was aggressive in attacking the opponent, deepening the dichotomy between friends and enemies in cyberspace. The central players in directing the tweets of the pro-Prabowo campaign were from the Islamist party Partai Keadilan Sejahtera (Prosperous Justice Party or PKS, for short) and the disbanded Hizbut Tahrir Indonesia (HTI).[11]

FIGURE 4.2
Patterns of Cyber Campaigning by the Jokowi-Ma'ruf team (JKW-MA) and the Prabowo-Sandiaga team (PS-SU)

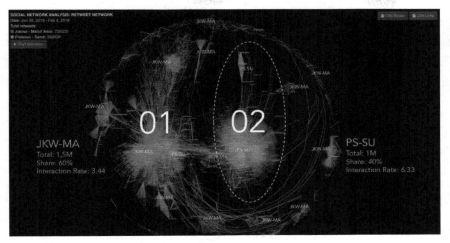

Source: Drone Emprit (2019).

In contrast, Jokowi's cyber campaign was flexible and elastic, or it could also be said that the team was multipolar, with loose coordination. Koster Rinaldi, the coordinator of the pro-Jokowi volunteer group known as Rumah Bersama Pelayan Rakyat (Community House to Serve the People or RBPR), acknowledged the uncoordinated nature of the Jokowi team's cyber activity and frequently highlighted that problem to the election campaign team members.[12] Usman Kansong, Jokowi's campaign communications director, said that the team created WhatsApp groups comprised of different groups of supporters and volunteers to coordinate cyber campaigns and also routinely conducted meetings with them.[13] Despite these efforts, the campaign's uncoordinated nature showed up in the social network analysis. This is partly because Jokowi himself did not want to force volunteers and volunteer groups with diverse backgrounds to take coordinated actions in cyberspace.[14] The Jokowi cyber team's tweets tended to be dispersed and its hashtags often failed to reach the top trending topics, especially in 2018. However, the campaign was inclusive, garnering support from different segments of society. Another merit of the looseness or multipolarity of Jokowi's cyber network was its resilience: the loss of one influencer's account was less devastating to the Jokowi's team than such a loss was to Prabowo's more centralized cyber team.

CYBER CAMPAIGNING 101: STRATEGIES EMPLOYED IN THE ELECTION

WhatsApp groups are most usually and frequently used by political campaigns for internal communication and consolidation of support. Therefore, both sides made efforts to penetrate the other side's WhatsApp groups, joining them by pretending to be a supporter and/or, as has been alleged, secretly joining a target group by taking advantage of a flaw in the WhatsApp communications programme.[15] On the other hand, owing to its concise and instantaneous format, Twitter is particularly suitable for a decisive short-term battle like the election. According to one survey, Twitter users drastically increased in January 2019 to 52 per cent of internet users aged 16–64, up from just 27 per cent a year earlier (We Are Social 2018 and 2019).

Typically, an influencer or buzzer of a team creates an eye-catching or evocative tweet, which successfully attracts netizens' attention. According to a confidential cyber team funded by Jokowi supporters,[16] the strategy to make a tweet go viral is to write it between 5:00 and 9:00 p.m. on a weekday, when Indonesians in the cities check their smartphones while commuting home. If a tweet goes viral online, the print media and TV will also give coverage to it, allowing it a wider social impact. Incessant creation and re-creation of viral tweets critical of a rival candidate was common during the election campaign. Whether a tweet became viral or not was often more valuable than whether the tweet was based on facts or not, because it could attract more attention and potential support for the candidate. Scholars and politicians in Indonesia started to raise the alarm that the rapid spread of (dis)information based on popularity rather than accuracy or truth had contributed to the deepening of social cleavages and the polarization of society (Ross 2019).

Another important method to make a topic dominant in the cyber discourse was to create an eye-catching hashtag that can rise to be ranked among the top one or two trending topics. If an influencer with a huge number of followers were to promote a hashtag and buzzers and/or bots intentionally and repeatedly spread it, that hashtag could rank as the top one or two hashtags. For example, a buzzer account from PKS, @R4jaPurwa (seemingly shared by some members and changed to @K1ngPurwa after it was shut down by Twitter) frequently appealed to followers through its tweets to spread certain hashtags critical of Jokowi or supportive of Prabowo in order to raise its ranking. During the 2019 election campaign, hashtags from the Prabowo side were often and continuously ranked at the top in the list of trending topics.[17] This created the impression that Prabowo was the more popular candidate.

Both sides had in-house influencers and buzzers, including Ulin Yusron in the Jokowi camp and Mustofa Nahra in the Prabowo camp,[18] and both actively attempted to co-opt established influencers. For example, each campaign battled fiercely to draw to its side Nissa Sabyan, a 19-year-old Muslimah singer with 9.6 million followers on her various social media accounts. Nissa eventually sided with Prabowo, posting a photo of him on her Instagram account to show her support (*Tempo.co* 2019). In order to raise the rankings of certain topics, both sides also employed professional and/or amateur buzzers (Reuters 2019), even though this strategy does not guarantee that a hashtag will remain in the top-ranked spot for a long time.

On average, the total mentions of any topic, including election topics, would peak on the third day after it had begun to go viral and fade away within five days, regardless of the social media platform.[19] Therefore, the constant revival of a trending topic was a must for both political campaigns. One of the most viral and successful hashtags of the 2019 election was "#2019GantiPresiden" (Change the President in 2019). Mardani Ali Sera, a PKS cadre, created the hashtag in March 2018 before contenders for the presidency against Jokowi had emerged. It went viral with the help of buzzers from PKS and HTI in early April 2018 and surpassed Jokowi's hashtag, "#Jokowi2periode", created in January 2018. Yet even this influential hashtag, which became viral on 5 April, faded away by 10 April 2018 (see Figure 4.3). However, continuous efforts and activities, such as creating a #2019GantiPresiden T-shirt, helped to make the hashtag popular and viral again and again (see Figure 4.4).

FIGURE 4.3
How the "#2019GantiPresiden" hashtag trended on Twitter, 1 April 2018–10 April 2018

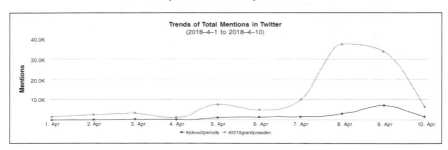

Source: Drone Emprit (2018).

FIGURE 4.4
Revived Fortunes of "#2019GantiPresiden" on Twitter

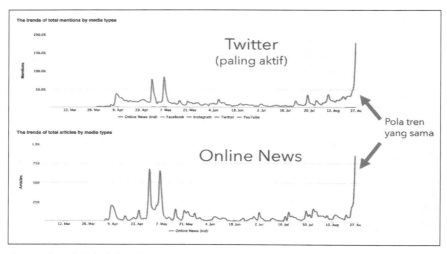

Source: Ismail Fahmi (2018).

Another important strategy for the campaigns was to shorten the viral period of a topic favourable to their rival as much as possible. The first way to do this was rapid risk management and the second was diversion of netizens' attention. The Prabowo team was quite good at these methods. The case of Ratna Sarumpaet, a famous actress and a Prabowo loyalist, is a good example. A photo of Ratna's swollen face was spread on the internet with the rumour that she was assaulted by Jokowi supporters in the parking lot of the airport in Bandung on 21 September 2018 and then hospitalized. Topics related to the case went viral, Ratna gained the sympathy of netizens, and the Jokowi team was harshly criticized without any proof that Jokowi supporters had actually assaulted her. Fadli Zon from Prabowo's Gerindra party tweeted, "It is true that Ms. Ratna Sarumpaet was assaulted, it was criminal and rude." Prabowo himself met Ratna and organized a press conference on 2 October 2018, saying that there was a political motive behind the assault. However, soon after the conference, the police investigation revealed that the alleged assault was a hoax to attack Jokowi. In fact, Ratna's face was swollen owing to a recent plastic surgery; she had pretended that her face was swollen because of an assault by Jokowi supporters (*Tempo.co* 2018; *Detik.com* 2019). When the hoax was uncovered, netizens began criticizing not only Ratna, but also Prabowo. Immediately after the criticism against Prabowo began, a totally different online discourse emerged that tried to shift blame away from Prabowo by criminalizing Ratna and presenting Prabowo as the victim of a lie and hoax. This victimization of Prabowo was in accordance with the narrative created by the Prabowo team and illustrates both the rapid risk management and diversion strategies of his campaign.[20]

Another example of risk management is the countermeasure against the hashtag "#PrabowoJumatanDimana" (where does Prabowo pray on Friday?) that (re)appeared in late December 2018 and questioned the Islamic piety of Prabowo. Just before the hashtag became viral, Andi Arief from the Democrat Party (part of Prabowo's coalition) wrote a diversionary rumour in Twitter and WhatsApp groups claiming that he was told there were seven containers of punched ballot papers in Tanjung Priok port and asking the group members to check whether their existence was true. Following this, Hermansyah, an IT specialist and alumnus of the Bandung Institute of Technology (ITB) from the Prabowo side, posted on his Facebook page that there were seven containers with 80 million punched ballot papers at Tanjung Priok port that "may have come from China". Although the story was false, it became viral (*Serambinews.com* 2019). This was a typical tactic to divert netizens' attention. It was not entirely effective, however, as #PrabowoJumatanDimana became viral again after some time.

Cyberspace is the realm of bots and profit-oriented buzzers. There are also so-called follower factories that create and sell follower accounts to customers who want to show they are popular online. Both presidential candidates' campaigns were said to use these tools. During the 2019 election "hot" topics were constantly changing as fake or dubious news and information flooded cyberspace. It was critically important for both camps to navigate this murky cyberspace and keep selling their candidates there. It was also important, or more important, for both camps to enlarge, strengthen, and stabilize their supporting bases via cyberspace and also to discern the conscious (or even unconscious) views and thoughts of voters in order to construct effective campaign strategies. To do this, they turned to big data, AI analysis, and micro-targeting. The following section describes the activities of the behind-the-scene teams on the Jokowi side.

BIG DATA ANALYSIS, AI SYSTEMS AND MICRO-TARGETING

The 2019 campaign marked the first serious introduction of big data into politics and the full-fledged politicization of IT specialists. Alumni of ITB, computer science graduates from other institutions and internet autodidacts joined both camps and became politicized. This section focuses on the Jokowi side because it was technologically more advanced than the Prabowo team. The official team leaders of Jokowi's digital campaigns, including the aforementioned Usman Kansong, Fiki Satari (director of content) and Arya Sinulingga (director of public information and social media), all ITB alumni, received data and analysis from several shadow teams (*tim bayangan*). For example, Arya Sinulingga constantly used his smartphone to check for both positive and negative sentiments expressed towards Jokowi and Prabowo on social media, and when Jokowi's popularity decreased even slightly, he immediately instructed the various teams to determine the reasons for the decline and deal with them. *Tim bayangan* would then analyse big data from social media and provide information for a response.[21]

Andi Widjajanto, Jokowi's former cabinet secretary and the son of Major General Theo Syafei (a politician from the Partai Demokrasi Indonesia Perjuangan or PDI-P and loyal to Megawati) was the head of the pro-Jokowi volunteer organization known as Cakra 19. He boasted that the Jokowi campaign had four teams with machines capable of processing big data. The first was operated by Cloud Team (*Tim Awan*) under the direction of Andi himself; the second by the political consultancy PoliticaWave under the direction of Yose Rizal (an ITB alumnus); the third by Corona Team under the direction of Hokky Situngkir (another ITB alumnus); and the fourth directly operated by the official Jokowi–Ma'ruf campaign team and coordinated by Wahyu Sakti Trenggono (also an ITB alumnus). These teams utilized the machines to (1) collect and analyse comments and chats on social media and online news sites; (2) calculate the positive and negative sentiments towards each candidate; and (3) estimate the electability of the candidates. On election day, algorithms programmed on each of the four machines drew on the collected data to predict the election results well ahead of the closure of balloting. Andi said that the predictions at 10:00–10:30 a.m. were nearly identical to the final election results (*Kumparan.com* 2019a, 2019b). That means that the Jokowi team was able to discern the approximate election results sooner than the quick counts done by pollsters. This marked a significant shift in the political importance of big data in Indonesia.

The following section describes how big data, AI and micro-targeting were utilized by three different teams on the Jokowi side—Corona Team and two volunteer groups, Jasmev 4.0 and RBPR.

Corona Team[22]

The Corona Team was named after the machine called Corona that the team used to crawl the internet, analyse big data and create simulations. The team was led by Hokky Situngkir (also the director of the Bandung Fe Institute) and had twenty staff members in Jakarta and thirty in Bandung (or a combined total of eight researchers, ten programmers and thirty-two data collectors). Since 2008, the Bandung Fe Institute had been amassing all manner of data, including election results from across Indonesia dating from 1999, various types of information on all the villages in the country, price information on staple items from twelve traditional markets across the country, traditional food recipes and traditional folk music, online and offline news, and data on social media usage. It has been using the Corona machine to analyse the data and predict future trends. The institute provides analytical reports to private companies and government offices for business purposes.

Hokky said he himself had no interest in politics and had never joined a political campaign, but at the request of a minister he decided to use the Corona machine to support the Jokowi team, mainly its Chakra 19 volunteer organization. He boasted that Corona uses AI to simulate election models and predict which presidential candidate or party will win even at the level of individual ballot boxes.

The new political strategy that the Corona Team introduced in the election was online micro-targeting. Micro-targeting is a marketing strategy used by businesses to analyse each person's online data, including gender, address, education, hobbies and consumption patterns, to suggest the most appropriate products and services to that individual. Barack Obama introduced this strategy in politics during the 2008 US presidential election campaign and the term "political micro-targeting" became familiar thereafter. The unexpected victory of Trump has since stirred controversy over political micro-targeting (Bodo, Helberger and de Vreese 2017). This was because of the activities of a political consultancy that the Trump team had contracted. Cambridge Analytica (CA), which specialized in data mining and analysis, had improperly gathered the digital footprints of 87 million Facebook users so that it could analyse their psychological attributes and use them to tailor election advertisements in support of Trump.[23]

Unlike CA's strategy, the political micro-targeting by the Corona Team was done at village level and did not attempt to change individual voter behaviour using data-informed personalized advertising. The team applied its method to Jokowi's campaign by identifying the merits, demerits and impact of visits to a particular village by either Jokowi or Uno Sandiaga (Prabowo's running mate). Based on a village index created from various village data, the Corona Team suggested the most appropriate campaign themes for a specific village before any visit by a Jokowi team. Corona even suggested where to put up campaign posters, based on information from Google Maps.

Jasmev 4.0[24]

In the 2009 presidential election, television commercials were the most important media for political campaigns (Okamoto 2010). This changed in 2012, when the online volunteer group Jasmev (Jokowi Ahok Social Media Volunteer) proved the political importance of cyberspace. At the request of Jokowi himself, Kartika Jumadi and friends established Jasmev in order to support him in the Jakarta gubernatorial election of 2012, and, indeed, Jasmev's efforts helped Jokowi win the governorship. Jasmev later supported Jokowi as a presidential candidate in 2014 and Basuki Tjahaja Purnama ("Ahok") in his bid in 2017 for a second term as governor of Jakarta.

Jasmev was not active at the start of the 2019 presidential election season. Alerted by the growing dominance of the Prabowo team on social media, ex-members of Jasmev did some political mapping in October 2018 and formally re-established Jasmev as Jasmev 4.0 in January 2019 to counter Prabowo's cyber army.[25] Fernando Senewe, an online commerce businessman, is the coordinator of the new Jasmev. Fernando and his friends analysed the online strategies of the Prabowo team, mainly of the PKS team, and found that while the campaign was proactive online, it was top-down in nature. They concluded that the Prabowo side focused too much on raising the trend rankings of certain topics. They assessed that this approach was no longer effective.[26] Their approach was to conduct a cyber campaign at lower levels, targeting first-time voters, "silent majority" voters and swing voters who had not yet clearly decided who to vote for and therefore had the potential to choose Jokowi.

Jasmev 4.0 employed a micro-targeting strategy to reach these voters. Unlike the Corona Team, Jasmev 4.0 combined online targeting with offline micro-targeting. They went to villages, mainly in Java, identified young active Twitter users who were pro-Jokowi and distributed to them various online pro-Jokowi information so that they could bring silent and swing voters in their communities to the Jokowi side. This strategy assumed that silent and swing voters put more trust in information they received from people they knew than in news from social media.

Jasmev 4.0 also created various volunteer groups and frequently communicated with them. These groups included: Jasmev Classic for supporters aged above 50 years; Jasmev Millennial for millennial-generation supporters; Jasmev Playground for women supporters with small children; Jasmev Hardcore for Jasmev volunteers since 2012; Jasmev Parahyangan for supporters in West Java Province; and Jasmev Glaring for socialites. Jasmev continuously delivered pro-Jokowi messages tailored to the behaviours, beliefs and interests of each group's members, and appealing to their emotions. They assessed that the micro-targeting strategy was quite effective in Yogyakarta, Solo and Semarang and had contributed to raising the percentage of those voting for Jokowi.

RBPR[27]

The RBPR (Rumah Bersama Pelayan Rakyat or Community House to Serve the People) was the successor to the pro-Jokowi volunteer group Komunitas Alumni Perguruan Tinggi (Community of University Alumni or KAPT, for short), one of the many volunteer groups that had supported Jokowi in the 2014 presidential election. Alumni of famous universities, such as the Bandung Institute of Technology (Bandung), University of Indonesia (Depok), Bogor Institute of Agriculture (Bogor), and the March 11 Institute of Technology (Surabaya), established KAPT in order to oppose Prabowo as a presidential candidate and support Jokowi instead. Koster Rinaldi, an activist and ITB alumnus, was the coordinator of KAPT. Koster and his friends realized that the volunteer groups that had supported Jokowi in 2014 had lost their volunteer spirit and had degenerated into mediocre social organizations (*ormas*) that seek money and power. Fearing the impact of internal conflicts for money and power among the members during the 2019 presidential election, Koster and his friends decided to transform KAPT into a facilitator-type of volunteer group and called it RBPR. The main purpose of RBPR was to monitor the election campaigns of both Jokowi and Prabowo and report the results to the Jokowi team as well as to facilitate communication within the Jokowi team, which was comprised of a diversity of people, organizations and groups. The RBPR had twelve offices (two in Jakarta, two in North Sumatra, two in East Java, five in West Java and one in Banten), where they held talk shows and workshops. Their main activity, however, was the monitoring of cyberspace.

In October 2018, RBPR began utilizing data crawling and analysis systems from three companies: Trans Media Social (a company under Chairul Tanjung, a pro-Jokowi business tycoon); Indonesia Indicator (created by an ITB alumnus); and Sasbuzz. Indicator had created a system called Intelligence Media Management (IMM), which was capable of collecting data from more than 1,000 online and offline news media outlets and TV and radio programmes by using AI to crawl the internet as well as human power. The IMM system could also collect data from social media platforms such as Facebook, Twitter, Instagram and WhatsApp groups. The system estimated that around four per cent of the social media accounts supporting both campaigns were bots and that this rate had increased to around seven per cent in the week before the election. Sasbuzz also used AI to analyse voting behaviour for seven months before the election. Its systems predicted the election results with high precision.

RBPR closely monitored developments in social media communication at all times and noticed the general trend that the Prabowo's cyber campaign ordered the dissemination of certain messages on Fridays and Saturdays. In fact, RBPR had infiltrated pro-Prabowo WhatsApp groups and it was through discussions in these groups that it managed to confirm this trend. Therefore, RBPR recommended that Jokowi's cyber groups disseminate their messages from Wednesday to Friday, when Prabowo's centralized cyber network was not active.

Excluding bot accounts, RBPR chose two million unique Twitter accounts as samples to analyse. It found that at any given time both teams had just 20,000 buzzers supporting the candidates. In other words, a mere 40,000 buzzers constituted the front line of the two cyber campaigns.

RBPR had its own system for analysing data and made daily and weekly reports to the Jokowi team based on its analyses. These reports contained the projected electability of Jokowi at particular junctures, the positive and negative sentiments circulating about both candidates and information on influential hashtags. The reports summarized the findings of the day or the week and provided recommendations (see Table 4.1 for the recommendations made on 9 April 2019 and for the week of 23–29 March 2019).

TABLE 4.1
Recommendations by RBPR

	Recommendations on 9 April 2019
1	Emotional expressions by Prabowo Subianto in his series of campaigns should be continuously reported critically in the media.
2	Negative reports on Prabowo's behaviour should be amplified in the media.
3	Efforts to provide space in the media for experts on social issues to criticize Prabowo's style of communication and the psychological risks it carries, thus signalling the negative consequences if he should attain power.
4	KH Ma'ruf Amin and the team should consistently address Islamic issues and approach Muslim communities in West Java, especially in the south.
5	KH Ma'ruf Amin should continuously consolidate the network of traditional Islamic bases and Islamic boarding schools.
	Recommendation from the Week of 23–29 March 2019
1	Continuously campaign to promote the wearing of white clothing as the Jokowi team's uniform.
2	Prepare materials for posting after the presidential candidates' debate on 30 March 2019.
3	Advise 01's [i.e., Jokowi's] netizen supporters to continuously post on the crowd attending his campaigns, the volunteers' canvassing activities, and Jokowi's friendliness and cheerfulness with the people (e.g., videos of his humourously communicating with the people when he gave away bicycles).
4	Advise Jokowi's supporters to refrain from reacting to, discussing or commenting on the controversial statements by Prabowo Subianto–Sandiaga Uno (PS–SU). Responding to these will increase the internet traffic of conversations and discussions relating to PS–SU.
5	Anticipate a scenario of 02 [i.e., Prabowo] trying to build a narrative of fraudulent elections and plotting to create social conflict.
6	Routine agenda-setting to be done at a continuous pace: Humanist: family-minded, the First Lady as the campaign's icon, harmonious family and closeness and warmth with the people should be emphasized as the difference of 01 from 02. Posting of Mrs Iriana's photos (plainness, cordiality and empathy), togetherness of Mrs Iriana and Jokowi, Jokowi's friendliness and warmth with the people, etc. Offensive: zeroing in on Prabowo as rough, unable to recite the Qur'an and be an *imam*, cannot pray, etc. Discussion and Narrative: Liars, traitors, hoax spreaders and those with legal problems are the ones on the 02 side.

Source: RBPR (2019a, 2019b).

EPILOGUE

The 2019 presidential election marked Indonesia's first full-fledged cyber election in the sense that concerted efforts were made to use big data, AI and online political micro-targeting. The use of these tools worsened the rampant negative campaigns by and against both candidates, which in turn deepened divisions between the supporters of the two teams. Some analysts even noted that this type of massive online campaigns was a clear sign of the emergence of post-truth politics in Indonesia and its deepening of social divisions, as had happened in the 2016 US presidential election and the United Kingdom's referendum for Brexit. However, whether the online campaigns have indeed divided Indonesian society as a whole has yet to be proven.

Nonetheless, a remarkable sign of post-truth politics, even though not many scholars and journalist noted the point, was the use of new political tools, big data, AI and micro-targeting, which the Jokowi camp utilized to discern the conscious (or even unconscious) views and thoughts of voters. We believe this is a notable sign of the coming age of new politics in Indonesia.

The question that remains, however, is how effective these new tools were in securing Jokowi's victory in 2019 even though the Corona Team, RBPR and other shadow teams correctly predicted the election results by analysing voters' online voices and other data through the machine learning aspect of AI. Their approach was quite different from that of pollsters, who directly ask respondents who they would vote for and then undertake statistical projections to determine the election results. The more digital footprints that voters leave behind, the more precise AI predictions of election results will be without voters even noticing. Political micro-targeting in the 2019 election was undertaken only at the village level, but it is highly possible that micro-targeting efforts online will be able to zero in on each voter who has a digital presence. The government can acquire the authority to access all the digital footprints of every voter in the name of security, which means there is a looming risk that these digital footprints can be utilized for political purposes. This is a gloomy scenario but it is just a possible situation. Whether it materializes depends on the type of technologies that the state and society are going to create and utilize and the resilience of civil society to break the state's surveillance powers.

We face a "black box" of unknowns as to how and why AI works the way it does. Yet, despite the unknowns, it is crystal clear that Indonesian politics has entered a new era of cyber politics. Big data, AI systems and micro-targeting are now integral to politics and daily life in Indonesia, and this reality has profound implications for Indonesian studies. Inter-disciplinary work on politics must be the new norm for future research.

NOTES

1. This paper is the revised version of a chapter in an online book in Japanese, *The 2019 Election in Indonesia: Deepening Social Cleavages and Re-election of Jokowi*, edited by Kawamura Koichi (Tokyo: IDE-JETRO, 2020).
2. A buzzer is a social media account that creates issues that can go viral in the social media. It can be an anonymous account or that of an identifiable individual or group. The term is quite commonly used in Indonesia. A buzzer is different from an influencer. An influencer is usually an identifiable person with a lot of followers who can make an issue viral to influence the views of certain groups of people in cyberspace.
3. We did not access detailed AI algorithms for this paper; the description of what both teams did with AI is mostly based on interviews. We only checked the plausibility of explanation in terms of political and information science.
4. Interview with Semuel Abrijani Pangerapan, Director-General of Informatics Application at the Ministry of Communication and Informatics, on 29 April 2019.
5. The total number of fake news items on politics in the election month of April 2019 was just 209. The number is small because it reflects only the number of fake news items on politics that the ministry managed to find each month and judged as fake news in consultation with the general election committee.
6. Twitter was picked for the analysis over platforms such as Facebook and WhatsApp because it is an excellent data source for network and non-network analysis. Twitter is explicitly structured as a network, and networks can be reconstructed by streaming or downloading data. Twitter also has a norm for public conversation that does not exist on Facebook (Steinert-Threlkeld 2018, pp. 4–6).
7. The keywords for the Jokowi camp were: Jokowi, Joko Widodo, Maruf Amin, makruf amin, kyai makruf, ma'ruf amin, kyai ma'ruf, maruf amin,

Kiai Ma'ruf, marufamin, jaenudin, nachiro and jkw. The keywords for the Prabowo camp were: prabowo, sandiaga, sandi and sandiuno.
8. The data used for this type of analysis are automatically collected based on keywords such as in note 6 through the application programming interface (API) of each platform such as Twitter.
9. The network structure between the tweets and retweets is assumed to have a significant correlation with the network structure of each presidential candidate's supporters.
10. Interview with Ismail Fahmi on 1 April 2019. It is not always easy to differentiate a unique account from a bot account because some unique accounts behave like bot accounts, almost automatically retweeting certain tweets. In Ismail's analysis, these bot-like unique accounts are regarded as bot accounts.
11. Interview with Koster Rinaldi on 30 April 2019 and with Irendra Rajawali, an IT consultant for the Partnership for Government Reform (Kemitraan), a non-profit organization to promote good governance between state, market and civil society in Indonesia, on 29 April 2019.
12. Interview with Koster Rinaldi on 30 April 2019 and on 13 June 2019.
13. Interview with Usman Kasong on 23 March 2019.
14. Interview with Ulin Yusron, a Jokowi influencer, on 29 April 2019.
15. Confidential interview on 29 April and 30 April 2019.
16. Confidential interview on 31 March 2019.
17. Interview with Ismail Fahmi on 1 April 2019 and Koster Rinaldi on 30 April 2019.
18. Interview with Ulin Yusoron on 29 April 2019 and Mustofa Nahra on 1 April 2019.
19. Interview with Rustika Herlambang, one of the co-founders of Indonesia Indicator, on 30 April 2019. Indonesia Indicator is an IT consulting company with expertise in social media analysis as well as online and offline news analysis.
20. Interview with Koster Rinaldi on 30 April 2019.
21. Interview with Arya Sinulingga on 11 February 2019.
22. Information based on interview with Hokky Situngkir on 13 June 2019 and on his presentation, "Kecerdasan Bangsa & Biopolitik: Membangun Manusia Indonesia Kebal Semburan Dusta", at the Big Question Forum 1 at Microsoft Indonesia, Jakarta, on 16 June 2019.
23. On CA, see Wylie (2019) and Kaiser (2019). Also see Sumpter (2018), Chapter 5, critcizing CA's exaggeration of the usefulness of psychological analysis. SCL Elections, the parent company of CA, came to Indonesia just after the fall of Suharto in 1998 and was tasked with managing growing

frustration with the administration of his successor, B.J. Habibie. Through a survey involving 72,000 respondents, SCL found that the principal instigators of the unrest were from the younger, "university"-age group. The company, therefore, proposed the establishment of rally committees in universities and sponsored organized avenues for protests. The company boasted that the strategy worked well and led to the election of Abdurrahman Wahid as the third president of Indonesia (Quartz 2018/3/29). It is doubtful whether SCL Elections' strategy indeed worked well.
24. Interview with Kurnia, Endi and Fernando from Jasmev on 25 April 2019.
25. Jasmev 4.0 signifies the fourth iteration of Jasmev (Jasmev 1.0 supported Jokowi as Jakarta governor in 2012, Jasmev 2.0 supported Jokowi as a presidential candidate in 2014, and Jasmev 3.0 supported Purnama as Jakarta governor for a second term in 2017).
26. Jasmev had employed this strategy in 2012 and 2014 and found it effective then.
27. Interview with Koster Rinaldi on 30 April 2019 and on 13 June 2019.

REFERENCES

Documents:

Rumah Bersama Pelayan Rakyat (RBPR). 2019a. *Monitoring dan Analisa Media Pilpres 2019: Laporan Harian 9 April 2019.*
_____. 2019b. *Monitoring dan Analisa Media Pilpres 2019: Laporan Mingguan 23 Maret–29 Maret 2019.*

Online Sources:

APJII and Indonesia Polling Indonesia. 2018. "Laporan Survei: Penetrasi & Profil Perilaku Pengguna Internet Indonesia: Survei 2018". https://diskominfo.purwakartakab.go.id/panel/assets/files/547e1e75b59e668bda451e92f9246d00.pdf.
Detik.com. 2019. "Hoax Ratna Sarumpaet: Foto-foto Usai Operasi Plastik, Ngaku Dipukuli Laki-laki", 28 February 2019. https://news.detik.com/berita/d-4447886/hoax-ratna-sarumpaet-foto-foto-usai-operasi-plastik-ngaku-dipukuli-laki-laki.
Drone Emprit. 2018. "#2019GantiPresiden vs #Jokowi2Periode", 10 April 2018. https://www.slideshare.net/IsmailFahmi3/2019gantipresiden-vs-jokowi2periode.
_____. 2019. "Laporan Analisis Media: JKW-MA vs PS-SU: 28 Januari-4 Februari 2019", 14 February 2019. https://pers.droneemprit.id/laporan-analisis-drone-emprit-jkw-ma-vs-ps-su-28-januari-4-februari-2019/.

Indikator Politik Indonesia. 2019. "Media Sosial, Hoaks, dan Sikap Partisan dalam Pilpres 2019: Temuan Survei Nasional, 16-26 Desember 2018", 15 January 2019. http://indikator.co.id/uploads/20190115095916.Materi_Rilis_Pilpres_dan_Medsos_Januari_2019.pdf.

Kumparan.com. 2019a. "Big Data: Senjata Andalan Jokowi", 22 April 2019. https://kumparan.com/kumparannews/big-data-senjata-andalan-jokowi-1qw5V7o3TBt.

──────. 2019b. "Andi Widjajanto: Big Data Jadi Terobosan Tim Jokowi di 2019", 22 April 2019. https://kumparan.com/kumparannews/andi-widjajanto-big-data-jadi-terobosan-tim-jokowi-di-2019-1qw9RNgcoMF.

Quartz.com. 2018. "From Indonesia to Thailand, Cambridge Analytica's Parent Influenced Southeast Asian Politics", 29 March 2018. https://qz.com/1240588/cambridge-analytica-how-scl-group-used-indonesia-and-thailand-to-hone-its-ability-to-influence-elections/.

Reuters. 2019. "In Indonesia, Facebook and Twitter are 'Buzzer' Battlegrounds as Elections Loom", 13 March 2019. https://www.reuters.com/article/us-indonesia-election-socialmedia-insigh/in-indonesia-facebook-and-twitter-are-buzzer-battlegrounds-as-elections-loom-idUSKBN1QU0AS.

Serambinews.com. 2019. "Saat ada kabar surat suara sudah tercoblos, KPU dan Bawaslu sempat panik, ini kronologi&temuannya", 3 January 2019. https://aceh.tribunnews.com/2019/01/03/saat-ada-kabar-surat-suara-sudah-tercoblos-kpu-dan-bawaslu-sempat-panik-ini-kronologi-temuannya.

Tempo.co. 2018. "Jebakan Hoaks Ratna Sarumpaet", 5 October 2018. https://kolom.tempo.co/read/1133717/jebakan-hoaks-ratna-sarumpaet.

──────. 2019. "Bersama Bobby Mengejar Anak Muda", 8 February 2019. https://majalah.tempo.co/read/157115/bersama-bobby-mengejar-anak-muda.

We Are Social. 2018. "Digital 2018: Indonesia".

──────. 2019. "Digital 2019: Indonesia".

Book Chapters/Articles in Journals/Periodicals:

Bodo, Balazs, Natali Helberger, and Claes H. de Vreese. 2017. "Political Microtargeting: A Manchurian Candidate or Just a Dark Horse? Towards the Next Generation of Political Marketing Research". *Internet Policy Review* 6, no. 4: 3-13.

Ismail Fahmi. 2018b. "Analisis: Pelarangan dan Penghadangan 4,7x Lebih Menguntungkan Gerakan", 27 August 2018. https://www.facebook.com/ismailfahmibdg/posts/10157654389586729.

Kaiser, Britney. 2019. *Targeted: The Cambridge Analytica Whistleblower's Inside Story of How Big Data, Trump, and Facebook Broke Democracy and How It Can Happen Again.* New York: HarperCollins Publishers.

Okamoto, Masaaki. 2010. "'Creation' of Parties and Candidates: Democratization and the Campaign Consulting Business". In *The 2009 General Elections in Indonesia and the Direction of New Government*, edited by Honna Jun and Karamura Kochi, pp. 73-90. Tokyo: IDE-JETRO in Japanese.

Populi Center. 2019. *Menakar Pengaruh Debat terhadap Keterpilihan Paslon*, 7 February 2019.

Steinert-Threlkeld, Zachary C. 2018. *Twitter as Data*. Cambridge: Cambridge University Press.

Sumpter, David. 2018. *Outnumbered: From Facebook and Google to Fake News and Filter-bubbles – The Algorithms That Control Our Lives*. London: Bloomsbury.

Tapsell, Ross. 2019. "The Polarization Paradox in Indonesia's 2019 Elections". *New Mandala*, 22 March 2019.

Wylie, Christopher. 2019. *Mindf*ck: Cambridge Analytica and the Plot to Break America*. New York: Random House.

5

DISINFORMATION, POST-ELECTION VIOLENCE AND THE EVOLUTION OF ANTI-CHINESE SENTIMENT

Quinton Temby

INTRODUCTION

Indonesia's 2019 elections culminated in protests and riots on 21–23 May 2021, as partisans of the Prabowo Subianto–Sandiago Uno opposition coalition rejected the results of the presidential election, alleging electoral fraud by incumbent Joko Widodo (Jokowi). During the unrest, eight people were killed in clashes with police and hundreds more were injured. The violence, perhaps the first of its kind in the capital since 1998, was followed by the ritual search for the *dalang* (puppetmaster) of the riots. But this search obscured the fact that a wealth of open source data indicated that many of those involved in the street violence had acted spontaneously, motivated by misleading or false information. In particular, militant oppositionists were motivated by a concatenation of fake news reports claiming the election had been stolen, which culminated in the belief that their communities were under attack.

The riots in Indonesia in 2019 may mark the first time in a democracy that social media-driven misinformation and disinformation led to violent unrest after a national election. The case of Indonesia serves as a warning to democracies with electoral systems that are vulnerable owing to weakened media institutions, high social media penetration and populist politics.

Although the violence in 2019 was tightly contained by the authorities and limited to clashes between police and opposition activists in Central Jakarta, the unrest was correlated with a large spike in online fake news and conspiracy theories targeting China and the ethnic Chinese community. The recent origins of anti-Chinese disinformation in Indonesia can be traced to the 2014 election, when popular outsider Jokowi was smeared in unofficial "black campaign" material as the son of ethnic Chinese communists (Tyson and Purnomo 2017). This birther-style conspiracy theory continues to circulate in Islamist circles and was at the centre of a 2016 propaganda screed widely circulated online, *Jokowi Undercover* (Bambang Tri 2016). Such racist narratives build on a history of anti-Chinese sentiment in Indonesia (Purdey 2006). Increasingly, however, contemporary disinformation narratives draw less on history and more on geopolitics, reflecting growing anxiety over the rapid rise of China as a major power in Southeast Asia. China's rising hegemony is now the meta-narrative within which anti-Chinese disinformation is embedded in Indonesia.

But historical patterns persist. Temporally, anti-Chinese disinformation in Indonesia is driven by the electoral cycle, a phenomenon supercharged by the 2017 Jakarta gubernatorial election in which Chinese Indonesian incumbent Basuki Tjahaja Purnama (Ahok) was defeated amid a blasphemy controversy (Setijadi 2017). Although election-corelated anti-Chinese sentiment appears to be generated organically online, it is fuelled by elements of the political elite. In 2019, coded rhetoric by senior opposition politicians reinforced the more explicit messages disseminated online, creating a seamless anti-Chinese narrative for audiences immersed in opposition echo chambers. The post-riot puppetmaster trope also served to distract attention from this more mundane reality of responsibility by sections of the establishment.

In this chapter, I examine the noise of the opposition echo chamber and how its volume peaked around the time of the riots, leading the government to impose restrictions on media uploads on social media platforms in order to limit the flow of "fake news". It is likely that this episode of socially mediated unrest followed by official censorship is merely the beginning of the era of digitally disrupted and polarized politics in Indonesia.

POPULISM AND ANTI-CHINESE SOCIAL PRIMING

During the Suharto regime, anti-Chinese sentiment in Indonesia focused on the economic power of a small but wealthy ethnic Chinese elite. Contemporary tropes draw on this background but shift focus to conspiracy theories about China "colonizing" Indonesia in collaboration with local ethnic Chinese, enabled by a corrupt and complicit political elite. This foreign-local conspiracy is referred to by the partial rhyming couplet *asing dan aseng*, with *asing* meaning foreigners and *aseng* being a derogatory term for Chinese Indonesians. The assonance of the phrase has served to encode *asing*—even when deployed alone—with anti-Chinese connotations, creating a pitch-perfect dog-whistle for populists to invoke xenophobia and ethno-nationalism in the one breath. Well before the 2019 election, Indonesian populists deployed anti-Chinese messaging such as this, in effect priming the population to respond to subtle cues by supplying their own anti-Chinese conclusions. Through this process, come election time, populists may trigger anti-Chinese sentiment while maintaining plausible deniability.

The most common anti-Chinese conspiracy narrative circulated online during the 2019 election campaign was that of colonization (*penjajahan*). Typically, the theory suggests that foreign workers are a disguised advance force sent to "flood" Indonesia prior to "neo-colonization" or "occupation". Images and videos purport to show foreign workers (*tenaga kerja asing* or TKA, for short, but also read as *tenaga kerja aseng*) deluging Indonesia or already secretly within the country. In this light, China's Belt and Road Initiative (BRI) is presented as a façade for occupation. One code word often used to signal the threat of Chinese hoards set to overwhelm Indonesia is the term "IndoChina". In its concision and grammar, it makes for the perfect hashtag. The colonization conspiracy theory may be recognized as a counterpart of the white nationalist "replacement theory" popular among far-right groups in Europe and the United States, which depicts Muslims as conspiring to demographically dominate whites (Bowles 2019).

During the election campaign, Prabowo often used language that resonated with the disinformation narrative of Chinese colonization. The theme of colonization had been set out in his 2017 book, *Paradoks Indonesia*, in which he writes:

> After more than 70 years as a nation, after our predecessors bravely rejected being re-colonized by foreign powers, now our country remains under threat of being colonized again. But now their colonization is cleverer, better, more subtle, more cunning. They don't send soldiers, they simply "buy" and bribe our leaders (Prabowo 2017, p. 66).

As chief populist-in-waiting, Prabowo has long sought to brandish some sort of existential threat to the nation from which he would be the only saviour. In 2018 he drew criticism for claiming that by 2030 Indonesia may no longer exist (BBC 2018). His source for this claim was a novel, *Ghost Fleet*, which imagines a future world war in which an expanding and belligerent China attacks America, and Indonesia has long since disintegrated into an archipelago of warring militias. Although the source was derided by critics in the media as merely fiction, Prabowo understood correctly that the authors are strategic analysts who offer the book as a form of FICINT or "fiction intelligence"—a genre that seeks to generate insights into plausible military scenarios through creative writing (Cole and Whitt 2019).

Colonization was a theme at Prabowo's centrepiece campaign event held at Gelora Bung Karno on 17 April 2019. Addressing the stadium crowd and live TV audience, he said Indonesia was being "raped" and its wealth "stolen" by the elite. "Once", he continued, "the Indonesian people expelled the colonizers. Now, the Indonesian people will expel the colonizers from within their own people." (*tvOne* 2019a). Who exactly these colonizers are is left to the imagination.

Earlier in the campaign, in a melodramatic performance on the same theme in Yogyakarta on 8 April, Prabowo had become so animated he dislodged a microphone. Delivering a pointed message to the military and police, he banged the lectern and yelled, "You are the people's military. You are the people's police. All the people of Indonesia. You must not serve only a handful of people. Much less defend foreign lackeys. We must seize back our sovereignty!" (*tvOne* 2019b). The performance, as polished as professional wrestling kayfabe, has since found immortality as an internet meme.

The anti-Chinese semaphore of Amien Rais, founder of Partai Amanat Nasional (National Mandate Party or PAN, for short) and a senior opposition coalition figure, was rather explicit. Since the Purnama controversy, Amien has often deployed the rhetoric of *"asing dan aseng"*—for example, when he plainly told Jokowi in 2017 "to not sell the country to *asing and aseng*" (Fahrizal 2017). One of his most dramatic uses of the phrase was at a May Day rally in front of the Indonesian parliament in 2018. Masks created out of an unidentified photograph of a man with Chinese features were distributed at the event. To avoid any ambiguity, the masks were emblazoned with the words "Unskilled Aseng Labour" (*Buruh Kasar Aseng*). From atop a mobile command post, Amien ceremonially held up one of the masks and tore it to pieces before scattering it into the air like confetti. He was joined in the mask-tearing ceremony by Fadli Zon, deputy leader of Prabowo's party, Gerindra, and other opposition figures (*Kumparan* 2018; *Liputan 6* 2018).

Amien invoked the colonization conspiracy theory early on in the election year, at a discussion forum in January. He warned that China had a plan in place to occupy Indonesia. He claimed to have special knowledge from an army general of a conspiracy to use Chinese troops to suppress the mass Islamist mobilizations known as the "Defence of Islam" protests. He reportedly said, "If [the demonstrations] result in shops and the like being damaged, security will be enforced not by the TNI [Indonesian military] but by the Chinese army that is present in Indonesia and has tens of thousands of weapons in the major cities. This is not a hoax. You can quote this." (*Merdeka.com* 2019).

Certain Islamist opposition leaders have been just as provocative and helped to seed the information ecosystem with anti-Chinese messages. At least since the mass Islamist mobilizations against then-Jakarta governor Purnama, Habib Rizieq Shihab, leader of the Front Pembela Islam (Islamic Defenders Front or FPI, for short), has raised the spectre of Chinese colonization. In September 2016, Rizieq called for Indonesians to "rise up" and save Indonesia from colonization by *"asing dan aseng"*, a threat he compared to Indonesia's occupation by the Dutch (*Era Muslim* 2016).

Claims of "dog-whistle" rhetoric in political speech can be overdone and can take the form of an unfalsifiable claim. But subtle anti-

Chinese priming is detectable in Indonesia if one looks at the pattern of rhetoric over time. The examples above are just a sample drawn from what I happened to observe perusing the Indonesian media. The point is that the electorate is socially primed to pick up on cues to anti-Chinese sentiment, even if these cues would be rejected by most Indonesians.[1] Much of the priming and cueing process travels below the radar of the international media and much of it is not reported by the local media because of the taboo around anti-Chinese sentiment. The subtlety of the rhetoric, however, is key to its power and how it evades criticism.

By the time of the 2019 election, multiple news events arose and played into already primed anti-Chinese themes. From March, perhaps the first major false narrative of the campaign emerged when claims circulated online that used ballot papers punched for Jokowi had been discovered in a shipping container from China. The disinformation was distributed on WhatsApp and various social media platforms. The false story developed into one of the largest hoax news stories of the election campaign after it was amplified online by Democrat Party politician Andi Arief (*Tempo.co* 2019a).

The most provocative rendition of the colonization trope of the 2019 election appeared in a video recording of a private post-election discussion group in May, featuring senior Gerindra politician Permadi Satria Wiwoho. In an impassioned monologue, Permadi called for "revolution" in the face of the threat of occupation by China. He anticipated violence at the announcement of the election result on 22 May. "On the 22nd when it is announced there will definitely be conflict. Whether Jokowi wins or Prabowo wins, there will still be conflict, because they [the opposition] are prepared to die. We are also prepared to die. The *ulama* and the *habaib* have declared jihad." (*Suara.com* 2019). Permadi was investigated by the police for hate speech for his comments. In defending himself, he said his remarks were made at a private Gerindra meeting at parliament, at the invitation of party founder Fadli Zon (*IDN Times* 2019a).

THE RIOTS

Historical tropes, social priming, and election disinformation set the stage for conflict in 2019. Acting on the belief that the presidential election had been stolen by incumbent Jokowi, thousands of supporters of Prabowo descended in protest on the office of the Election Supervisory Agency (Bawaslu) on 21 May. The protests were triggered by the official declaration of Jokowi as the winner early that same morning, a timing chosen to minimize attention and the potential for backlash. Protesters, marching under the banner of the National Movement for People's Sovereignty (GNKR), demanded that Bawaslu disqualify Jokowi and his running mate, Ma'ruf Amin, for electoral fraud that was "structured, systematic and massive"—the legal threshold to overturn an election result under Indonesia's electoral law (CNN Indonesia 2019).

After nightfall, as the protests outside the Bawaslu office dissipated, smaller numbers of people began to throw rocks and Molotov cocktails at the police. Skirmishes between rioters and police broke out in the Tanah Abang area of Central Jakarta, an area adjacent to the Bawaslu office that is historically associated with Jakarta's street gangs. A violent incident occurred outside the headquarters of FPI, also in Tanah Abang. A nearby police dormitory came under attack. By the end of 23 May, eight civilians were dead, hundreds had been injured, and over 400 people had been arrested in the worst street violence in Jakarta since the fall of Suharto in 1998.

In the weeks leading up to and during the riots, partisans of the government and of the opposition appeared to have been inhabiting almost completely separate information ecosystems. Opposition audiences were exposed to a social media echo chamber teeming with accounts of election rigging, vague but ominous threats of violence and foreign intervention, and suggestions that the TNI would be deployed to defend the nation. Fake and misleading reports of this nature circulated on YouTube, some videos with millions of views.[2] As a result of YouTube's suggestion algorithm, viewers of such videos found that they were served an increasingly rich diet of similar fake news—a classic case of the so-called YouTube "rabbit hole" phenomenon (*New York Times* 2019).

In this context, at the outbreak of street violence, pro-opposition message groups on encrypted chat platforms WhatsApp and Telegram became deluged with paranoid fake news and misinformation. The master frame of such misinformation was the allegation of massive electoral fraud (*kecurangan*). But a high proportion of message traffic consisted of anti-Chinese disinformation and conspiracy theories, even if this messaging was less visible in the public and on open platforms. On 22 May, in order to reduce fake news traffic, the Ministry of Communications and Information blocked the ability to upload media (video and photo) to several social media platforms, including WhatsApp, Facebook, Instagram and Twitter. This temporary move, however, appeared only to drive more activity to chat groups on the Telegram platform, where the traffic in anti-Chinese disinformation continued apace.

ANTI-CHINESE DISINFORMATION

Online disinformation that the election had been stolen helped to engender the volatile atmosphere in which the riots took place. Meanwhile, fake news and conspiracy theories drawing on anti-Chinese tropes raised the risk of racially motivated violence. The level of risk is impossible to specify but it would have been higher had the police not drastically constrained protester movement, both from surrounding regions into Jakarta and within the city itself. Fortunately, no anti-Chinese violence eventuated. The elevated level of anti-Chinese disinformation, however, persisted beyond the immediate post-election period and formed the background noise to a murky plot to bomb ethnic Chinese targets in North Jakarta, a plot disrupted by police in September (*Majalah Tempo* 2019).

The primary false narrative circulating during the riots was that of Chinese "colonization". Message groups became deluged with false claims that soldiers from mainland China had infiltrated the Indonesian National Police (Polri) and were being allowed by the Jokowi government to repress opposition protesters. Some versions of the conspiracy theory suggested the (non-existent) Indonesian Communist Party was colluding with the Chinese Communist Party in the plot.[3]

Out of context, reports of Chinese troops on the street of Jakarta might sound implausible. But within the militant opposition social media echo chamber, the false narrative was the logical extension of months, if not years, of conspiracy theories on the theme of Chinese neo-imperialism. In addition to feeding into anti-Chinese sentiment, the "Chinese soldiers" hoax contributed to a dangerous false narrative that accused the police of communist sympathies and sought to play the police off against the army.

Animosity between the Islamist opposition and the police had developed in Indonesia since the mass mobilizations against Purnama, after which a number of Muslim opposition leaders were investigated or charged. A common claim, made by FPI and others, is that the government is "criminalizing" Muslim leaders. Since 2016, an Islamist conspiracy theory has asserted that the police have communist sympathies. A foundational document of this false narrative is the 1963 text of several speeches by Indonesian Communist Party leader D.N. Aidit to Indonesian police officers in order to raise their revolutionary consciousness, published under the title *PKI dan Polisi* (Aidit 1963). The PDF of the booklet continues to circulate in Islamist circles.

During the riots of 21–23 May, a stream of messages and discussions appeared on Facebook, WhatsApp and Telegram suggesting that Chinese troops had infiltrated the police deployed to counter the rioters. One message, circulated on Facebook on 22 May, commented on an image taken from television footage of mobile brigade police (Brimob) forcing back rioters. The message by "Khumayra" said, "The language spoken by these Brimob members is Chinese. So it is not a hoax that Brimob has been infiltrated by the Chinese military."[4] Another user, active on Telegram, wrote in response to the "Chinese soldiers" hoax, "I thought only foreign workers were being brought from China; in fact [Chinese] are also being brought to kill the people."

In one of its regular reports, the Ministry of Communications and Information notes a different iteration of the same conspiracy narrative circulating as a series of messages on WhatsApp. The messages warned of "mass kidnapping" by Chinese troops, one of them stating:

> Take care those who want to travel to Jakarta [for the protests]. If there is a free lift and you don't know the driver, don't accept it. Because there is a plot to kidnap en masse and Chinese soldiers are on standby with weapons in strategic places. This info is from Koramil [Indonesian military]. Spread to your groups, the info is validated by a Gerindra candidate. (Kementrian Kominfo 2019)

The ministry report adds that fake news about Chinese soldiers infiltrating Indonesia has circulated online for some time. It refers to the case of a Facebook post on 19 December 2018 that claimed "as many as 500 thousand soldiers from China are already inside Indonesia and they are ready to burn the whole of Indonesia" (Kementrian Kominfo 2019).

During the riots, the "Chinese soldiers" hoax was disseminated and discussed incessantly on Telegram chat groups where militant opposition activists and Islamists congregated. The stream of disinformation was striking for its images of masked Indonesian police who were said to be Chinese soldiers, identifiable by their facial features, deployed against the protesters. Some posts elicited threatening messages by other users, including calls to behead the troops and steal their rifles.

Although the disinformation narrative spread mostly on private groups and encrypted chats, the Indonesian police correctly saw it as presenting a risk to its officers. On 24 May at the National Police Headquarters, the Polri public relations unit held a press conference in which three officers whose images had been used in the hoax were presented to the public. In a dramatic scene made for live television, the officers unmasked themselves before the cameras and proceeded to give their names and birthplaces in order to prove that they were Indonesian—not Chinese—citizens (*Liputan 6* 2019).

"MOSQUE ATTACK" DISINFORMATION

Compounding the "stolen election" and "Chinese soldiers" narratives, after the outbreak of violence on the night of 21 May, fake news was spread that a historic mosque located not far from the protests had been attacked by the police. The Al-Makmur mosque, which had been at the centre of the post-Purnama mass Islamist mobilizations, was one of dozens of mosques in the area where protesters from outside Jakarta had stayed overnight (*Tempo.co* 2019b). One version of the false story claimed that the police involved in the "attack" were ethnic Chinese (Reuters 2019); other versions appearing within the stream of messages and photographs in opposition chat groups were less specific, depicting the national police as having been infiltrated by "Chinese soldiers".

The origins of the hoax can be traced to the night of 21 May, when violence first broke out in front of the Bawaslu building. As police forced protesters back from the building towards the Central Jakarta suburb of Tanah Abang, their rounds of rubber bullets and tear gas appear to have come in close proximity to the mosque, which is located along the route. Panic appears to have been sparked among protesters, who feared that the mosque was being targeted. In a brief, shaky video circulated on messaging apps not long after the incident, titled "Tanah Abang Mosque Situation", an unidentified voice says "Al-Makmur mosque in Tanah Abang is being fired on by inhumane police, we are being fired on here...."[5] The video circulated widely on opposition message groups and those of militant Islamist groups—including pro-ISIS groups—that rapidly took up the opposition cause. In one crossover pro-opposition jihadist message group, the "mosque attack" hoax video was forwarded with the comment, "the masses are being massacred by police at the Al Ma'mun [sic] Mosque, Tanah Abang". Someone in the same group then commented, "Al-Makmur mosque is being shot at exactly like at Al-Aqsa", in reference to the mosque in Jerusalem, the third holiest site in Islam, often a target in the Israel-Palestine conflict.[6]

Jejak News Agency, a recently emerged jihadist Telegram account styled as a newswire, also reported the "mosque attack", spreading the disinformation across the Indonesian jihadist community. The article stated: "Reportedly the riots grew bigger last night after many of the Aksi 212 [Islamist mobilisation] masses were injured and even reportedly died; moreover police and Brimob shot at the masses inside a mosque and caused the mosque to be damaged." (Jejak News Agency 2019).

A video that circulated on the night of 21 May and morning of 22 May spread the hoax by using prominent local Muslim figures to add credibility. Titled "Siaga Jihad" (Jihad Alert), the video featured three Tanah Abang Muslim figures standing in the street with the burning and exploding debris from the riots in the background. One of the men, a prominent community leader, Fachry Al-Habsyi, was identified in the credits.[7] In the brief recording the men called for people to join them to defend the mosque against the attack. Fachry Al-Habsyi shouts: "Defend Tanah Abang! Tanah Abang is the bastion of the Muslim community. I invite all to join us—all!—tonight. The Al-Makmur mosque is the pride of the Muslim community in Tanah Abang; not just Tanah Abang, even in West Sumatra they know this mosque."[8]

In fact, the mosque had not been damaged and the reports of an attack were denied by the police and debunked in a detailed account by the online news site Tirto (Fahri Salam 2019). But in one of the most provocative moments of the post-election conflict, the following day, Amien Rais visited Al-Makmur mosque, where he made a statement that further perpetuated the hoax. In a video posted to his official Instagram account, Amien waved a bullet jacket as he stood in the mosque, declaring, "My brothers, I'm crying. I'm very, very sad, but also angry that the police, who I think smell like PKI [Communist Party of Indonesia], have crudely shot at the Muslim community."[9]

Following the riots, police investigators and journalists focused on the premeditated and coordinated aspect of the violence. Indeed, there is evidence that a degree of preparation and coordination by bad actors helped to turn the peaceful protest into a street battle, employing Tanah Abang gang figures with connections to Prabowo (*IDN Times* 2019b). Despite much speculation, however, a "puppetmaster" or *dalang* who could be blamed for orchestrating the whole episode was never found. That there is always a *dalang* behind an outbreak of political violence is one of the most tired clichés in Indonesian politics. But what if, in an age of social media flash mobs, a *dalang* is no longer even necessary to coordinate events like the post-election riots? What if, in Indonesia as elsewhere in the world, the internet creates the conditions for emergent phenomena—like protests and riots and all kinds of new swarming behaviour—that arise and subside without anyone taking the lead?

In any case, seen against the background I have outlined in this chapter, a puppetmaster is not necessary to explain the post-election violence in Indonesia in 2019. All the necessary ingredients are in plain sight, on the public record or in the online chat records. A cocktail of false information and local grievances created a fertile environment for spontaneous post-election violence.[10] Beneath the platitudes from the authorities and some organizations, including FPI, that the rioters were an unknown "third force", there is abundant evidence that many individuals who got caught up in the violence were motivated by false or misleading information. These included FPI members (*RMOL Bengkulu* 2019; *Radar Tasikmalaya* 2019). But they also included an assortment of mosque youth, street toughs, locals who saw themselves as defending their *kampung* (village), and a number of underage youth from West Java and other regions who had been sent to Jakarta by their religious teachers to join the protest of the election results (*Rakyat Merdeka* 2019).

As *Tempo* magazine found in its first detailed report on the riots, although some people were paid to join the unrest, others were motivated by disinformation, such as the "mosque attack" story:

> There were those who attacked the police because they were victims of misleading information after watching a viral video on social media. In that video Mobil Brigade [police] members were suspected of shooting at a mosque in Tanah Abang while in pursuit of demonstrators. Sapto Putra Permana, 22 years, who was provoked after watching the video, decided to go to the streets and fight the police without checking the accuracy [of the video]. "I couldn't accept that my religion was being meddled with", said the man from Radio Dalam, South Jakarta. (*Majalah Tempo* 2019, p. 37)

Sapto was hospitalized after being shot by police in the leg with a rubber bullet.

CONCLUSION

Much of the details of the 2019 election riots remain murky. Conveniently, government and opposition figures alike have found a scapegoat in the notion of unknown "third actors". The puppetmaster and "third actor" tropes are particularly useful given that Prabowo ultimately transitioned from contesting the election results to entering the Jokowi cabinet as minster for defence—setting him up for a run for the presidency in 2024. Yet, with Indonesia's establishment now in a ritual "reconciliation" phase, the lessons of the post-election violence must not be lost in the "fog of peace".

It is impossible to know what proportion of the violence against police and property was caused by cynical actors and paid provocateurs, and what proportion was motivated by genuinely held grievances generated by fake news and disinformation. There may have been a complex interplay of both factors that developed in dangerous and unpredictable ways on the streets of the capital. But Indonesia in 2019 has given the world a salutary example of how ethnic and religiously motivated disinformation can spiral out of control on social media and lead to offline violence.

Election disinformation gathered force in 2019 within a nested sequence of conspiracies—"stolen election", "Chinese soldiers", "mosque attack". No ethnic violence eventuated, but the risk was apparent.

There may have been some close calls. For example, the police alleged that Yunarto Wijaya, the prominent director of a polling institute, was targeted for assassination along with four senior government officials. Yunarto believes he was singled out as the only non-official target owing to his Chinese heritage—a heritage he is outspoken about on social media (Najwa Shihab 2019). An equally murky plot to bomb Chinese-Indonesian targets was disrupted by the police in September. Both plot allegations are highly disputed, but both are correlated with the election-cycle spike in anti-Chinese disinformation.

The risk of anti-Chinese violence, however small, is likely to recur at the next election if three key background factors remain present in Indonesia: populism, anxiety over the rise of China as a force in Southeast Asia, and social media disinformation. Anxiety over Chinese influence increasingly plays a role in uniting right-wing nationalists and Islamists against the Jokowi government. The 2019 presidential election cycle is over, but political phenomena emerging from dark corners of the internet and fuelled by social media are just beginning.

NOTES

1. To be clear, I am not making a claim about how effective such priming is on the Indonesian public and I note that social priming theory in psychology is one of the high-profile casualties of the "replication crisis". See Chivers (2019).
2. These videos have since been removed.
3. Photo and WhatsApp message screenshot, "Kami Partai Komunis Indonesian Telah Bekerjasama dengan Partai Komunis China", 22 May 2019.
4. Khumayra, screenshot of Facebook post, 22 May 2019.
5. Kondisi masjid Tanah Abang
6. Telegram messages, 22 May 2019.
7. Siaga Jihad, mp4 recording, 21 May 2019.
8. Ibid.
9. Instagram, @amienraisofficial, 22 May 2019, https://www.instagram.com/p/BxvlRSiA28J/.
10. For other aspects of why Tanah Abang was volatile, see Ahmad Syarif Syechbubakr (2019).

REFERENCES

Ahmad Syarif Syechbubakr. 2019. "The Urban Poor in the Jakarta Riots". *Indonesia at Melbourne*, 11 June 2019. https://indonesiaatmelbourne.unimelb.edu.au/the-urban-poor-in-the-jakarta-riots/.

Bambang Tri. 2016. *Jokowi Undercover: Melacak Jejak Sang Pemalsu Jatidiri*.

BBC. 2018. "Cek fakta seputar pernyataan Prabowo bahwa Indonesia bubar pada 2030", 24 March 2018. https://www.bbc.com/indonesia/indonesia-43490128.

Bowles, Nellie. 2019. "'Replacement Theory,' a Racist, Sexist Doctrine, Spreads in Far-Right Circles". *New York Times*, 18 March 2019. https://www.nytimes.com/2019/03/18/technology/replacement-theory.html.

Chivers, Tom. 2019. "What's Next for Psychology's Embattled Field of Social Priming". *Nature*, 11 December 2019. https://www.nature.com/articles/d41586-019-03755-2.

CNN Indonesia. 2019. "Gerakan Nasional Kedaulatan Rakyat Satroni Bawaslu 21-25 Mei", 19 May 2019. https://www.cnnindonesia.com/nasional/20190519014515-32-396089/gerakan-nasional-kedaulatan-rakyat-satroni-bawaslu-21-25-mei.

Cole, August and Jacqueline E. Whitt. 2019. "'Ficint': Envisioning Future War Through Fiction & Intelligence". *War Room*, 22 May 2019. https://warroom.armywarcollege.edu/special-series/indo-pacific-region/ficint-envisioningfuture-war-through-fiction-intelligence-indo-pacific-series/.

Era Muslim. 2016. "Habib Rizieq: Selamatkan NKRI Dari Penjajahan Asing dan Aseng!", 29 September 2016. https://www.eramuslim.com/berita/nasional/habib-rizieq-selamatkan-nkridari-penjajahan-asing-dan-aseng.htm.

Fahri Salam. 2019. "Benarkan Polisike Menembak ke Arah Masjid Al Ma'mur, Tanah Abang?". *Tirto.id*, 29 May 2019. https://tirto.id/benarkah-polisi-menembak-ke-arah-masjidal-mamur-tanah-abang-d9hZ.

Fahrizal Fahmi Daulay. 2017. "Sindiran Kecebong Amien Rais, Minta Jangan Jual Negara Pada Asing dan Aseng di Reuni 212". *Tribun Medan*, 2 December 2017. https://medan.tribunnews.com/2017/12/02/sindiran-kecebong-amien-rais-minta-jangan-jualnegara-pada-asing-dan-aseng-di-reuni-212.

IDN Times. 2019a. "Permadi Batal Diperiksa Setelah Tunggu Penyidik 2,5 Jam", 27 May 2019. https://www.idntimes.com/news/indonesia/axel-harianja/permadi-batal-diperiksasetelah-tunggu-penyidik-25-jam/full.

_____. 2019b. "Terkait Kerusuhan 22 Mei, Polisi akan Panggil Eks Anggota Tim Mawar", 11 June 2019. https://www.idntimes.com/news/indonesia/axel-harianja/terkait-aksi-22-meipolisi-panggil-eks-anggota-tim-mawar/.

Jejak News Agency. 2019. "Kericuhan Terjadi Diwilayah Jakarta Pusat, Dimana Masa Aksi 22 Menuntut Untuk Menggunlingkan Rezim Jokowi", 22 May 2019.

Kementerian Kominfo. 2019. "Laporan Isu Hoaks Terkait Kerusuhan", 25 May 2019.

Kumparan. 2018. "Amien Rais Sobek Topeng Bertulis Tenaga Kerja Aseng", 1 May 2018. https://www.youtube.com/watch?v=zsfmOcAHxC4.

Liputan 6. 2018. "Amien Rais hingga Fadli Zon Hadiri Aksi Buruh di Depan DPR", 1 May 2018. https://www.liputan6.com/news/read/3495860/amien-rais-hingga-fadli-zon-hadiri-aksiburuh-di-depan-dpr.

_____. 2019. "Bantah Hoaks 'Polisi Impor' dari China, 3 Brimob Dipamerkan di Mabes Polri", 24 May 2019. https://www.liputan6.com/news/read/3974925/bantah-hoaks-polisiimpor-dari-china-3-brimob-dipamerkan-di-mabes-polri.

Majalah Tempo. 2019. "Skenario Bom Supermi di Aksi 212", 5 October 2019. https://majalah.tempo.co/read/hukum/158531/skenario-bom-supermi-di-aksi-212.

Merdeka.com. 2019. "Amien Rais Tuding Tentara China Siap Duduki Indonesia", 15 January 2019. https://www.merdeka.com/politik/amien-rais-tuding-tentara-china-siap-dudukiindonesia.html.

Najwa Shihab. 2019. "Soal Cina dan Jilbab: Blak-blakan Merawat Indonesia", 15 July 2019. https://www.youtube.com/watch?v=_aUfAHtT8-E&t=2448s.

New York Times. 2019. "The Making of a Youtube Radical", 8 June 2019. https://www.nytimes.com/interactive/2019/06/08/technology/youtube-radical.html.

Prabowo Subianto. 2017. *Paradoks Indonesia: negara kaya raya, tetapi masih banyak rakyat hidup miskin*. Pasar Minggu, Jakarta: KGN, Koperasi Garudayaksa Nusantara.

Purdey, Jemma. 2006. *Anti-Chinese Violence in Indonesia, 1996–1999*. Honolulu: University of Hawaii Press.

Radar Tasikmalaya. 2019. "Jakarta Rusuh, Laskar FPI Tewas Diduga Tertembak", 22 May 2019. https://www.radartasikmalaya.com/jakarta-rusuh-laskar-fpi-tewas-diduga-tertembak/.

Rakyat Merdeka. 2019. "Bunut Peristiwa Kerusuhan 22 Mei Yang Diduga Melibatkan Anananak", 11 July 2019.

Reuters. 2019. "'We're not Chinese officers': Indonesia fights anti-China disinformation", 24 May 2019. https://uk.reuters.com/article/uk-indonesia-election-fakenews/were-not-chineseofficers-indonesia-fights-anti-china-disinformation-idUKKCN1SU1QI.

RMOL Bengkulu. 2019. "Seorang Laskar FPI Peserta Aksi Dikabarkan Tewas Di Tanah Abang", 22 May 2019. http://www.rmolbengkulu.com/read/2019/05/22/16721/Seorang-Laskar-FPI-Peserta-Aksi-Dikabarkan-Tewas-Di-Tanah-Abang-.

Rmol.id. 2019. "Daftar 34 Masjid Di Jakarta Yang Bisa Disinggahi Peserta Aksi Kedaulatan Rakyat", 17 May 2019. https://politik.rmol.id/read/2019/05/17/390164/daftar-34-masjid-dijakarta-yang-bisa-disinggahi-peserta-aksi-kedaulatan-rakyat.

Setijadi, Charlotte. 2017. "Chinese Indonesians in the Eyes of the Pribumi Public". *ISEAS Perspective*, no. 2017/73, 27 September 2017. https://www.iseas.edu.sg/images/pdf/ISEAS_Perspective_2017_73.pdf.

Suara.com. 2019. "Sebut Revolusi dan Jihad, Inikah Video Permadi yang Berujung Dipolisikan?", 10 May 2019. https://www.suara.com/news/2019/05/10/144048/sebutrevolusi-dan-jihad-inikah-video-permadi-yang-berujung-dipolisikan.

Tempo.co. 2019a. "[Fakta atau Hoax] Benarkah Surat Suara Dikirim dengan Kontainer dari Cina?", 12 March 2019. https://cekfakta.tempo.co/fakta/145/fakta-atau-hoax-benarkah-surat-suara-dikirim-dengankontainer-dari-cina.

———. 2019b. "Waktunya Semakin Dekat, Inilah Lima Hal tentang Aksi 22 Mei", 19 May 2019. https://nasional.tempo.co/read/1206926/waktunya-semakin-dekat-inilah-lima-haltentang-aksi-22-mei/full&view=ok.

tvOne. 2019a. "Orasi Politik Prabowo Subianto Pada Kampanye Akbar di Stadion Utama GBK, Jakarta", 7 April 2019. https://www.youtube.com/watch?v=5kY7mAmphOs.

———. 2019b. "Kampanye Akbar Prabowo-Sandi di Kridosono Yogyakarta", 8 April 2019. https://www.youtube.com/watch?time_continue=2&v=3xmacrLkN0w.

Tyson, Adam and Budi Purnomo. 2017. "President Jokowi and the 2014 Obor Rakyat Controversy in Indonesia". *Critical Asian Studies* 49, no. 1: 117–36.

PART II:

Constituencies

6

THE POLITICAL ECONOMY OF POLARIZATION: MILITIAS, STREET AUTHORITY AND THE 2019 ELECTIONS

Ian Wilson

"Joining Pemuda Pancasila has been great for business. I now have over 100 staff, an expanding portfolio and owe a lot of it to them." Heru pauses to sip his whisky on the rocks. "This ice is supplied by Pemuda Pancasila, best quality in Jakarta." He was sitting in an upmarket bar in a five-star Jakarta hotel owned by a mid-ranking member of the paramilitary organization Pemuda Pancasila. The venue and its clientele, consisting largely of fashionable upper middle-class millennials, is seemingly far removed from the street-level thuggery or seedy "nightlife" with which many still associate the paramilitary group and others like it. In his late-twenties and an ethnic Chinese, Heru constitutes the changing face of Pemuda Pancasila, part of a younger generation of an old organization still synonymous for many with political gangsterism and the violent excesses of the New Order regime.

Heru's motivations for membership, situated within the context of what many have argued is Indonesia's deep political polarization around sectarian identity, are both self-servingly pragmatic and "idealistic". The group's extensive networks, influence and muscle have been an eminently practical means for gaining strategic business advantage in the push and shove of Jakarta's hyper-competitive financial services market. Affiliation with the group has also, he claims, afforded protection at a time when anti-Chinese sentiment has regained political traction. This protection is corporeal but also "ideological", to the extent that Pemuda Pancasila has long represented itself as a frontline defender of the state ideology of Pancasila from an array of real and imaginary threats, the most historically salient of which has been "communism". It has been reconfigured in current times as defenders of a "Pancasila-prescribed notion of communal pluralism" and "moderation" in the face of Islamist radicalism and politicized "intolerance". The irony of seeking protection from an organization with a well-documented history of the targeted persecution of ethnic Chinese was not lost on Heru. "I've seen the movie *Act of Killing*, but you know times have changed. The lines of division and what is at stake are different from the old days."

For Heru and many others, the huge Islamist mobilizations in 2016–17, pivotal in the electoral defeat and conviction for blasphemy of Jakarta's former governor, Basuki Tjahaja Purnama ("Ahok"), constituted something of a turning point moment. In contrast to their relatively peripheral role in 2014, the Islamist group Front Pembela Islam (FPI)—the prime mover behind the anti-Purnama mobilizations—became central to presidential candidate Prabowo Subianto's 2019 campaign as articulators of the rhetorical parameters of an identity-based polarization. Some of its members held key positions in the campaign team while Habib Riziq Shihab, known to his followers as grand imam of FPI, emerged as a rallying figure in exile and "spiritual" guide to the opposition. Long-time actors associated with street-level vigilantism and morality racketeering, the FPI has from its inception deployed as its central strategy a mode of polarizing politics and discourse revolving around identifying threats to an imagined *ummah* (Islamic community) against which it offers militant protection. With the mobilizations against Purnama, the FPI found its moment in the sun. Its rising influence, political prominence and assertiveness as part of the Prabowo 2019 campaign, however, not only produced deep anxieties among those subject to the FPI's vitriol, such as ethnic and religious minorities, but also served to antagonize, alienate and polarize many of their fellow militias and paramilitary groups, often referred to as "social organisations" or *ormas*, including those in the Prabowo camp.

As many commentators have noted, deepening polarization has become a defining feature of Indonesian electoral contestation, although there remains much debate over its parameters and depth. This polarization has been variously described as geocultural (Lane 2019), reflective of socioreligious ideological cleavages such as pluralist-Islamist (Aspinall 2019) and as social media-driven identity politics providing superficial points of differentiation between otherwise ideologically similar candidates (Tapsell 2019). As Warburton (2019) has argued, polarization has been relatively contingent on circumstances, peaking around periods of electoral conflict and then mellowing, but by no means disappearing. It is nonetheless at the level of society that it has arguably been felt most acutely, rather than at the level of contesting political elites, where "reconciliation" efforts through the offer of key government positions to opposition figures typically take place in the immediate post-election period.

This chapter examines some of the dynamics of political polarization via the shifting politics of *ormas* in the lead-up to the 2019 national elections, focusing on Jakarta. After examining the historical relationship of *ormas* with electoral democracy in Indonesia, it considers the rise of the FPI and its role in shaping the parameters of electoral polarization. It is suggested that FPI's role generated significant tensions among and within militia groups previously united in their support for Prabowo, leading some to reassess where their best interests lay. Based on the case of *ormas*, the paper argues that polarization has been not only experienced as an identity-based cleavage but also reflected in shifting and contesting patterns of patronage, economic interest and modes of authority. The rise of FPI and militias on the Islamist right has had reverberating effects in parts of Jakarta, challenging existing political economies of protection and the modes of authority underpinning these. This has produced new alliances and political recalibrations by rival militia groups to protect their economic interests, a development that has seen deepening ties between these groups and state-owned enterprises and political mobilization on behalf of the Jokowi administration.

ORMAS IN ELECTORAL DEMOCRACY

Ormas, militias, paramilitary and street organizations have been a staple but changing feature of Indonesian electoral democracy. In the immediate post-New Order period, political parties reproduced New Order-style militarism via so-called *satgas*, party paramilitary groups that blurred the lines between party functionary and political protection racket. From the mid-2000s the role of *satgas* declined significantly after the introduction of regulations restricting their use, combined with the drain they placed on party resources. Instead, parties and politicians have formed more fluid, contingent and contractual-type alliances with an array of "social organizations" or *ormas*, an ambiguous term that encompasses a broad array of religious, communal, ethnic, nationalist and "youth"-oriented organizations, but which is commonly used as shorthand for often predatory militia-like groups (Wilson 2015).

Ormas of this kind have often blurred the line between vigilantism, political entrepreneurship, campaign vehicle and opportunity structures for the socio-economically marginal, considering that the bulk of the membership of many groups such as the FPI, Pemuda Pancasila, Forkabi, Laskar Merah Putih and Forum Betawi Rempug (FBR) have consisted of poor and working-class men. In the context of local and national elections, *ormas* can and have provided various services and strategic advantages, ranging from security, intimidating rivals, mobilizing crowds and voters, and brokering deals between constituencies they claim to represent and the political elites. Some *ormas*, as in the case of the FPI, have the ability to significantly shape the parameters of political and electoral discourse. *Ormas* have also been significant vehicles through which popular political agency is channelled, co-opted and shaped. In return *ormas* have gained financial and political rewards, including economic opportunities, exemptions and in some instances pathways to formal power (Wilson 2015).

With mass and localized mobilizations increasingly a key feature of Indonesian electoral politics, as seen in the series of so-called 212 Movement rallies in Jakarta, *ormas* have become crucial logistical partners for aspirants to power. This is underpinned by patterns of clientelist and contractual alliances that have become increasingly complex and contingent.

The 2014 presidential elections saw something of a political reorganizing of *ormas*. A key architect of the Indonesian military's use of militias and civilian proxies as a third arm of the state, Prabowo utilized this expertise as part of his electoral campaign strategy. While he established his political vehicle, Gerindra, in 2011, an entity known as Gerakan Rakyat Indonesia Baru (GRIB) was also set up (Wilson 2015). Led by the East Timorese "celebrity gangster" Hercules Rosario Marcal with whom Prabowo had a long, albeit troubled relationship, GRIB operated as the organizational umbrella for Prabowo's extensive networks of gangsters, local strongmen, Islamist vigilantes, ex-militias and martial arts groups. Despite its claimed independent status as a "supporter" organization, GRIB was firmly wedded, politically and economically, to Prabowo's political ambitions. On the ground GRIB, provided logistical support for grassroots campaigning and operated as an organizational hub for an array of *ormas* and local strongmen (Wilson 2015).

For groups that reproduced forms of militarism, from their uniforms to the territorial command structure, Prabowo's military pedigree and New Order strongman heritage made him the "natural" choice for many *ormas* (Wilson 2015). Groups such as Pemuda Pancasila, for example, considered Prabowo the flag-bearer for the kind of post-New Order authoritarianism they desired, framed ideologically as a "return" to the 1945 constitution (Bourchier 2019). On the other hand, President Joko Widodo (Jokowi), with his brand of everyman populism, presented to many, at least at the time, the possibility of a new kind of reformist and liberal democratic politics that could potentially threaten the interests of groups embedded in clientelist and predatory relations. In particular, perceptions of Jokowi as a liberal reformer, while unfounded, generated a degree of alarm, exacerbated by sustained black campaigning, in which many *ormas* were active participants, portraying him as the son of a communist and a closet Christian.

Prabowo's 2014 electoral loss saw the almost immediate unravelling of GRIB as a coherent organization. Hercules, after completing a pre-election stint in prison on charges of extortion and assault, returned to his previous career of debt-collection and land brokering. His role at the forefront of street-level campaigning as a so-called "war commander" (*panglima perang*) generated animosity among rivals who perceived his revived prominence as disruptive to existing street economies. These included the Jakarta police, who launched a crackdown on Hercules's networks that eventually led to his imprisonment.[1] Despite the loss, many *ormas* who had aligned behind Prabowo in 2014, such as Pemuda Pancasila and the ethnic militias Forum Betawi Rempug and Forkabi, remained ostensive political supporters while simultaneously working pragmatically to consolidate their interests under the Jokowi administration.

FPI AND THE 212 EFFECT

GRIB's post-2014 decline as a useful campaigning tool in Prabowo's strategic arsenal paved the opening for new contenders, and these would emerge from the turmoil of Jakarta City politics. Jokowi's decision to run for the presidency in 2014, which ruptured his relationship with Prabowo, saw his deputy, Purnama, take over the governorship, also much to the consternation of his former party boss. Purnama's confrontational style combined with his double minority status as ethnic Chinese and Christian quickly shifted the nature of the opposition to him, from one initially focused in part on public policy issues such as his aggressive evictions regimes to an overtly sectarian campaign.

At the forefront of vocal opposition to Purnama from early on, the FPI and a swag of Islamist and ethnic Betawi organizations such as the Forum Umat Islam (FUI) and FBR were key drivers of the Gerakan Masyarakat Jakarta (GMJ), a "moral" movement established in early 2014 in opposition to Purnama's ascendancy to the governorship. Symbolically appointing their own preferred "alternative governor", Kyai Fahrurozi Ishaq, a religious scholar and former politician of the Partai Persatuan Pembangunan (the Islam-based United Development Party or PPP, for short), the GMJ was crucial in developing the networks, mobilization patterns and ideological framing that would expand significantly in 2016 into the 212 Movement. The FPI had offered conditional support to Prabowo in the presidential elections in 2014, but it was with Purnama's defeat in the 2017 Jakarta gubernatorial election on the back of massive street mobilizations, and his subsequent conviction for blasphemy, that the alliance consolidated. Purnama's ouster was considered a major strategic success for the FPI, with its years of agitation, smear campaigns and street-level mobilizing finally gaining the degree of recognition and support it believed it deserved. Having succeeded in Jakarta in deposing Purnama, the 212 Movement that it had spearheaded provided a strategic and organizational template to be reproduced on the national stage, with the main target now being the Jokowi administration. Subsequent rallies continued to attract large crowds, drawn by diverse and often conflicting motives, but with organizers framing these in overtly political and unified terms.

As Aspinall (2019) notes, while in 2014 the Nahdlatul Ulama (NU) traditionalist Islamic organization was divided in its support for Jokowi, in 2019 it was largely unified in its backing for Jokowi, becoming a central component of his successful campaign. With the loss of NU support for Prabowo, FPI and FUI moved to occupy the space as self-appointed representatives of the *ummah*. A populist discourse portraying the Muslim majority as a victim of state repression and criminalization was helped in part by government actions. These included the banning of Hizbut Tahrir, the pan-Islamist organization aspiring to re-establish the Islamic caliphate, in 2017 and the clumsy orchestration of pornography charges against Rizieq, resulting in his finding safe haven in Saudi Arabia, where he remained until November 2020. From Saudi Arabi, Rizieq established himself as de facto religious leader in exile, delivering regular YouTube sermons and directives to followers while receiving a steady stream of high-profile visitors from Indonesia. His claim that he was a victim of state persecution fed into an already established discourse that *ulama* (Islamic scholars) were being targeted for criminalization by the Jokowi administration. A key rationale of the FPI from its inception has been that Islam is under sustained attack from social and political forces bent on its destruction. Historically it has benefitted from periods of government crackdown, which have served to underscore this narrative, amplifying its visibility and leading to spikes in applications for membership. Rizieq's alleged persecution in defence of the faith took this narrative to an unprecedented new level, drawing support and sympathy from new quarters, such as a conspicuously pious middle class.

POLARIZING VISIONS

The prominence of the FPI in political campaigning and Prabowo's seemingly open embrace of them posed dilemmas for other *ormas* in his coalition and was, ultimately, instrumental in driving some, such as Pemuda Pancasila, Forum Betawi Rempug and Laskar Merah Putih to shift their allegiances in support of the incumbent.

It was not until March 2019 that Pemuda Pancasila officially declared its support for Jokowi's re-election. The shift was driven by the intersection of a growing and lucrative material investment in the Jokowi administration and concerns for self-preservation and relevancy in the rhetorically polarized political context. The consolidation of an alliance of conservative and hardline Islamist groups as a central component of Prabowo's campaign and what Bourchier refers to as the "Islamization of Pancasila" had, for Pemuda Pancasila, reached a point too far (Bourchier 2019). This view was underscored by what had been their increasingly peripheral role in Prabowo's coalition, already evident in 2014. Senior members recounted how Prabowo had snubbed a major rally organized for him by Pemuda Pancasila in Kalimantan at which its chairman and a Prabowo family friend, Yapto Soerjosoemarno, was present. Prabowo's non-attendance was considered not just deeply insulting to Yapto but also a clear signal of how little importance he attached to the organization's support and by extension what they aimed to potentially gain from his presidency.

Unlike the FPI, who had committed themselves completely to a Prabowo victory, assuming the fate of their grand imam-in-exile was to an extent dependent upon it, Pemuda Pancasila worked pragmatically to secure opportunities available from the Jokowi administration. It found that the administration, mobilizing in preparation for the 2019 campaign, was highly receptive. As an organization that had made a career as ostensive defenders of the state ideology, Jokowi's statements that Pemuda Pancasila had a significant role to play in defending the nation, not just from the well-worn spectre of communism but also the contemporary threat of those advocating a caliphate, were considered something of a political lifebuoy for the organization. Notwithstanding its deep economic and social roots, Pemuda Pancasila was experiencing difficulties in finding its place in "post-Pancasila" Indonesia.[2] Within the organization the threat of "creeping radicalism" was linked explicitly to the polarization of the elections, with the political opposition recast as encompassing elements whose commitment to the Pancasila was, at best, "suspect".[3]

Beneath the rhetoric of shared commitment to upholding the Pancasila in the face of ideological and political threats that characterized the association between Pemuda Pancasila and the Jokowi administration was a raft of significant economic concessions and exclusive deals offered to Pemuda Pancasila by government ministries and state enterprises. These included an agreement guaranteeing discounted work-based health insurance from the state-managed Employees Social Security System (BPJS Ketenagakerjaan) for all Pemuda Pancasila card-carrying members in Jakarta and plans to roll out the scheme for members in the rest of the country (Dahuri 2018). It covered all Pemuda Pancasila members variously working in the informal sector. The first agreement of its kind, it was later extended to Banser, the paramilitary-type arm of Ansor, the youth wing of NU, which had also supported Prabowo in 2014 but switched camps in 2018, providing work insurance related to their role in so-called "state security" (Wibowo 2018).

Another was the signing of an agreement between the national leadership of Pemuda Pancasila and the state-owned company the Indonesian Bureau of Logistics (Bulog). This gave Pemuda Pancasila access to cost-price basic goods (*sembako*) such as rice, sugar and meat, ostensibly to disrupt "cartels" alleged to be manipulating market prices. These goods were then sold through cooperatives run by local Pemuda Pancasila branches at prices set by Bulog (Heriansyah 2016).

Unlike Pemuda Pancasila, the ethnic militia FBR, which claims to represent the interests of Jakarta's indigenous ethnic group, the Betawi, had been intimately involved in the 212 Movement. It had also frequently collaborated with the FPI in various vigilante actions, protests and political projects (Wilson 2015). Increasingly however, the FBR's leadership grew uneasy with the politicization of the movement. The FBR's grand imam, Lutfi Hakim, expressed concern that what he characterized as a "moral movement" was being "hijacked" and turned into a national entity and a campaign vehicle for Prabowo's political aspirations.

More problematically, after its success in removing Purnama from power and his subsequent blasphemy conviction, the religious leaders at the centre of the movement—the *ulama*, *habaib* and *ustadzes*—sought to assert themselves as a new centre of religious authority in competition with those of mainstream religious organizations, including NU. In Lutfi's view, the 212 Movement was a legitimate response to the "fascist, foul mouth" of Jakarta's governor. It was, however, never meant to be "either a political campaign vehicle nor something to be reproduced on a national stage. It was about Jakarta." Doing so was, in his view, dangerous, deeply divisive, and religiously contentious.

Tensions over the objectives of the 212 Movement reached a peak, when at its congress in December 2017 the movement declared Rizieq not just the grand imam of FPI, but of all Indonesian Muslims. The declaration was laughed off by mainstream Islamic organizations such as NU and Muhammadiyah as delusional, but within the broader "212 alumni" and pro-Prabowo movement it had as much a polarizing effect as it did of ostensibly producing organizational and ideological unity. Prabowo would later affirm the declaration in what appeared a strategic move designed to tighten his alliance with hardliners while attempting to further inculcate the perception of his coalition as the "minoritized majority" for Indonesian Muslims.[4] This was despite Prabowo's own lack of conspicuous faith and without offering anything in the way of significant policy concessions. For many within his broader coalition, Prabowo's endorsement generated alarm bells as it pointed to the possibility that under a Prabowo presidency Rizieq's claimed religious authority as the grand imam of Indonesian Islam, a title unknown in the country, could be formalized in some way, and with it the role and influence of the FPI.

The FBR's central leadership decided to conspicuously realign towards NU, a move largely facilitated by a senior member in its legal aid division who was a NU functionary. According to Lutfi, FBR did not have strong institutional links to NU but was culturally aligned with its religio-cultural traditions. It was warmly welcomed by NU as a key ally in Jakarta in the face of often heated contestations in mosques in FBR's heartland in Jakarta's east and north, contestations between traditionalists, on the one hand, and *habaib* and *ustadzes* aligned to the 212 Movement and FPI, on the other hand.

The decision regarding where FBR would stand in the 2019 elections was done in accordance with its established processes, which gave decision-making autonomy to its regional commands. The West Jakarta branch was the first to declare support for Jokowi and his running mate, Ma'ruf Amin, followed soon afterwards by North Jakarta and Bekasi. Then, once something resembling a consensus had emerged, and after meetings with Jokowi, the central leadership declared its position. What was considered at stake was the basis of the sociocultural authority of the FBR's leadership, but also socio-economic "stability" in its heartland.

The leadership's position nonetheless provoked discontent among some in the rank and file of the organization. Many had been deeply involved in the various mobilizations against Purnama and had "drunk the Kool-Aid" that 212's leaders were the representative of the true will of the *ulama* and, by extension, Islam. The leadership's apparent about-face prompted internal rumours that it had been "bought out" by the Jokowi administration. A short-lived leadership coup was launched by Muhammad Fajrudluha, also known as Ustadz Fajar. The son of FBR's founder, the late Fadloli el-Muhir, Fajar claimed he had the hereditary right to lead the organization and that the *arus bawah* (grassroots) of the organization was firmly in support of Prabowo. This contention intersected with the strong support for Rizieq as the grand imam of Indonesia and as charismatic oppositional figure. Ultimately, however, it failed to gain traction beyond a handful of FBR branches in East Jakarta.

The FBR joined a loose alliance of formerly Prabowo-supporting *ormas* consisting of Pemuda Pancasila, Laskar Merah Putih, the Communication Forum of the Sons and Daughters of Military and Police Retirees (FKPPI), Kembang Latar and two NU-affiliated groups, Ansor and Banser.[5] These combined forces in Jakarta were, nonetheless, considered to present an effective street-level counter to potential agitation and intimidation in campaigning in Jakarta from the FPI, FUI and others in Prabowo's coalition, as well as crucial additional components. Banners around Jakarta featuring this *ormas* alliance made no mention of their political preferences but rather emphasized the importance of a peaceful and fair process, with hashtags such as #NoIntimdasi and #NoHoax, underscoring the alliance as a "moderate" and stabilizing force in the city. FBR was asked to monitor Jakarta's north, home to large populations of ethnic Chinese, in order to ensure that the people there were not intimidated at voting stations, as had occurred in some districts in the gubernatorial elections in 2016, nor tempted to leave the city before voting, considering that election day was a national holiday.

A consequence of the FPI's rise to the centre of national politics, at least in Jakarta, was a partial abandoning of its grassroots social infrastructure. It had emerged in 1998 as a street-based vigilante group deeply embedded in *kampung* (village) life, and part of its resilience and popularity over the years is attributable to its conscious reaching out to *kampung* youth otherwise largely ignored by mainstream religious and political organizations. This social infrastructure in Jakarta's *kampung* became integral to the FPI's ability to quickly mobilize significant crowds in the capital, the strength and power of the organization judged, in part, by this. The FPI, however, had come to increasingly rely upon branches outside of Jakarta for its mass mobilizations, in particular, in West Java, whose members have been driven by often different motives from those of the politically expedient Jakarta leadership and constitute a new, often chaotic cohort of Rizieq devotees. The impacts of this new focus were on display during the riots that broke out in Jakarta after the announcement of the election results in May 2019, where the FPI was neither able to effectively mobilize organized masses at a crucial political moment, nor confirm its claimed credentials as a source of order: it failed to mitigate rioting, even during Ramadhan and in its organizational heartland of Petamburan, which witnessed some of the worst violence (Wilson 2019). This failure speaks to a broader problem of FPI having become a victim, of sorts, of its own success, with its rhetorical bombast outstripping its organizational capacity to exercise effective control over what is done in the grand imam or the organization's name.

In contrast, FBR and, to a lesser extent Pemuda Pancasila, had maintained a more low-key grassroots social infrastructure such as networks of "command posts" or *gardu* and sectoral associations, and also had the sustained street-level presence that comes from being embedded in street economies and businesses such as parking, security and small-scale enterprise. As a senior FBR member recounted, "the 212 Movement gave an inflated perception of the size of the FPI.

They bused in people from all around the country. When it comes to *kampung*-level presence in Jakarta, the FPI is no match to us and our friends." These networks and street-level presence served to elevate the groups' political usefulness for the administration, and especially the security agencies, at a time when rumours of the possibility of widespread violence had put the city on edge. They also helped to reshape their image in the eyes of many middle-class voters as "moderate" *ormas*, alongside groups such as Ansor and Banser.

OLD GAME, NEW ALIGNMENTS

The 2019 elections showed that street *ormas* are and will remain significant players in Indonesian electoral democracy into the foreseeable future—both as articulators and mobilizers of oppositional discourse and sentiment and as key "partners" with the state in securing the status quo. Polarization proved to bring opportunity and benefits, with renewed relevancy and constituents for *ormas* on both sides of the electoral contestation. The benefits for candidates were more mixed. Both contenders in the presidential election allocated significant resources to consolidate their alliances with *ormas* despite the political risks of doing so. In Prabowo's case, the open embrace of the FPI and the 212 Movement, in particular, at key political moments during the campaign proved in the end to be a strategic mistake, serving to frighten and alienate crucial constituencies and groups. As he had done with GRIB after his electoral defeat in 2014, Prabowo has shown little loyalty to those who campaigned on his behalf. As minister for defence in Jokowi's "unity" administration, he has been conspicuous in his lack of interest in the FPI or the fate of its grand imam. Both had served their purpose.

The shifting allegiances of *ormas* that had been previously united in their support for Prabowo points to the political economy underpinnings of social and identity-based polarization. In 2019 this was inseparable from the role and influence of the FPI, playing on a national stage the kind of politics it has peddled locally for over twenty years. While groups such as the FBR and Pemuda Pancasila may have been able to "coexist" with the FPI on the streets and in a loose political coalition in 2014, its rapid political ascendancy, together with Rizieq's de facto grand imam-in-exile role and the starkness of the polarized discourse, presented distinct threats, but also opportunities. FPI's die-casting of itself as an oppositional group may have facilitated its frontline role in campaigning. However, this in turn opened the opportunity for others to realign themselves as defenders of the status quo, both materially and ideologically.

Jokowi's re-election has already produced significant ongoing impacts from these realignments. Pemuda Pancasila has enjoyed a renewed political relevancy, together with the benefits that flow from this, and the organization no doubt holds expectations that these will continue to grow, such as an expansion of BPJS coverage and further Bulog "cartel busting" deals. For Heru and Pemuda Pancasila affiliates, business is booming as they enjoy high-level patronage and access to power, including through their secretary-general, Bambang Soesatyo, who is the current chairman of the People's Consultative Assembly (MPR). In return, the organization's renewed political relevancy is likely to amplify its ideological role as defenders of the Pancasila from claimed internal and external threats, at a time when the government shows signs of engaging in a purge of "religious radicalism" (McBeth 2019). Pemuda Pancasila has already been invited by the National Counterterrorism Agency (BNPT) to play an active role in preventing the spread of radicalism, intolerance and terrorism (Saputra 2020), which may even see the organization tasked with keeping an eye on their former electoral allies, the FPI.

The FBR has consolidated its self-proclaimed role as a "stabilizing" presence in Jakarta in contrast to the demonstrations and unrest of FPI and is likely to enjoy renewed access to state patronage. It is also well placed to regain its previous dominance of the umbrella Betawi organization, Badan Musyawarah Betawi, or Bamus, whose belligerent support of Prabowo now appears as something of a strategic miscalculation. If there are positives to be gained from this, we may see a further reduction in the reliance of the grassroots memberships of both organizations upon predatory and illicit businesses. In place of such business activities, both have flagged small-enterprise programmes for rank-and-file members that could be eligible for a sizeable allocation of government micro-credit loans.

The longer-term post-election fate of FPI remains less clear. Having played its hand and lost, its leadership descended into disarray, with some long simmering tensions emerging to the surface as they scrambled to negotiate their way through the political impasse. With its elite backers, including Prabowo, quickly moving on, the 212 Movement losing coherence, and key supporters purged from the influential council of *ulama*, Majelis Ulama Indonesia, the FPI is now politically exposed. The Jokowi administration has shown a willingness to ruthlessly pursue political opponents through targeted criminalization, and it appears likely the FPI will suffer the same fate (Fealy 2020). Soon after his eventual return to Indonesia from self-exile in November 2020, Rizieq and other senior FPI leaders were charged with incitement to breach Covid-19 social-distancing protocols after they had held several mass gatherings, with Rizieq detained in police custody. The FPI's attempt to renew its status as a state-recognized *ormas* has remained in limbo since June 2019, with the Ministry of Home Affairs stating that its application "doesn't fulfil the necessary criteria" (CNN Indonesia 2020a). More alarmingly, on 7 December 2020 a violent incident involving the police and bodyguards of Rizieq left six FPI members dead (Fachriansyah, Sutrisno and Loasana 2020). Several weeks earlier, the police had circulated a list of thirty-seven former and current FPI members allegedly linked to terrorist groups, in what appears as an attempt to represent the group as a gateway to terrorism and hence a serious security threat (CNN Indonesia 2020b). A key component of the FPI's strategy has been to capitalize on periodic state sanctions to boost its popularity and legitimacy as a militant oppositional group, portraying itself as a victim of government persecution. It remains uncertain, however, if and how it will be able to negotiate and survive more sustained and far-reaching state securitization.

NOTES

1. Despite Hercules' incarceration, figures within his network continued to work on the ground with elements of Prabowo's coalition. These included Abdul Ghani Ngabalin, known as Kobra, who was later arrested on allegations of playing a mobilizing role in the Jakarta riots of 21–23 May 2019, as part of a then alleged conspiracy to overthrow the Jokowi government. He was eventually charged for an unrelated incident and sentenced to a six-month imprisonment, including time already served. See Pramono (2019). Hercules would later re-emerge in early 2020 as chairman of a reconstituted GRIB with a senior Gerindra politician, Eka Gumilar, as its secretary-general.

2. Pemuda Pancasila's efforts to secure its relevance included an unsuccessful attempt at establishing its own political party, Partai Patriot, which failed to win any seats in either the 2004 or 2009 elections.
3. For an organization with economic interests embedded in the nightlife and entertainment industry, the possibility of an empowered or even state-sanctioned FPI or Islamist coalition targeting "immorality" caused a certain degree of unease despite the bravado of its members. The unease was less over the likelihood of broad Shari'a-like restrictions being imposed than over a shift in power dynamics possibly requiring forms of *jatah* (tribute payments) already imposed on the more vulnerable.
4. Muhammad al-Kathath, the secretary-general of the Forum Umat Islam, which was a key part of the 212 Movement alliance, implored fellow alliance members to pledge loyalty to Rizieq, carrying out his commands and remaining committed to what he called "constitutional jihad". See CNN Indonesia (2018).
5. This alliance was by no means "organic", with the FBR and Pemuda Pancasila having a long history of bloody inter-group turf wars in Jakarta, which resumed soon after the elections.

REFERENCES

Aspinall, Edward. 2019. "Indonesia's Election and the Return of Ideological Competition". *New Mandala*, 22 April 2019.

Batubara, Herianto. 2019. "Kecewa, FBR Buka-bukaan Alasan Tinggalkan Prabowo-Sandi dan Dukung Jokowi". *Detik.com*, 9 March 2019. https://news.detik.com/berita/d-4459860/kecewa-fbr-buka-bukaan-alasan-tinggalkan-prabowo-sandi-dan-dukung-jokowi.

Bourchier, David. 2019. "Two Decades of Ideological Contestation in Indonesia: From Democratic Cosmopolitanism to Religious Nationalism". *Journal of Contemporary Asia* 49, no. 5.

CNN Indonesia. 2018. "Al Khaththath Serukan Sumpah Setia untuk Rizieq di Aksi 212", 2 December 2018. https://www.cnnindonesia.com/nasional/20181202094628-20-350464/al-khaththath-serukan-sumpah-setia-untuk-rizieq-di-aksi-212.

―――. 2020a. "FPI Anggap Status Ormas di Kemendagri Tak Bermanfaat", 21 November 2020. https://www.cnnindonesia.com/nasional/20201121144058-20-572749/fpi-anggap-status-ormas-di-kemendagri-tak-bermanfaat.

―――. 2020b. "FPI Tak Tahu Soal 37 Anggota Diduga Terlibat Aksi Teror", 16 December 2020. https://www.cnnindonesia.com/nasional/20201216180753-12-583073/fpi-tak-tahu-soal-37-anggota-diduga-terlibat-aksi-teror.

Dahuri, Deri. 2018. "Anggota Pemuda Pancasila Dirangkul Jadi Peserta BPJS-TK". *Media Indonesia*, 22 March 2018. https://mediaindonesia.com/read/detail/150742-anggota-pemuda-pancasila-dirangkul-jadi-peserta-bpjs-tk.

Fachriansyah, Rizki, Budi Sutrisno, and Nina Loasana. 2020. "Observers call for independent investigation into killing of six FPI members in alleged clash with police". *The Jakarta Post*, 8 December 2020. https://www.thejakartapost.com/news/2020/12/07/observers-call-for-independent-investigation-into-killing-of-six-fpi-members-in-alleged-clash-with-police.html.

Fealy, Greg. 2020. "Jokowi in the Covid-19 Era: Repressive Pluralism, Dynasticism and the Overbearing State". *Bulletin of Indonesian Economic Studies* 56, no. 3.

Gusti, R. 2018. "Bulog Gandeng Pemuda Pancasila Kawal Stabilitasi Harga Pangan Di Sumut". *Republika Merdeka*, 30 October 2018. http://www.rmolsumut.com/read/2018/10/30/59776/1/Bulog-Gandeng-Pemuda-Pancasila-Kawal-Stabilitasi-Harga-Pangan-Di-Sumut.

Heriansyah. 2016. "BULOG dan Pemuda Pancasila Kerjasama Cegah Pemainan Kartel Komoditi". *Aceh Journal Network*, 31 January 2016. https://www.ajnn.net/news/bulog-dan-pemuda-pancasila-kerjasama-cegah-pemainan-kartel-komoditi/index.html.

Inur Arifah, Iffah. 2019. "Cegah Pimpinan Berpaham Radikal, BNPT Dilibatkan Dalam Proses Seleksi Calon Pimpinan KPK". ABC News, 18 June 2019. https://www.abc.net.au/indonesian/2019-06-18/pansel-kpk-libatkan-rekam-jejak-pendaftar/11219062.

Lane, Max. 2019. "The 2019 Indonesian Elections: An Overview", *ISEAS Perspective*, no. 2019/49, 14 June 2019.

McBeth, John. 2019. "Widodo Strikes Back at Extremists in his Midst". *Asia Times*, 28 June 2019.

Prabowo, Dani. 2014. "Mirip Gajah Mada Alasan Banser Dukung Prabowo". *Kompas*, 24 June 2014. https://nasional.kompas.com/read/2014/06/24/1156408/Mirip.Gajah.Mada.Alasan.Banser.Dukung.Prabowo.

Pramono, Stefanus. 2019. "Bau Mawar di Jalan Thamrin". *Tempo.co*, 8 June 2019. https://majalah.tempo.co/read/157812/bau-mawar-di-jalan-thamrin.

Saputra, Muhammad. 2020. "BNPT dorong ormas kepemudaan aktif cegah paham radikal". *Merdeka.com*, 3 July 2020. https://www.merdeka.com/peristiwa/bnpt-dorong-*ormas*-kepemudaan-aktif-cegah-paham-radikal.html.

Warburton, Eve. 2019. "Polarisation in Indonesia: What if Perception is Reality?". *New Mandala*, 16 April 2019. https://www.newmandala.org/how-polarised-is-indonesia/.

Wibowo, A. 2018. "Pemerintah Jamin Tugas Banser Dengan Jaminan BPJS Ketenagakerjaan". *RMOL Jateng*, 3 December 2018. http://www.rmoljateng.com/read/2018/12/03/14586/Pemerintah-Jamin-Tugas-Banser-Dengan-Jaminan-BPJS-Ketenagakerjaan-.

Wilson, Ian D. 2014. "The Perils of Loyalty". *New Mandala*, 4 July 2014. https://www.newmandala.org/the-perils-of-loyalty/.

———. 2015. *The Politics of Protection Rackets in Post-New Order Indonesia*. London: Routledge.

———. 2019. "Between Throwing Rocks and a Hard Place". *New Mandala*, 2 June 2019. https://www.newmandala.org/between-throwing-rocks-and-a-hard-place-fpi-and-the-jakarta-riots/.

7

UNIONS AND ELECTIONS: THE CASE OF THE METAL WORKERS UNION IN ELECTIONS IN BEKASI, WEST JAVA

Amalinda Savirani

The labour movement—particularly, the metal workers union, Serikat Pekerja Metal Indonesia (SPMI)—is the most active social movement in Indonesia post-*Reformasi*. SPMI has been involved in electoral politics since 2004. It labels such involvement as *Buruh Go Politik* ("Workers Go Politics"). This is a programme set up by the national federation that SPMI is a member of Federasi Serikat Pekerja Metal Indonesia (or FSPMI, for short) to support union members to run as legislative or executive candidates at any level of government. Starting from the industrial areas of Batam in Sumatra during the 2004 local legislative elections, the labour movement's involvement in politics represents one form of non-elite participation in Indonesian electoral democracy (Ford 2014). Such participation also marks a new era for the unions after a long period of isolation from electoral politics during the New Order period, when the labour movement was heavily restricted (Hadiz 1997).

The SPMI's political participation is situated in two main contexts in Indonesia: the decline of the manufacturing sector (World Bank 2016, p. 17) and increased political restrictions. Before the economic crisis of 1997, the manufacturing sector had contributed 9 per cent to the Indonesian economy but its contribution steadily declined after the crisis. For example, between 2003 and 2015, the rate of decline was 4.9 per cent (Tadjoedin et al. 2016). As of 2015, the sector absorbed 22 per cent of manpower, compared with the 47.8 per cent absorbed by the services sector. The decline has increased the vulnerability of workers in the sector (Tadjoedin et al. 2016).

The second context within which the SPMI operates today is increased government restrictions on political participation by labour unions since 2015. At the root of the restrictions is a series of labour protests in West Java in 2012 demanding an increase in the minimum wage. The protesters blocked a toll road leading to a manufacturing estate in Bekasi, causing significant economic losses.

The economic malaise and political constraints should have pushed the labour movement into political quiescence; instead, it thrived through political participation (Caraway and Ford 2014). In particular, in the 2014 legislative elections in both Bekasi District (*kabupaten*) and Bekasi City, SPMI members ran for election and two of them secured seats at the district level. (Although Bekasi City and Bekasi District are administratively two separate entities, and SPMI has branches in both areas, they are well coordinated when their members run for election to legislative or executive bodies.) In 2017, Obon Tabroni, the former head of SPMI's Bekasi office, ran for the position of district head (*bupati*) but lost to the incumbent. In the 2019 national legislative election, however, Obon secured a seat as a representative of the Gerindra Party, becoming the first labour union member to be represented in the national parliament.

This chapter explores the political strategies adopted by SPMI to influence policies through the electoral process by running for legislative and executive positions in the 2014, 2017 and 2019 elections. It argues that participation in the electoral process has strengthened union politics, at least symbolically, yet it has also weakened the SPMI in terms of the energy spent in campaigning for elections. In addition, securing seats in the legislature does not automatically guarantee the advancement of labour demands. This is due to the existing power structure within the political parties, known to be dominated by small elite circles, the power structure within parliament, which is controlled by the ruling parties and their allies, as well as the government bureaucracy's technocratic roadblocks that impede the ability of union members to advance their interests through the parliamentary process.

SPMI IN BEKASI ELECTIONS

Bekasi District is the largest industrial complex in Southeast Asia. It is located to the east of Jakarta and has a population of more than 2.8 million, mostly immigrants. More than 60 per cent of the population work in the manufacturing sector (BPS Kabupaten Bekasi 2019). The metal workers union is the largest union in the area: SPMI membership there stands at 82,000, constituting its largest base within the country.

The size of labour unions and the power arising from their organized nature make them politically attractive to politicians. Political candidates often seek out union leaders for electoral support, making deals to support the latter's union agendas in exchange if they get elected. There are several main factors, one internal and three external, that explain why labour unions like SPMI get directly involved in electoral politics. The internal factor relates to the increased awareness that unions have significant power during elections that they can capitalize on. The first external factor relates to political parties and their members' behaviour to win elections using any strategies possible. Experience has shown that deals struck with political candidates running for various executive positions were rarely honoured by the latter. In 2012, for instance, SPMI supported Neneng Hasanah in exchange for her promising to help increase the minimum wage in Bekasi if she won the election for *bupati*. Neneng won, but she never stuck to her deal. Such experiences prompted SPMI members to run for election themselves so that labour could have a direct voice in parliament. However, as I explore later in this chapter, SPMI members who secure seats in parliament often feel obliged to discipline their union and put a damper on its demands.

The second external factor is the political restrictions on street protests that cause huge economic loss. The government is likely to block any future attempts to stage such protests as it needs a controlled political environment that provides certainty and security for businesspeople. To curb protests, the government has, for instance, issued regulations declaring many industrial areas as "strategic objects"

(*Obyek Vital Nasional*), meaning demonstrations are not allowed in such areas as they would "endanger strategic objects", including toll roads and industrial areas, where street demonstration usually occur. Military officers are allowed to be deployed to areas marked as "strategic objects".

The third external factor revolves around wage negotiations. In 2015, Government Regulation (Peraturan Pemerintah or PP) 78/2015 was issued on a minimum wage formula. Under this regulation, trade unions could no longer be involved in wage negotiations; the minimum wage formula was to be henceforth based on economic growth and the rate of inflation. Previously, the minimum wage was calculated based on the minimum needs for a decent life (*Kebutuhan Hidup Layak* or KPL, for short). PP 78/2015 also ruled out the tripartite forum process consisting of representatives from employers, labour unions and the government in determining the minimum wage. This forum was where the aspirations of both employers and workers were previously negotiated, facilitated by the government. In Bekasi, at least, labour interests could always be accommodated in the forum. By dissolving the tripartite forum and ruling that wage levels are to be determined nationally by the government using a formula based on the gross domestic income and the rate of inflation, the law of 2015 has effectively re-centralized labour matters. (More recently, the Omnibus Law—the job creation bill passed by parliament in October 2020—sparked off massive protests by the labour movement, which considers the law a further setback to its interests, given declining wages and welfare rights.) With demonstrations being prohibited and a forum for collective wage negotiations dissolved, labour unions found themselves with limited options to advance their interests other than "go politics" (Interview, Obon Tabroni, 5 January 2017). This meant unions needed to re-adjust their long tradition of mobilization involving just union members to political mobilization aimed at all citizens beyond their factory complexes and based on causes other than just labour issues.

I. Legislative Election, 2014

Five SPMI members participated in the 2014 local legislative elections. Members Nurdin and Nyumarno were elected in the electorate areas (*dapil*) where they stood, garnering 10,891 and 6,092 votes, respectively.

Their total votes were small compared with the number of unionists residing in their electoral areas (*dapils* I and VI). This meant that not all SPMI members voted for their union colleagues. One of the reasons for this is an administrative issue. Many union members do not have Bekasi District identity cards (*Kartu Tanda Penduduk* or KTP, for short). They still hold KTPs from their respective hometowns. By law, only those with Bekasi KTPs are allowed to vote for parliamentary elections in Bekasi District, although those without are allowed to vote in national parliamentary elections. Despite this limitation, the success of these two candidates has made SPMI members confident that they can do well in electoral politics (Savirani 2016).

In terms of political parties, there were at least five different ones on whose ticket SPMI members ran, including, Partai Amanat Nasional (National Mandate Party or PAN, for short), Partai Demokrasi Indonesia Perjuangan (Indonesian Democratic Party of Struggle, PDI-P), Partai Keadilan dan Persatuan Indonesia (Indonesian Justice and Unity Party, PKPI), Partai Keadilan Sejahtera (Prosperous Justice Party, PKS) and Partai Persatuan Pembangunan (United Development Party, PPP). These parties were picked because they did not ask the unionists to pay a fee for candidacy, a common practice among other parties, particularly if the candidates are not party cadres. This was one of the union's principles for running for election in 2014, namely, no money politics, including paying to secure candidacy. Member Suparno had planned to run on a PDI-P ticket, but the party requested a "donation". Nyumarno, however, got a ticket from the party without having to pay for it because he had served as an assistant to a PDI-P politician, Rieke Dyah Pitaloka, at the national parliament. Two SPMI members ran for provincial and national legislative seats. They were Rustan (PDI-P) and Iswan Abdullah (PKS). In addition, two members ran for the Bekasi City parliament (Hendi Suhendi and Masrul Zambak) from PAN and PDI-P, respectively.

Indonesia's electoral laws do not allow individuals to run for legislative office without membership in a parliamentary party; neither are union members allowed to run as representatives of their unions. As noted above, in 2014, union members ran on the tickets of five different parties for election to three different levels of government. This made it difficult for these members to formulate their own campaign strategies. Parties usually prefer a "one package" campaign

TABLE 7.1
Votes Garnered by SPMI Members in the 2014 Legislative Election in Bekasi District

Candidate	Electoral area (*dapil*)	Party	Votes	Outcome
Nurdin Muhidin	I	PAN	10,981	Elected
Nyumarno	VI	PDI-P	6,092	Elected
Suparno	II	PKPI	5,600	Unsuccessful
Aji Narwi	III	PAN	2,200	Unsuccessful
Susanto	V	PKPI	2,700	Unsuccessful
Total votes			27,483	

Source: Bekasi Office, Federasi Serikat Pekerja Metal Indonesia (FSPMI).

strategy applicable to all their candidates, regardless of whether they are running at the national, provincial or district/city levels since this minimizes campaign costs. Each SPMI candidate adapted the "one package" strategy provided by the party he was running for but the problem was that, on the whole, the union was promoting the interests of different parties at the various levels of government that its members were running for. The parties concerned were not happy with this situation because the union was identifying with different parties' interests at different levels. Their complaints to the union were ignored.

The union's relations with the parties became further complicated after Nurdin and Nyumarno were elected. The union demanded that these cadres advocate its special interests; the parties, on the other hand, demanded party loyalty. As a solution, during their five-year tenures, the loyalties of the two union legislators were divided into two phases: the first three years were devoted to union interests, while the remaining two years were devoted to party interests. Despite this informal arrangement, however, the union's volunteers (*relawan*) complained that Nurdin and Nyumarno were just like ordinary politicians: once they were elected, they forgot about the people who had supported them. Tensions between these politicians and the union remained unresolved until the 2019 election. The resentment on the part of union members was also the main reason why Nyumarno later shifted his support base from union members to non-union voters.

Apart from problems with the parties, the SPMI candidates faced the problem of campaign resources. One of the avenues for mobilizing voters from among union members was its workplace leadership unit (Pimpinan Unit Kerja or PUK, for short). PUKs played roles in providing campaign funding for their fellow members who were running for election. For instance, Aji Narwi, who worked for PT NSK Bearing Indonesia, received assistance from the PUK in his factory in terms of funding and campaign personnel. Suparno's PUK, namely PT Aisin, did likewise. The candidate without a PUK, Nyumarno, whose PUK (PT Kymco Lippo Motor Indonesia) went bankrupt in 2010 before the election, had to find resources himself. He received a small amount of support from the union in terms of funding for campaign material (Interview, Nyumarno, February 2014).

The union's "no money politics" policy was adhered to during the campaign. Candidates had few problems adhering to the policy as far as union members were concerned. But in dealing with non-union members, that is, Bekasi residents in general, candidates frequently found themselves faced with requests for *uang cendol*, or "snack money", something the union candidates had no resources for (Savirani 2016). This was the reason they focused more on unionized residents for their votes. The candidates' strategy to reach out to union members was to form a voluntary team in the *dapil* each ran in. They generated money themselves by selling "Go Politics" merchandise and used the money raised towards the costs of voter mobilization (meetings and canvassing). Similar volunteer teams were set up later during the 2017 *bupati* election and for the 2019 elections.

II. Executive Election, 2017

Obon Tabroni ran for election as an independent candidate in the 2017 election for *bupati* of Bekasi District. His running mate was Bambang Sumaryono, an unpopular figure, according to many union members. The reason Obon chose to run as an independent candidate was to cut a cycle of political dependency on parties and establish political freedom.

Being an independent candidate requires significant logistical support, compared with running as a party candidate. The law requires that to run as an independent candidate, he must produce copies of the identity cards (IDs) of 10 per cent of the population in his place of residence as proof of their support. Obon's volunteers successfully managed to collect 130,000 IDs, constituting political support for his nomination. To mobilize the people for this effort, Obon was supported by a special unit that he set up, "Obon Tabroni Centre" (OTC), which predominantly consisted of union members serving as volunteers. Obon, however, lost his bid to incumbent Neneng Hasanah (see Table 7.2).

TABLE 7.2
Election for *Bupati* of Bekasi District, 2017

Candidate	Parties	Votes	Votes (%)
Meilina Kartika Kodir and Abdul Kholik	PDI-P, PKB, PPP	113,664	9.6
Sa'adudin and Dhani Ahmad Prasetyo	PKS, Partai Demokrat, Gerindra	309,205	26.12
Obon Tabroni and Bambang Sumaryono	Independent	207,940	17.57
Iin Farihin and KH Mahmud	Independent	81,496	6.88
Neneng Hasanah Yasin and Eka Supria Atmaja	Golkar, PAN	471,483	39.83

Source: Komisi Pemilihan Umum. n.d., "Hasil Hitung TPS (Form C1) Kabupaten Bekasi", https://pilkada2017.kpu. go.id/hasil/t2/jawa_barat/bekasi.

Most of the votes that the Obon-Bambang team garnered came from people who lived in the relatively urban and industrial areas of Bekasi (see Map 7.1). In five main urban areas, namely, Serang Baru, Cikarang Selatan, Cibitung, Cikarang Barat and Cibarusah, Obon and Bambang scored second among the candidates. The population of these areas are predominantly working-class people who work in factories. The team performed most poorly in areas where agriculture is the main economic activity, such as Muara Gembong, Sukawangi, Tarumajaya, Pebayuran and Cabangbungin. Pebayuran is the sub-district where the incumbent comes from.

To win, the Obon-Bambang team needed to reach out to voters from outside the union as well. Strategies to reach out to the non-unionized residents involved working through Jamkeswatch, a volunteer group consisting of union members which specifically assisted Bekasi residents who did not have access to free healthcare. However, Obon confronted a different reality: the majority of residents courted by Jamkeswatch volunteers through free healthcare, in fact, voted for other candidates. As in the 2014 election, vote-buying was rampant in Bekasi, particularly in rural areas where native Bekasis lived. The

MAP 7.1
Map of Bekasi District Showing Breakdown by Type of Economic Activity

Source: Bekasi District General Elections Commission (KPU); visualized by Galih Kartika.

Obon-Bambang team stuck to their policy of "no money politics", just like in 2014. Their unwillingness to collaborate with politicians who could support them caused frustration among their volunteers (Interview, Amier Mahfouz, Bekasi, 30 March 2017).

The incumbent, on the other hand, courted voters by disbursing money and instituting government programmes throughout many rural areas. Several days before the election, coupons bearing the photographs of Sa'adudin, another candidate and a former *bupati* of Bekasi, as well as his running mate were distributed. The coupons allowed the bearer to obtain 3 kg cooking gas tanks for free. This was part of the candidates' vote-buying programme. Vote-buying efforts by other candidates included giving away one hen per vote and bribes of Rp5,000 (less than US$0.50). Unverified estimates claimed that the incumbent spent more than Rp150 billion (US$11 million) on vote-buying. The result was expected: Obon-Bambang lost the race.

III. Legislative Election, 2019

More SPMI candidates ran for election to the Bekasi District parliament in 2019 than in 2014 (see Tables 7.1 and 7.3). There were both old and new faces. The old ones included Nurdin Muhidin (*dapil* I). Another old face was Nyumarno, but he was no longer a union member. The new faces were Baris Silitonga, Nono Kartono, Eko Purnomo, Sulaeman and Moh Nurfahroji. Because of the complicated relations between the union and many of the political parties in the 2014 election, in 2019 the union decided on working with only one political party, the Gerindra party. The reason for picking Gerindra was that the party was institutionally weak in Bekasi although it seemed to be strong at the national level. The union calculated that its ability to contribute votes to Gerindra would give it bargaining power over the party (Interview, Amier Mahfoudz, 30 March 2019). There was also a pragmatic reason why the union allied itself with Gerindra: there was more room for negotiation with the young political party than with the more established and institutionalized parties.

Unlike in the 2014 election, in 2019 the union had maps showing their candidates' comparative performance at *dapil* level in the 2014 legislative election and in the 2017 election for *bupati*. This combined data become the basis for predicting the constituencies worth contesting and who among the union members could run. For example, in *dapil*

I, where Nurdin won in 2014, Obon had garnered more than 20,000 votes in 2017. Based on this data, it was estimated that two union members could run in *dapil* I and split Obon's 20,000 votes among them (Interview, Baris Silitonga, 7 January 2019). This would be sufficient to secure two seats. Two union members—Nurdin and Baris Silitonga (a former coordinator of the paramilitary wing of SPMI or *Garda Metal*)—ran there. Similar strategizing was done for the other electoral areas. For instance, the union had identified *dapil* IV, where Moh Nurfahroji was fielded, as a *dapil neraka* ("hell *dapil*"). It meant that not many SPMI members lived there. When Obon ran from there for the national election, he did not garner many votes either. SPMI was aware of this but nevertheless still fielded Nurfahroji there owing to his strong connections with community leaders in the constituency.

TABLE 7.3
Votes Garnered by Union Members in the 2019 Legislative Election in Bekasi District

Candidate	Electoral area (*dapil*)	Party	Votes	Outcome
Nurdin Muhidin	I	PAN	5,649	Lost
Baris Silitonga	I	Gerindra	7,750	Lost
Nono Kartono	II	Gerindra	5,517	Lost
Eko Purnomo	III	Gerindra	3,260	Lost
Moh Nurfahroji	IV	Gerindra	4,103	Lost
Sulaiman	VI	Gerindra	4,530	Lost
Nyumarno	VI	PDI-P	11,782	Won
Total votes			42,591	

Source: FSPMI.

The union's political calculations for *dapil* I proved to be off the mark: both candidates (Nurdin and Baris Silitonga) lost their bids there. All the other candidates for the other *dapils* lost as well. Nyumarno was the only one who could secure a seat—in *dapil* VI—but he had distanced himself from the union, claiming that his voter base had expanded to non-unionized residents and that his votes could no longer be considered votes from union members. The union's assumption that all of its members in *dapil* I who voted during the 2017 *bupati* election for Obon—a popular candidate among unionists—would automatically vote for either Nurdin or Baris was too optimistic and had no basis in reality; the considerations that influence voters to cast votes for *bupati* and for legislative positions are different. Despite these losses, the total number of votes cast for union candidates in local legislative elections in 2019 increased by 30 per cent compared with the votes they had secured in the 2014 elections, as can be seen in Table 7.4. If Nyumarno's votes are included, the increase in total votes in 2019 compared with 2014 was 40 per cent.

Apart from eyeing the local parliament, union members also ran for election in the national parliament in 2019. As noted earlier, Obon successfully ran as a candidate for the national legislative on a Gerindra ticket. His seat was *dapil* VII of West Java, where he garnered more than 130,000 votes. The *dapil* consists of three districts, namely, Bekasi, Purwakarta and Karawang. While Obon was beaten in the latter two districts by another candidate who was known to be close to union members—Rieke Dyah Pitaloka—it was his performance in

TABLE 7.4
Comparative Performance of Union Candidates in the 2014 and 2019 Bekasi Legislative Elections

Electoral area (*dapil*)	2014 Candidate	Votes	2019 Candidate	Votes
I	Nurdin Muhidin	10,891	Nurdin Muhidin	5,649
	–	–	Baris Silitonga	7,750
II	–	–	Nono Kartono	5,517
III	Suparno	5,600	Eko Purnomo	3,260
IV	Aji Narwi	2,200	Moh Fahroji	4,269
V	Susanto	2,700	–	
VI	Nyumarno	6,092	Nyumarno	11,782
	–	–	Suleman	4,530
Total votes		27,483		42,757

Source: Bekasi District General Elections Commission (KPU), 2014 and 2019.

Bekasi District that was pivotal to his victory. There, he beat all other candidates and garnered more than 112,000, which constituted more than 85 per cent of the total votes that he obtained in the *dapil*.

VOLUNTEERS AS A POLITICAL MACHINE AND THE ROLE OF NON-UNION VOTERS

In their bids for political office, SPMI candidates mostly relied on *relawan*. During the 2017 *bupati* election, when Obon ran as a candidate, there were two ways that voters were mobilized, as mentioned earlier: through the candidate's political machine, namely, the aforesaid OTC, and through Jamkeswatch (healthcare monitoring). According to their own data, the OTC had 1,500 registered volunteers and 10,000 unregistered ones (Interview, OTC coordinator, Bekasi, 7 April 2019). These volunteers served as genuine *relawan* in supporting OTC and Obon's candidacy. They were not paid; in fact, the volunteers contributed their own time and money. To cover the daily running costs incurred in supporting Obon, volunteers sold merchandise. As noted earlier, the volunteers' role was collecting copies of voter IDs from the time Obon officially announced his independent candidature in 2016. They had about 96 days in total between 2016 and early 2017 to collect these endorsements. The OTC volunteers collected IDs every Saturday and Sunday during their day off work. In one day, six volunteers could cover one village for this task. The volunteers I met during my field work were still wearing their factory uniforms most of the time they went around to collect voter IDs. In total, the amount spent by the OTC to support Obon's candidature was more than Rp5 billion (US$350,000). This sum excludes the funds the volunteers raised themselves to support their own expenses.

The second political machine was the volunteers of Jamkeswatch. The group was formed by SPMI as an advocacy unit for Bekasi residents to access healthcare facilities in the region. If OTC's aim was to mobilize union members to vote for Obon, Jamkeswatch's aim was to reach out to non-union residents to show that the union did care about ordinary people in the area. It aimed to demonstrate to the public that the union did not only focus on wages and the welfare of its own members. It hoped that this message would garner sympathy and support from the non-unionized residents for both the labour movement and Obon as a candidate, which would in turn eventually increase Obon's electability.

Approaching every single household, providing information about the candidate and canvassing for votes was another of Jamkeswatch's strategies to secure votes for Obon from non-union residents. The volunteers referred to this strategy as *ngaprak*, a local term that means "approaching people". I joined one of the *ngaprak* sessions, going on a walkabout with the volunteers in one of the housing complexes. The volunteers were garbed in orange, the campaign colour of their candidate. I noticed that the volunteers lacked confidence in properly introducing Obon to the residents. They had no experience in approaching ordinary citizens and merely handed out posters and flyers to individual households in the complexes instead of engaging the voters and trying to persuade them to vote for their candidate. My impression was that they had not been properly trained for the task.

GROWING DISCONNECT BETWEEN UNION LEGISLATORS AND UNION MEMBERS

The labour union movement differs in character from other formal democratic institutions such as political parties and legislative bodies. There are at least three basic features that limit the labour union's capacity to engage in electoral politics: (1) in terms of scale, labour unions are strong only in industrial areas; (2) in terms of issues, labour union have a single issue, namely, the welfare of their members; and (3) in terms of membership profiles, labour unions are relatively homogenous. These three features limit their ability to mobilize voters, particularly non-unionized voters.

Electoral politics, however, requires vastly different characteristics. It requires a much larger scale of membership than that of the various unions and a variety of issues and interests to cater to. These requirements make the playing field rather complex for unions that seek a role in politics. Unions would need a high level of flexibility and a willingness to deal with a variety of public issues that may not be core to the union or may even contradict the union's interests. Once they are elected, they confront several layers in the policy-making process, starting with the legislative and the executive and then the multiple layers within the government itself. This political process can indirectly lead to a disconnect between union members and their representatives in parliament.

Because of these features, union members who assume legislative positions cannot always directly advocate union issues, which crop up quite frequently in an industrial area like Bekasi. For example, violations regarding work safety, wages and incentives, and overtime pay occur quite frequently in Bekasi. Given the multiple institutions and multiple layers of authorities involved in the legislative and the executive branches, elected legislators would find it hard to promote their special interests at will. Every legislative body has a number of commissions, each taking care of several set sectors. For example, commission "A" of the national parliament works on issues of law, government, social order, human resources and people's empowerment, and there are other commissions with their own areas of responsibility. These commissions work in coordination with the respective offices (*dinas* or *kantor*) at the executive level.

In addition, becoming a member of the legislative body means representing a party which has its own hierarchy, from the head of the party to the coordinator of its caucus or faction (*fraksi*) in the legislative body. Members of SPMI sitting in the legislative, who politically represent their union but formally represent the party on whose ticket they ran, find it exceptionally hard to navigate their way in these bewildering political and institutional configurations.

This has been very much the case with Nyumarno and Nurdin, who have had considerable experience in mobilizing union members to protest rather than in crafting policies within a specific institutional setting. This shortcoming has created difficulties in establishing a political connect between these union legislators and their supporters. The former have been accused of forgetting their supporters, the union members. There is an informal political agreement that union legislators must contribute to union interests. But such contribution, if any, has been difficult to monitor (Interview, Sukamto, SPMI senior member, January 2019). Consequently, a disconnect has arisen between union members/supporters and their newly elected representatives in the Bekasi parliament. More importantly, it has caused union members to distrust their legislators.

Union members who have become legislators have had to instruct themselves on how to deal with what is a new political terrain for them, with multiple layers of institutions. Owing to their lack of training on how to function effectively as members of parliament, union members who became legislators in Bekasi District responded to their challenges variously. Nyumarno adapted well to his new political environment owing to his personal skills, while Nurdin struggled with the transition. Nyumarno tended to show greater loyalty to his party than to his former union, which created further tension between him and the union and culminated in Nyumarno's claim to have aligned himself with non-union voters in the 2019 election (Interview, Nyumarno's team, 29 March 2019).

CONCLUSION

This chapter has focused on how Indonesian politics has been coloured by grassroots involvement (Tomsa and Setijadi 2018), notably the involvement of the labour movement (Caraway and Ford 2014). It has shown how the metal workers union in Bekasi has navigated the new terrain of electoral politics. Through SPMI's participation in three elections in Bekasi since 2014, the union has tried to adapt to political realities. It has become aware of the challenges of upholding its idealistic objection to money politics amid the prevalence of vote-buying in Indonesia, including in Bekasi (Aspinall and Sukmajati 2016). SPMI unionists have also realized the importance of affiliating themselves with a political party in the business of elections in Indonesia and the complexity of the various institutions of democracy that they have to deal with once they have decided to *"go politik"*.

While SPMI candidates managed to attract more votes in the 2019 legislative election than in the two other elections its members had participated in since its foray into electoral politics in 2014, it was not able to increase its representation in the local parliament. The union miscalculated the support it had in each *dapil*. It failed to realize that voters are influenced by different considerations when voting for *bupati* and for legislators. It nominated more candidates for the 2019 local legislature than in the 2014 election, which only led to its losing seats that it had won earlier. Although Obon, owing to his personal popularity and his militant volunteer groups, garnered a much higher number of votes when he ran in the 2017 election for *bupati* of Bekasi than members of the union collectively obtained in the 2019 local legislative election, his bid in that election failed. This leads to the conclusion that, in spite of the union's ability to mobilize the support of its members, it still lacks the support of non-union voters. Reaching out to non-union voters has been a struggle owing to the union's idealistic antipathy to vote-buying, a practice that is rampant in Bekasi (Savirani 2016).

Nonetheless, the union's experiment with electoral politics, especially Obon's ability to secure a seat in the national parliament in the 2019 election, has strengthened the union's standing, at least symbolically, and has brought confidence to other union members to fight in the 2024 election.

REFERENCES

Adjie, Moch. Fiqih Prawira. 2020. "Labor Unions Plans More Protests Against Omnibus Law, to Prepare Legal Challenge". *The Jakarta Post*, 24 October 2020. https://www.thejakartapost.com/news/2020/10/24/labor-union-plans-more-protests-against-omnibus-law-to-prepare-legal-challenge.html (accessed 21 January 2021).

Aspinall, Edward and Mada Sukmajati, eds. 2016. *Electoral Dynamics in Indonesia: Money Politics, Patronage and Clientelism at the Grassroots*. Singapore: NUS Press.

Badan Pusat Statistik Kabupaten Bekasi. 2019. *Kabupaten Bekasi Dalam Angka 2019*. Bekasi: BPS.

Caraway, Teri and Michele Ford. 2014. "Labor and Politics under Oligarchy". In *Beyond Oligarchy: Wealth, Power and Contemporary Indonesian Politics*, edited by Michele Ford and Thomas Pepinsky, pp. 139-56. Ithaca: Cornell Southeast Asia Program.

_____. 2019. *Labor and Politics in Indonesia*. New York: Cambridge University Press.

Ford, Michele. 2014. "Learning by Doing: Trade Unions and Electoral Politics in Batam, Indonesia, 2004-2009". *South East Asia Research* 22, no. 3: 341-57.

Hadiz, Vedi. 1997. *Workers and the State in New Order Indonesia*. London: Routledge.

Komisi Pemilihan Umum. N.d. "Hasil Hitung TPS (Form C1) Kabupaten Bekasi". https://pilkada2017.kpu.go.id/hasil/t2/jawa_barat/bekasi.

Komisi Penyelenggara Pemilu Daerah. 2017. "Hasil Pilkada Kabupaten Bekasi 2017". https://pilkada2017.kpu.go.id/hasil/t2/jawa_barat/bekasi (accessed 12 December 2017).

_____. N.d. "Hasil Pemilu 2014 dan 2019 di Kabupaten Bekasi". Press Release.

Nurmatari, Avitia. 2015. "Hasil Penetapan UMK 2016: Karawang Tertinggi, Pangandaran Terendah". *Detik News*, 21 November 2015. https://news.detik.

com/berita-jawa-barat/d-3077193/hasil-penetapan-umk-jabar-2016-karawang-tertinggi-pangandaran-terendah (accessed 9 October 2020).

Pojok Bekasi. 2019. "Obon Raih Suara Terbesar di Kabupaten Bekasi, Dominasi Rieke Tergeser", 15 May 2019. https://bekasi.pojoksatu.id/baca/obon-raih-suara-terbesar-di-kabupaten-bekasi-dominasi-rieke-tergeser (accessed 19 November 2020).

Savirani, Amalinda. 2016. "Bekasi, West Java: From Patronage to Interest Group Politics?". In *Electoral Dynamics in Indonesia: Money Politics, Patronage and Clientelism at the Grassroots*, edited by Edward Aspinall and Mada Sukmajati, pp. 184–202. Singapore: NUS Press.

Statista. 2019. "Employment by Economic Sector in Indonesia 2018". https://www.statista.com/statistics/320160/employment-by-economic-sector-in-indonesia/ (accessed 30 October 2019).

Tadjoeddin, Mohammad Zulfan, Ilmiawan Auwalin, and Anis Chowdhury. 2016. *Revitalizing Indonesia's Manufacturing: The Productivity Conundrum*. Arndt-Corden Department of Economics, Crawford School of Public Policy, ANU College of Asia and the Pacific, Working Paper No. 2016/20. https://acde.crawford.anu.edu.au/sites/default/files/publication/acde_crawford_anu_edu_au/2016-11/2016-20_chowdhury_manufacturing_in_indonesia-productivity_23nov16.pdf (accessed 28 October 2019).

Tomsa, Dick and Charlotte Setijadi. 2018. "Redefining the Nexus between Electoral and Movement Politics". *Asian Survey* 58, no. 3: 557–81.

World Bank. 2016. *Indonesian Economic Quarterly: Resilience through Reform*. Jakarta: The World Bank.

8

THE POWER OF *EMAK-EMAK*: WOMEN AND THE POLITICAL AGENDA OF ISLAMIC CONSERVATIVES IN INDONESIA'S 2019 ELECTION[1]

Dyah Ayu Kartika

INTRODUCTION

Women have long been left out of the policy debate and politics in Indonesia. At the beginning of the New Order era (1966-98), politically active women were accused of being members of Gerwani, an organization affiliated with the Indonesian Communist Party (PKI). The New Order military government depicted Gerwani members as evil and immoral; as a consequence, women were afraid of voicing their opinions publicly and coming across as outspoken (Wieringa 2002). The Suharto government pursued other ways to depoliticize women and steer them towards being active in state-approved movements that reinforced the important roles played by obedient mothers and wives in the country's development (Suryakusuma 2011). In its later years, however, the New Order government became more tolerant of women's activism, which grew rapidly and became more vibrant after *Reformasi*. Nevertheless, the progressive women's movement grappled with reaching out to the broader grassroots level because it was mainly run by small, issue-specific, and donor-dependent organizations without mass bases (Rinaldo 2019).

The picture seems to have shifted with the 2019 election. More women actively participated in politics and defended their preferred presidential candidates at the grassroots level. Those who supported the presidential candidacy of Prabowo Subianto and his running mate, Sandiaga Uno, (popularly known as the Prabowo-Sandi team) referred to themselves as *emak-emak* (mothers), projecting themselves as strong-willed mothers in fighting for whatever they think is right. They claimed to represent struggling women from the middle-to-low socio-economic class, who care primarily about economic stability and having more job opportunities for their children. On the other side, those supporting the team of Joko Widodo (Jokowi) and Ma'ruf Amin called their women supporters *ibu bangsa* (mothers of the nation), referring to the term used in the 1935 conference of the International Council of Women (ICW), which has a more inclusive and uplifting meaning compared to *emak-emak* (Khalika 2018). These women supporters were mainly led by those from the middle-upper class who fear growing intolerance in Indonesia.

We have also seen greater diversity among women candidates in the legislative elections. They came from varied backgrounds such as former activists, entrepreneurs or even relatives of party bigwigs who paved the way for them to participate in the election. There were about 93,975 women candidates at all levels of the legislative election, slightly over 38 per cent of all candidates registered (IFES 2019). The national parliament also set a record by having the highest ever representation of women at 20.5 per cent, and for the first time in Indonesia's history it is led by a woman, Puan Maharani from Partai Demokrasi Indonesia Perjuangan (Indonesian Democratic Party of Struggle or PDI-P, for short).

However, the rise of identity politics and political Islam, particularly since the 2017 gubernatorial election for Jakarta, suggests a new challenge for those fighting for equal rights for women.[2] As a report from the Institute for Policy Analysis of Conflict (2019) states:

> If the 212 movements reinvented Muslim political identity in majoritarian terms, it also activated women's political agency along conservative lines: mothers must mobilize against Jokowi in order to protect their children from un-Godly communism, homosexuality, and other moral threats associated with Jokowi's camp.

Thus, the new challenge for women activists is located in the rise of a religiously ultra-conservative women's movement, which works to challenge the feminist ideas of women's emancipation. The 2019 election highlighted the growing influence of anti-feminist female candidates, mostly coming from ultra-conservative Islamic groups, who have excellent leadership qualities, the ability to present clear and convincing arguments, and organizational skills to mobilize the grassroots. These candidates actively engaged with Muslim *emak-emak* to fight against the perceived moral crisis in society.

This situation raises two questions. How did the *emak-emak* and ultra-conservative candidates interact and how did the latter utilize social networks to disseminate conservative narratives? While answering these questions, it is important to highlight the essential roles of social media and *majlis taklim* as political space to propagate their message. *Majlis taklim* are regular, community-organized Islamic study groups that branch out to the village and neighbourhood levels. They are open to every Muslim, and although they have separate groups for men and women, the women's groups are often more active.

This chapter aims to analyse Indonesian women's political participation in the 2019 election, in which ultra-conservative women were particularly vocal. It further examines how feminist and conservative narratives will affect Indonesia's public and policy discourse beyond 2019. In doing so, I will use my observations of women supporters of both presidential candidates and of Islamic ultra-conservative candidates in the 2019 general election to explain how social media and *majlis taklim* became critical drivers of the moral issues centred on women. Then, I invite readers to look at the modalities adopted on the other side—digital feminist activists—in response to the conservative narratives. I will close the chapter with a discussion of the challenges feminists will face after 2019.

PARTISAN WOMEN'S GROUPS

The women supporters of Jokowi and Prabowo each had distinct policy priorities during the campaign. The views held by pro-Jokowi women on various issues, including economic enhancement, protection from sexual violence, and gender-inclusion, were relatively close to what would be considered normative positions. Prabowo's *emak-emak* supporters, by contrast, had a more unified agenda of achieving economic stability. Although their aspirations were secular on the surface, the *emak-emak* were influenced by robust networks of local religious groups and were particularly targeted by conservative Islamic activists at the grassroots level.

Jokowi was immensely popular among women voters. The electability survey by the Jakarta-based Centre for Strategic and International Studies in March 2019 showed 50.8 per cent of women respondents would vote for Jokowi and 33.9 per cent for Prabowo (Santosa and Sihaloho 2019). During the campaign, Jokowi often played the "perfect family man" card to attract women voters: a humble father, a beautiful wife, successful children, and a cute grandson (Cook 2019). He also successfully created a pro-gender-equality image by handpicking eight professional women for his first-term cabinet, the highest number of women ministers in Indonesia's history. Furthermore, his national campaign team established a special division for women's outreach to secure women's votes as they competed against the rhetoric of the Prabowo-Sandi *emak-emak*.

Jokowi had a more diverse, albeit fractured, base of women supporters compared with Prabowo's. Some of the pro-Jokowi women's groups used more explicit gender perspectives in their appeals to female voters; for instance, the women's wing of Bravo-5 argued that women should not be limited to doing domestic chores.[3] Other women's groups, however, kept a focus on economic appeals. Pertiwi, another women's volunteer group, was founded by Putri K. Wardhani, the president-director of the cosmetics company Mustika Ratu. It draws its membership from educated urban women and tasked them to distribute social assistance to women at the grassroots level. Pertiwi's campaign to promote Jokowi was based largely on highlighting his micro-finance policy, MEKAAR, which was designed to help poor women access capital and open home-based businesses. Pertiwi claimed it had aided more than four million women in 2015–19.[4]

Jokowi also had on his side Muslimat, the women's wing of Nahdlatul Ulama (NU), the country's largest Islamic organization. In March 2019, Jokowi attended the anniversary of Muslimat, with more than 100,000 members and high-profile NU women. Two NU women figures, Yenny Wahid, the daughter of former President Abdurrahman Wahid, and Khofifah Indar Parawansa, then East Java governor, declared their support for Jokowi (Sapiie 2019).

Realizing the significance of women's voices, Prabowo's team tried to create a pro-women image in the 2019 election. The effort started when Sandiaga, Prabowo's running mate and Jakarta's former vice-governor, registered his candidacy at the general election office on 10 August 2018. Sandiaga declared at that time: "We want to fight for *emak-emak*; we want goods to be affordable." (Mediani 2018).

With good looks and armed with an entrepreneurship programme known as OKE-OCE, Sandiaga was confident he could attract more women's votes in the presidential election. OKE-OCE is the abbreviated form of One Kecamatan (sub-district), One Centre of Entrepreneurship. It provided micro-business support for small-medium enterprises, one of the main programmes undertaken by Jakarta Governor Anies Baswedan and Sandiaga Uno in Jakarta Province.[5] Sandiaga acknowledged the programmes needed substantial improvement, but he thought people demanded such programmes across the country (Bomantama 2018). Although not specifically targeting women, OKE-OCE's beneficiaries were predominantly women, and it was they who later became the driving force in the *emak-emak* movement. In August 2018, a group of middle-class women in Jakarta declared the formation of Partai Emak-Emak Pendukung Prabowo–Sandi ("Party" of Mothers Supporting Prabowo–Sandi), popularly known as PEPES. The initiative was coordinated by Wulan, a Prabowo supporter in the 2014 election, and an entrepreneur-coach for Sandiaga's OKE-OCE programme. PEPES claimed to have more than 3,000 members, with representatives in each province. In line with the Prabowo–Sandi campaign team, it voiced the need for price stability and more job opportunities. It targeted the group most affected by economic fluctuations, middle-to-low-income women, believing that even the most apolitical women would demand change, considering the prevailing economic circumstances.

Another active women's group supporting Prabowo-Sandi was the Gerakan Rabu Biru (Blue Wednesday Movement or GRB, for short).

Led by a former colleague of Sandiaga's at the Indonesian Chamber of Commerce and Industry (KADIN), the movement visited traditional markets around Jakarta every Wednesday throughout the campaign period. GRB welcomed men and women, although the most active members were women.[6] PEPES was often invited to its activities, but PEPES members were not comfortable with the GRB movement. The class distinction was the primary reason for this discomfort: GRB targeted the middle-upper class women who have little in common with the *emak-emak*. As PEPES' Wulan told me: "The unstable price of goods is affecting [GRB members financially], but it is not as severe as for our members; that's why our language is different [from that of GRB's]".[7] Nonetheless, PEPES saw the difference as beneficial since both groups could target different voter constituencies.

PEPES had a highly active social media presence, continuously posting updates of its activities with bold hashtags like #PEPESKepung ("PEPES surrounds the village") and #PEPESDatangKelar ("once PEPES goes to a village, everything will be settled"). It defended its candidates vehemently, denying accusations against them and attacking their opponents in turn. All these attacks were undertaken deliberately to threaten the incumbent's supporters and expand the influence of Prabowo–Sandi. In contrast, Jokowi's women supporters did not rely on social media as the campaign's primary tool. They mainly utilized the established network of women from the 2014 election to go into *kampungs* (villages).

PEPES rarely used identity politics as the main element of its campaign message. It was open to anyone who supported Prabowo-Sandi, including non-Muslims, as long as they shared the same vision of economic stability. However, in February 2019, a viral video surfaced of three women, identified as members of PEPES, going door-to-door in Karawang, Bekasi, telling people that if Jokowi were re-elected, he would allow same-sex relationships. He would also, they said, prohibit the Islamic call for prayer (*azan*), Qur'anic study groups for children, and veils for women (Prabowo 2019). These claims indicate how the message of the Islamists became intertwined with that promoted by other pro-Prabowo groups. IPAC (2019) further explained: "Many OKE-OCE mentors were *ustadz* [Islamic preachers] who specialized in shari'a economy, which enabled the overlap between Sandi's campaign team with the 212 movement."

ULTRA-CONSERVATIVE FEMALE CANDIDATES

Over the years, Indonesia has adopted several mechanisms to reinforce female representation in the political sphere. These include requiring political parties to have a minimum of 30 per cent women candidates, implementing the zipper rule[8] and ensuring female representation in election offices (Cakra Wikara Indonesia 2018; Prihatini 2018). However, the significant increase in the number of women in parliament does not necessarily mean better policies for women. Many female members of parliament hold conservative values regardless of their religion. Even if they support women-centred bills, they are tied to the decisions of their respective political parties, and parties generally tend to avoid controversy.

The affirmative action policies in the election system, however, facilitated the entry into the race of women from diverse political backgrounds, including anti-feminists, who were able to mobilize their masses. I met three female candidates who were openly against feminism: Nur Azizah Tamhid and Sri Vira Chandra from Partai Keadilan Sejahtera (Prosperous Justice Party or PKS, for short) and Fitriah Abdul Aziz from Partai Bulan Bintang (Crescent Star Party or PBB, for short). Both of these are considered Islamist parties that support the formal application of Islamic law. Nur Azizah Tamhid was a PKS candidate running for the Dewan Perwakilan Rakyat (house of representatives or DPR, for short) in an electoral district that includes Bekasi and Depok City. She is the wife of Nur Mahmudi Ismail, who was mayor of Depok from 2006 to 2016. As the head of the Pendidikan Kesejahteraan Keluarga (Family Welfare Programme) and sitting on the board of Al-Mubarokah, a *majlis taklim* group with hundreds of members, she has an extensive network in the constituency.

Fitriah Abdul Aziz, who ran on the PBB ticket, is the vice-chair of the women's wing of Dewan Dakwah Islamiyah Indonesia (DDII), a long-standing Islamist outreach organization. She has wide experience with other organizations as well. She focused on international affairs as she represented the Jakarta II electoral district, a constituency that includes overseas voters. Her main platform was the protection of migrant workers and the role that Indonesia's Muslim diaspora could play to tackle the growing Islamophobia in the West. Notwithstanding her wide experience, she failed to secure a seat because her party could not reach the four per cent vote threshold to be represented in parliament.

The other candidate I met, Sri Vira Chandra from PKS, also known as Umi Vira, ran in the election for Jakarta's provincial legislative. She is an Islamic preacher and is active in Aliansi Cinta Keluarga Indonesia (Family Love Alliance or AILA, for short). Umi Vira has been working with women at the grassroots for twenty-five years. The main reason she entered politics was her concern that Muslim women who understood the real issues affecting women were underrepresented in parliament. She once told *emak-emak* in her religious study circle:

> Ladies, in *majlis taklim* we cannot produce regulations; we need to be involved in politics. If you want to fight for what's right and important [and] you want to put it in the form of regulations, you have to choose your representative in politics.[9]

The three candidates claimed that the moral crisis in society, involving extra-marital sex and the presence of the LGBT community, was the main problem that women must address in parliament. One proposed law they felt must be debated was the bill on the Elimination of Sexual Violence (Rancangan Undang-Undang Penghapusan Kekerasan Seksual, or RUU-PKS, for short). Women activists advocated the bill because it aimed to prevent sexual violence, a growing problem in Indonesia, and it called for better law enforcement and the rehabilitation of victims. Candidates like the three I met thought otherwise. They believed the bill could threaten the morality of the nation and disrupt family values. It could promote LGBT tendencies, abortions and free sex. As Nur Azizah Tamhid said in an interview:

> The proposed Elimination of Sexual Violence bill ought to be rejected because it weakens the family. If it is applied, we cannot report pre-marital sex cases [to the police]. No law prohibits adultery or alcohol, but parents can be jailed [for enforcing their daughters to wear the *hijab*]. That's what they mean by sexual violence. They want to eliminate it; they want to be free, and they are disrupting family values.[10]

Such widespread disinformation efforts perpetuated misunderstanding of the bill during the campaign period. A social media campaign was launched to spread a fake version of the draft bill stating that a wife could sue her husband for non-consensual sex and parents could be jailed for forcing their daughters to wear the veil. Furthermore, Tengku Zulkarnain, a well-known preacher and deputy to the general secretary of the Indonesian Council of Islamic scholars, Majelis Ulama Indonesia (MUI), said on a YouTube video that the content of the bill was worrying. He said one clause in the bill requires the government to provide contraception for students and young people, a claim which was later proven to be false (CNN Indonesia 2019).

Leading the propaganda against the proposed RUU-PKS bill was the Aliansi Cinta Keluarga (AILA) or Family Love Alliance. The organization was founded in 2013 by several Islamist organizations, including the Council of Indonesian Muslim Intellectuals and Young Ulama (MIUMI), Muslimah Community for Islamic Studies (KKMI), and the Centre for Gender Studies (CGS). All of the board members were women except for the adviser, Bachtiar Nasir, a Salafi leader[11] who also played a pivotal role in the 212 Movement.[12] AILA first came to public attention in 2016, when it proposed a judicial review of three articles in the Criminal Code claiming to "allow" adultery, immoral behaviour and homosexuality. Although the Constitutional Court rejected its case, AILA's popularity rose since that development and the alliance continued being critical of enlightened gender policies, such as RUU-PKS.

One element that makes AILA more influential than other conservative organizations is its criticism of gender policies *within the existing legal system*, similar to the Family Research Council, a conservative Christian research and advocacy organization in the United States. Such an approach has never been used before by Indonesia's anti-feminists (Hermawan 2016). AILA crystallizes conservative reasoning for policy advocacy, providing intellectual support through studies and analysis from an Islamic worldview to influence public discourse on anti-feminist agendas.

AILA's main argument in rejecting RUU-PKS, and feminism in general, is that it is derived from a secular and Western-influenced worldview instead of an Islamic one. It problematizes the concept of consent in the definition of sexual violence, which in its view indicates that sexual activity outside marriage is permissible. AILA believes that gender justice exists in Islam because men and women are equal in the eyes of God albeit with different roles in society. As AILA member Sri Vira Chandra said in March 2019:

> I am not a feminist. I am a Muslimah who understands that in Islam women have a noble place. A woman has the authority to do good deeds to her country, and this starts with the family. A woman has a spiritual value to uphold so that the whole family can be together in heaven. Does feminism count that? I don't think so. On that point, we disagree.

AILA worked with lawmakers from PKS to propose the Family Resilience Bill. The bill was aimed at tackling moral ills in society, including sexual violence and homosexuality, through the smallest unit of society, the family. Its proponents believed that the state needs to provide assistance to strengthen families, especially the underprivileged ones. Such assistance could help families focus on the internalization of noble values and thereby become immune to social problems. The bill received massive criticism because it includes provisions for the state's interference in the private lives of citizens, perpetuates traditional patriarchal culture and discriminates against sexual and gender minorities (*Jakarta Post* 2020). After long debate and discussion, in November 2020, parliament decided to reject the bill owing to its overlap with law no. 52/2009 on family and population development (Nugraha 2020).

Nonetheless, women still have a long way to go in achieving gender justice. As of January 2021, two policies advocated by progressive women activists for years, the Domestic Workers Protection bill (RUU-PRT) and the aforesaid RUU-PKS, were left hanging. The former has not had much progress in sixteen years of advocacy, being barely listed among priority bills in parliament. As for RUU-PKS, in July 2020, parliament decided to delay its discussion because it was "too complicated". It re-entered the list of priority bills in January 2021. The on-off interest in the bill has been going on since its first submission in 2016, and the decision on its passing seems to be dependent on political dynamics rather than the victims' dire need to access justice.

ONLINE AND OFFLINE ARENAS FOR POLITICAL CAMPAIGNING

The huge number of people gathered in the 212 protests boosted the confidence of the Islamists regarding their impact on the political arena, which they further utilized during the 2019 election with the main goal of establishing a more Islamic Indonesia. Supporting Jokowi was not an option. He was seen as an ally of Basuki Tjahaja Purnama ("Ahok") and accused of being anti-Islam after the state initiated criminal charges, not related to the protests, against many of the religious leaders involved. The government further stigmatized the Islamist organizations involved as "radical" (IPAC 2019). Organizations in the 212 coalition used all possible channels to boost Prabowo's campaign and extend its reach to broader audiences. For instance, they used the popular hashtag of #2019GantiPresiden (Change the President in 2019) and waged a fear-mongering campaign about the supposed moral crisis in society. Social media and *majlis taklim* became two of the most important mechanisms for spreading the conservative narrative from offline channels to online channels and vice versa. Each had different target audiences and strategies.

The online-to-offline mechanism tended to target tech-savvy young Muslim girls who spent much of their time online. One researcher observes how Muslim women's social media accounts turned into a political movement during the 2017 Jakarta gubernatorial election (Beta 2019). These social media accounts often started with posts that encouraged self-transformation (*hijrah*) by depicting the ideal Muslim women: successful mothers who can balance their public and private lives and still make money to support their financial needs. During the mass mobilization against Purnama on the blasphemy accusation, some of these accounts and influencers started to participate in an online campaign bearing the hashtags #AksiBelaQuran and #MuslimvoteMuslim.

Social media became a key channel for Islamists to spread their conservative narrative, especially to young women. In April 2019, an Instagram account named "Indonesia Tanpa Feminis" (Indonesia Without Feminism) went viral, targeting young girls with the hashtag #UninstallFeminism and promoting the message "my body is not mine, but Allah's" to counter the feminist concept of body autonomy. It was part of a series of online campaigns by conservatives targeting the younger population. Some of the movements involved in the campaign included "Pemuda Hijrah" (Young Men Transforming to Better the Self) and "Indonesia Tanpa Pacaran" (Indonesia Without Dating or ITP).[13] The narrative was reproduced and amplified by Islamist student groups under the umbrella body Aliansi Cerahkan Negeri (Brightening the

Nation Alliance or ACN, for short).[14] These groups brought the online debate into offline discussions, seminars and regular public protests on Sunday mornings when a central avenue in Jakarta was transformed into a car-free street fair for pedestrians and cyclists.

The constant disinformation campaign fed into WhatsApp groups and was bolstered by the same narrative played offline as peers tried to convince friends that the threat of moral crisis was real (Lim 2017). It brought a sense of imagined community owing to constant online interactions with people from a perceived shared identity in their algorithmic bubble. An in-group began to think of the out-group as an existential threat. These feelings were followed by in-group favouritism and the possibility of hostile reactions against the out-group. The situation was worsened by Indonesia's generally low trust of mainstream media, lack of critical skills and low digital literacy (Tapsell 2018).

The offline-to-online mechanism was more effective for mothers and housewives who regularly attended local *majlis taklim*. The *majlis taklim* are not always political. They serve as a place for women to exchange information about their daily lives and religious learning (Winn 2012). Usually, the *majlis taklim* would get religious preachers and counsellors to speak on topics requested by members. The recent development of conservative Islamic politics has turned the *majlis taklim* into a significant political campaign arena (Bayu 2018).

IPAC (2019) describes how this mechanism worked in the network of Neno Warisman, a TV-personality who became a prominent Islamic preacher in the 212 Movement. Neno's team began by identifying potential *majlis taklim* in the neighbourhood, usually those with a large number of members or attended by women with a mass base, such as the heads of midwives associations or of small-enterprises networks. Neno would offer herself as a one-off preacher in their sessions or give them free courses on micro-business with speakers from the OKE-OCE programme. Her team would add the selected *majlis taklim* members to her WhatsApp group and then regularly update them on the #2019GantiPresiden campaign.

A similar strategy seemed to have been adopted by PKS candidate Sri Vira Chandra. While running for election, she continued her work as a preacher, going from one *majlis taklim* to another, providing spiritual advice, teaching life skills, and empowering women according to Islamic norms. Her lectures provided a conservative Islamic perspective on parenting and other morality issues, including LGBT issues. Some of these lectures were recorded and uploaded to YouTube to amplify her campaign.[15]

DIGITAL FEMINIST ACTIVISM TO COUNTER CONSERVATIVE NARRATIVES

Despite the gloomy description of how identity politics and conservative narratives were employed in the 2019 election, there is a brighter side involving digital feminist activism to push for a more gender-equal Indonesia. The rapid progress of feminists in Indonesia in the past years was largely achieved through online activism. The worldwide Women's March and #MeToo campaigns have spurred Indonesian feminists to build an alliance and attract more people to join their force. At least 4,000 people joined the 2019 Women's March in Jakarta—double that over the previous year—urging Indonesia's parliament to legalize the anti-sexual violence bill (Cahya 2019). Dhyta Caturani, an Indonesian feminist, asserts:

> This is the biggest feminist movement in Indonesia I've ever seen in my twenty-five years of activism. There are many self-proclaimed feminists, individuals and groups, including those institutions that promote human rights. When I started "One Billion Rising" in 2013, many were not comfortable with the term "feminism". I urged them that we need to reclaim the word for the movement.[16]

Most of these feminists are young, well-educated and well connected to the global Women's March movement. They also show social-media savvy and use such media as primary tools to educate, engage and mobilize their followers. Consequently, more online initiatives have emerged to respond to the growing demand for feminist education. *Magdalene*, a feminist online magazine established in 2013, publishes short articles, interviews and podcasts. Its website has become a medium for young feminists to share their personal experiences and analyses of how Indonesia's sociopolitical environment affected their gender expression and sexual orientation. It gets, on average, 150,000 page views each month (Soetjipto 2018). Aside from that, many online-based initiatives have emerged introducing feminist concepts to the young. These include Lawan Patriarki, Indonesia Feminis and Konde.co.

Unlike conservative women's movements that promote a single narrative of religion, feminists focus on a wider range of policies, from body autonomy, the right to work and the environment, without suggesting a single overarching solution for these problems. Diverse topics entail different approaches and strategies. While one group prefers to be bold, including being outspoken on taboo topics like sexual activities and LGBT rights, other groups are more comfortable using subtler messages to advocate for their concerns.

Muslim feminists, for example, are not comfortable using terms like "gender equality" and "feminism" in their platforms since these will provoke controversy within their community. They prefer to promote "gender justice", a value that Islam upholds, i.e., that men and women are equal before God. The same concept has been adopted by the conservatives but with different interpretations, that is, with the qualifier that men and women have different roles in society. Progressive Muslims and Muslim feminists tend to take more egalitarian interpretations of Qur'anic verses and Prophetic sayings (*hadith*) relating to equality before God for the two sexes and equal rights for women. They believe that Islam is pro-women's rights, but that years of male domination in the Islamic world led the religion to be seen otherwise (Rinaldo 2019).

The Muslim feminist movement is an important and evolving space and crucial for the overall gender rights movement in Indonesia. Fahmina, Rahimah, and Alimat are Muslim women organizations with expanded grassroots networks that strive for gender justice in Islam. They are loosely associated with the biggest Muslim organizations in the country, NU and Muhammadiyah. In 2017, they initiated Kongres Ulama Perempuan Indonesia (Indonesia's Women Ulama Congress, or KUPI, for short), involving about 2,000 women *ulama* (Islamic scholars) and academics across Indonesia gathering in Cirebon, West Java. The gathering was vital in proving that the narrative of gender and Islam does not belong only to the conservatives. The congress resulted in the condemnation of three major issues: sexual violence, child marriage and environmental degradation (Robinson 2017).

The young Muslim feminist movement is actively countering conservative narratives online. One of their biggest channels in this endeavour is mubadalah.id on Instagram. The young Muslim feminists employ the same strategy used by the conservatives—simplifying the discussion of daily issues such as dating, wearing the veil, education, work, sexuality and parenting through attractive infographics and distributing them on Instagram, one of the most popular social media platforms among youngsters. Another of their platforms is islami.co, a website that promotes peace and tolerance by publishing articles and short analyses from progressive Islamic perspectives.

CONCLUSION

The increasing political engagement of women in Indonesia is generally a cause for celebration. However, we need to understand that the policies that women seek to promote are as diverse as Indonesian society. Not all women are in favour of expanding women's rights and gender equality: the effort to expand women's participation has also brought more ultra-conservative women onto the political stage. We need to critically examine the implications of policies that women are fighting for and situate them in today's political climate.

The work of feminists and women's rights activists in the coming years will not be easy. Decisions made thus far by the government and parliament show that their commitment to women's rights is still weak despite the tremendous support women have given political candidates during elections. Women would need to strive hard to break the deeply entrenched patriarchal system. Some of the key policy challenges ahead are the passing of the aforesaid anti-sexual violence bill and Domestic Workers Protection Bill. Women may also find themselves having to counter the growing number of discriminatory local bylaws that include calls for controlling women's body autonomy.

While feminists have made tremendous progress in recent years, the old problem of consolidation at the grassroots level remains. The issue is not just that of the scale or funding, as Rinaldo (2019) assumes, but the narrative used by feminists. They would need a strategy to challenge conservative narratives that call for restricting women's roles to that of wives and mothers and conservative efforts to tighten widely accepted social norms, such as those on women's dress and women's activities outside the home. The secular feminists may not be recognized as having the locus standi to come up with re-interpretations, but Muslim feminists could delve deep into the classical Islamic juristic discourse to look for interpretations that show the compatibility of Islam and feminism to win the hearts of potential supporters whose views on the subject are still inchoate.

NOTES

1. This chapter is an extension of my articles in *New Mandala*, "What will Indonesian Women Win in this Election?", published on 4 March 2019; "An Anti-Feminist Wave in Indonesia's Election?", published on 14 April 2019, and "The Post Election Challenges for Indonesia's Feminist Movement", published on 25 July 2019.
2. The two candidates in the 2017 Jakarta gubernatorial election were Basuki Tjahaja Purnama alias "Ahok", a Christian and ethnic Chinese, and Anis Baswedan, a Muslim of Arab descent. Purnama's candidacy had been controversial because of his minority background. During a public campaign in Thousand Islands, a chain of islands to the north of Jakarta, Purnama made a controversial statement involving a Qur'anic verse. Conservative Muslim groups, often referred to as Islamists, used this statement to gain momentum for delegitimizing Purnama's candidacy and enhancing their own public support. They flooded social media platforms with the campaign hashtags of #AksiBelaQuran (The Act of Defending the Qur'an) and #MuslimvoteMuslim. They also held a series of peace protests, the biggest being on 2 December 2016, leading to the formation of what has since been called the 212 Movement.
3. Bravo-5 is a volunteer group of pro-Jokowi retired generals and high-ranking military officials that backed him both in the 2014 and 2019 elections. The group was founded by Luhut Binsar Pandjaitan in 2014 and is led by Fachrul Razi. Both hold cabinet positions in Jokowi's second term of office, the former as coordinating minister for maritime affairs and investment and the latter as minister of religious affairs. The head of the group's women's wing is Kartika Sjahrir, a feminist intellectual and Luhut's sister.
4. Interview with Pertiwi's coordinator, Putri K. Wardhani, 4 February 2019.
5. Sandiaga was elected as vice-governor with Anies Baswedan in 2017. He left the position on 27 August 2018 after accepting Prabowo's offer to be his vice-presidential candidate in the 2019 election.
6. Interview with coordinator of Gerakan Rabu Biru, Vivi Susanti, 30 January 2019.
7. Interview with coordinator of PEPES, Wulan, 24 January 2019.
8. The zipper system is part of the proportional representation system that intended to increase females' electability. It obliges parties to put up a

minimum of one female for every three candidates on their ballot list. Indonesia's General Elections Commission started implementing this system in the 2009 election, which led to women's electability prospects standing at a significant 18.12 per cent. It enforced sanctions for parties that could not meet this requirement from the 2014 election onwards (Prihatini 2018).
9. Interview with Sri Vira Chandra, 29 March 2019.
10. Interview with Nur Azizah Tamhid, 24 March 2019.
11. Salafis are orthodox Muslims advocating a return to Islam as practised by the pious ancestors or first generation of Muslims but in recent years have been associated with extremism.
12. See endnote 2 for a description of the 212 Movement.
13. Pemuda Hijrah and ITP began as social media campaigns, which then evolved into social movements. Pemuda Hijrah was founded by a Bandung-based Islamic preacher, Hanan Attaki. He was deliberately recruiting urban youth groups who were often seen as non-religious, such as musicians and bikers. The goal was to repackage Pemuda Hijrah as a cool and trendy movement (Temby 2018). Meanwhile, ITP was rooted in a WhatsApp group started in 2015 by La Ode Munafar, who believed dating before marriage has negative implications, such as distracting oneself from God and other responsibilities. The group's message revolved mainly around conservative views on how young girls must behave and conduct their lives (Adisya 2018).
14. The Islamist student groups include groups such as Indonesia Tanpa JIL (Indonesia without Liberal Islam, ITJ), Kesatuan Aksi Mahasiswa Muslim Indonesia (National Front of Indonesian Muslim Students, KAMMI) and Aku Cinta Islam (I love Islam, ACI). For more details, see the website of ACN, https://medium.com/@aliansicerahkannegeri.
15. See her videos on YouTube titled "Lesbian, Gay, Bisexual dan Transgender dalam Pandangan Islam", posted on 15 January 2015, and "Menyelamatkan keluarga dari Api Neraka: cukupkah hanya mengandalkan peran orangtua?", posted on 4 November 2018.
16. Interview with Dhyta Caturani, 18 May 2019. Dhyta initiated the Indonesian branch of "One Billion Rising", a global initiative founded in 2012 to end rape and sexual violence against women. See the website of the organization, https://www.onebillionrising.org.

REFERENCES

Adisya, Elma. 2018. "Indonesia Without Dating: Get Married Young, Lest You Sin". *Magdalene*, 18 April 2018. https://magdalene.co/story/indonesia-without-dating-get-married-young-lest-you-sin.

Bayu, Dimas Jarot. 2018. "Dibandingkan NU, Jaringan Majelis Taklim Lebih Penting Dalam Pemilu". *Katadata*, 18 October 2018. https://katadata.co.id/berita/2018/10/18/dibandingkan-nu-jaringan-majelis-taklim-lebih-penting-dalam-pemilu.

Beta, Annisa R. 2019. "Commerce, Piety and Politics: Indonesian Young Muslim Women's Groups as Religious Influencers". *New Media & Society* 21, no. 10: 1–20.

Bomantama, Rizal. 2018. "Akui OKE OCE Gagal Total, Sandiaga Uno: Tapi Diminta di Seluruh Indonesia". *Tribun News*, 16 October 2018. https://wartakota.tribunnews.com/2018/10/16/akui-oke-oce-gagal-total-sandiaga-uno-tapi-diminta-di-seluruh-indonesia.

Cahya, Gemma Holliani. 2019. "Thousands Join Women's March in Jakarta for Justice, Gender Equality". *The Jakarta Post*, 27 April 2019. https://www.thejakartapost.com/news/2019/04/27/thousands-join-womens-march-in-jakarta-for-justice-gender-equality.html.

Cakra Wikara Indonesia. 2018. *Menyoal Data Representasi Perempuan di Lima Ranah*. Jakarta: Cakra Wikara Indonesia. http://cakrawikara.id/publikasi/buku/menyoal-data-representasi-perempuan-di-lima-ranah/.

CNN Indonesia. 2019. "Tengku Zulkarnain Minta Maafsoal RUU PKS, MUI SebutCeroboh". *CNN Indonesia*, 13 March 2019. https://www.cnnindonesia.com/nasional/20190313165306-20-376954/tengku-zulkarnain-minta-maaf-soal-ruu-pks-mui-sebut-ceroboh.

Cook, Erin. 2019. "Jokowi's Cute Political Ploy Has Become a Campaign Sensation". *The Interpreter*, Lowy Institute, 10 April 2019. https://www.lowyinstitute.org/the-interpreter/jokowi-s-cute-political-ploy-has-become-campaign-sensation.

Hermawan, Ary. 2016. "Why AILA is a Bigger Threat to Freedom than the FPI". *The Jakarta Post*, 30 August 2016. https://www.thejakartapost.com/news/2016/08/30/commentary-why-aila-is-a-bigger-threat-to-freedom-than-the-fpi.html.

IFES (International Foundation for Electoral Systems). 2019. "Elections in Indonesia: 2019 Concurrent Presidential and Legislative Elections". IFES, 9 April 2019. https://www.ifes.org/sites/default/files/2019_ifes_indonesia_concurrent_presidential_and_legislative_elections_faqs_final.pdf.

IPAC (Institute of Policy Analysis and Conflict). 2019. *Anti-Ahok to Anti-Jokowi: Islamist Influence on Indonesia's 2019 Election Campaign*. IPAC Report 55, 15 March 2019.

Jakarta Post, The. 2020. "Indonesia's Parliament Continues Deliberation of Controversial Family Resilience Bill". *The Straits Times*, 21 September 2020. https://www.straitstimes.com/asia/se-asia/indonesias-parliament-continues-deliberation-of-controversial-family-resilience-bill.

Khalika, Nindias Nur. 2018. "Emak-Emak Vs Ibu Bangsa, Mengapa Istilah Jadi Masalah?" *Tirto.id*, 26 September 2018. https://tirto.id/emak-emak-vs-ibu-bangsa-mengapa-istilah-jadi-masalah-c2Cy.

Lim, Merlyna. 2017. "Freedom to Hate: Social Media, Algorithmic Enclaves, and the Rise of Tribal Nationalism in Indonesia". *Critical Asian Studies* 49, no. 3: 411–27.

Mediani, Mesha. 2018. "Sandiaga, Bisikan SBY dan 'The Power Of Emak-Emak'". CNN Indonesia, 15 August 2018. https://www.cnnindonesia.com/nasional/20180815074634-32-322363/sandiaga-bisikan-sby-dan-the-power-of-emak-emak.

Nugraha, Ricky Mohammad. 2020. "DPR House Majority Rejects Family Resilience Bill". *Tempo.co*, 24 November 2020. https://en.tempo.co/read/1408341/dpr-house-majority-rejects-family-resilience-bill.

Prabowo, Haris. 2019. "Pepes Hanya Korban Narasi Elite Prabowo-Sandi?". *Tirto.id*, 27 February. https://tirto.id/pepes-hanya-korban-narasi-elite-prabowo-sandi-dhQi

Prihatini, Ella S. 2018. "On the Same Page? In Indonesia, Some Male Lawmakers are Skeptical of Quotas for Women in Politics". The Conversation, 21 June 2018. https://theconversation.com/on-the-same-page-in-indonesia-some-male-lawmakers-are-sceptical-of-quotas-for-women-in-politics-90824.

Rinaldo, Rachel. 2019. "The Women's Movement and Indonesia's Transition to Democracy". In *Activists in Transition: Contentious Politics in the New Indonesia*, edited by Thushara Dibley and Michele Ford, pp. 135–52. New York: Cornell University Press.

Robinson, Kathryn. 2017. "Female Ulama Voice a Vision for Indonesia's Future". *New Mandala*, 30 May 2017. https://www.newmandala.org/female-ulama-voice-vision-indonesias-future/.

Santosa, Dwi Argo and Markus Junianto Sihaloha. 2019. "Survei CSIS: Emak-emak Lebih Banyak Pilih Jokowi-Ma'ruf". *Berita Satu*, 28 March 2019. https://www.beritasatu.com/politik/545536/survei-csis-emakemak-lebih-banyak-pilih-jokowimaruf.

Sapiie, Marguerite Afra. 2019. "Rival Camps Woo Different Women's Group". *The Jakarta Post*, 30 January 2019. https://www.thejakartapost.com/news/2019/01/29/rival-camps-woo-different-womens-groups.html.

Soetjipto, Tomi. 2018. "Meet the Team Behind Magdalene: Indonesia's Feminist Website Covering 'Taboo' Subjects on Gender and Sexuality". *The Splice Newsroom*, 1 March 2018. https://www.thesplicenewsroom.com/magdalene-indonesia/.

Suryakusuma, Julita. 2011. "Ibuisme Negara—State Ibuism: Konstruksi Sosial Keperempuanan Orde Baru". Depok: Komunitas Bambu.

Tapsell, Ross. 2018. "Disinformation and Democracy in Indonesia". *New Mandala*, 12 January 2018. https://www.newmandala.org/disinformation-democracy-indonesia/.

Temby, Quinton. 2018. "Shariah, Dakwah, and Rock N Roll: Pemuda Hijrah in Bandung". *New Mandala*, 30 June 2018. https://www.newmandala.org/shariah-dakwah-rock-n-roll-pemuda-hijrah-bandung/.

Wieringa, Saskia. 2002. *Sexual Politics in Indonesia*. The Hague: Palgrave Macmillan.

Winn, Phillip. 2012. "Women's *Majelis Taklim* and Gendered Religious Practice in Northern Ambon". *Intersections: Gender and Sexuality in Asia and the Pacific*, no. 30 (November). http://intersections.anu.edu.au/issue30/winn.htm.

9

CHINESE POLITICAL PARTICIPATION SINCE INDEPENDENCE: BETWEEN NATIONAL IDENTITY AND ETHNIC IDENTITY

Leo Suryadinata

Indonesia held simultaneous elections for president and both the national and regional parliaments on 17 April 2019. According to information available on the ethnic backgrounds of successful candidates, at least eleven Indonesians of Chinese descent have been elected into the national parliament, the Dewan Perwakilan Rakyat (DPR);[1] also, several Chinese Indonesians have been elected into regional parliaments or the Dewan Perwakilan Rakyat Daerah Provinsi (DPRD). These numbers show clearly that there was Chinese political participation in Indonesia.[2]

POLITICAL PARTICIPATION AND ETHNIC CHINESE-BASED POLITICS

Political participation is defined here as "activity by private citizens designed to influence governmental decision-making". It includes electoral activity, lobbying, organizational activity, contacting and violence (Huntington and Nelson 1976, p. 4). In my view, political participation can be divided into formal political participation and informal political participation. Formal political participation involves participating through political parties while informal political participation refers to political activity through non-governmental organizations, civil society organizations or pressure groups.

Ethnic Chinese political participation in Indonesia has occurred at both the formal and informal levels. However, Chinese political activity is designed not merely to influence governmental decision-making but also to strengthen the national identity of the Chinese minority. It is through political participation, especially through formal participatory processes, that the Chinese minority has become recognized as part of the Indonesian national polity.

The Chinese have been involved in politics since the colonial period. It is important to note here that the Chinese in Indonesia were not—and still are not—a homogeneous group. They can be divided into two categories, *peranakan* and *totok* (*singkeh*). The former refers to the local-born and Indonesian-speaking Chinese while the latter refers to China-born, Chinese-speaking Chinese. The latter were newcomers in relative terms. Their direct descendants were often Chinese-educated and preserved the culture of their migrant fathers, so culturally they were often considered as *totok*. The Chinese who were involved in local politics were usually the *peranakans*. Nevertheless, owing to the absence of significant numbers of Chinese new migrants into Indonesia during the Suharto period, Chinese Indonesians, especially the younger generations, have been highly Indonesianized.

Prior to World War II, Chinese political participation was on ethnic terms, i.e., the Chinese took part in politics mainly through ethnic organizations. This was due to colonial society being race-based and the refusal on the part of the indigenous parties—with the exception of the illegal Partai Komunis Indonesia (PKI) and a small left-wing party, Gerindo—to accept the Indies Chinese. There were three Chinese political groups/parties then: the China-oriented Sin Po, the Dutch Indies-oriented Chung Hwa Hui (CHH) and the Indonesia-oriented Partai Tionghoa Indonesia (PTI).

Only after Indonesia had attained independence did parties dominated by indigenous Indonesians welcome Chinese Indonesians to join them. At the same time, Chinese Indonesians also began establishing their own political parties and associations. The largest was Persatuan Tionghoa (PT), which was established in 1948 by Thio Thiam Tjong, an ex-CHH leader who belonged to a moderate group. After the Dutch transferred sovereignty to the Indonesian nationalists in December 1949, PT changed its name to Partai Demokrat Tionghoa Indonesia (PDTI), while Liem Koen Hian, the leader of the pre-World War II PTI, set up a new PTI in February 1950, namely Persatuan Tenaga Indonesia (Indonesian Union of Forces), which was a multi-ethnic party.[3] However, the new PTI was unable to develop as those who were interested in multi-ethnic politics joined parties dominated by indigenous Indonesians.[4]

The PDTI, too, encountered difficulties as members began to split: some wanted to remain in the ethnic-based party while others wanted to join indigenous-dominated parties, but the PDTI constitution prohibited dual party membership. As time passed, the PDTI began to face an internal crisis. Meanwhile, the Indonesian government was preparing a new Indonesian citizenship law that would make it more difficult for the Chinese to maintain Indonesian citizenship. This caused concern among the Chinese. In addition, the government was planning to hold the first parliamentary election. The PDTI and other smaller Chinese associations consequently decided to merge. A new sociopolitical organization called Badan Permusyawaratan Kewarganegaraan Indonesia (Indonesian Consultative Citizenship Body or Baperki, for short) was formed in March 1954. Its chairman was the Dutch-educated Siauw Giok Tjhan, a left-wing politician who was close to the PKI.

Baperki decided to contest the 1955 general election, but before the election took place a major split occurred within the organization owing to ideological differences. Those who disagreed with Siauw's ideological leaning left the organization. It is important to note that only two ethnic Chinese were successfully elected into parliament in the 1955 election: one was Siauw himself and the other was Tjoo Tik Tjhoen, a member of the PKI (Somers 1965, pp. 150–51). As a minority group, the ethnic Chinese found it difficult to be voted in. However, soon after the election seven more Chinese became members of parliament (MPs) but they were appointed by the government in consultation with the major Indonesian political parties.

Nonetheless, Baperki became the largest ethnic Chinese sociopolitical organization. It became quite influential not because of its size but because of its alliance with President Sukarno. Siauw, who was close to Sukarno, gained the president's support to fight against racial discrimination. But owing to Siauw's close association with and even dependence on Sukarno, and also his association with the PKI, Baperki met its end when Sukarno was overthrown by the Indonesian military in the so-called G30S (Gerakan Tiga Puluh September) movement in 1965. This also marked the sudden end of ethnic Chinese-based politics.

THE DEMISE OF ETHNIC CHINESE-BASED POLITICS AND ITS RE-EMERGENCE?

The result of the G30S affair was the dissolution of the PKI, the fall of Sukarno and rise of General Suharto. Once Suharto came to power, he abolished the three Chinese cultural pillars: Chinese organizations, Chinese schools, and Chinese newspapers/periodicals. Initially, there were ten Indonesian political parties that contested the general election of 1971 under the New Order, but following the election the ten parties were reorganized into three parties, namely Golkar (the party of functional groups), the Partai Demokrasi Indonesia (Indonesian Democratic Party or PDI, for short) and the Partai Persatuan Pembangunan (United Development Party or PPP, for short, which comprised a fusion of Islamic parties). Chinese Indonesians could only join one of these three indigenous-dominated parties if they wanted to enter formal politics. A few did join Golkar and PDI but they did not represent the Chinese community.

In 1968, a think tank called the Centre for Strategic and International Studies (CSIS) was established by a number of military generals such as Ali Murtopo and Sudjono Humardhani and Chinese political activists. Former student leaders and politicians such as Harry Tjan Silalahi (Tjan Tjoen Hok), Jusuf Wanandi (Liem Bian Kie) and Sofian Wanandi (Liem Bian Khoen) were the backbone of the CSIS. They were closely involved in New Order politics, at least up to 1978. Nevertheless, they did not represent the Chinese community. Neither did Yap Thiam Hien, a leading human rights lawyer known for his courage and his dedication to defending human rights. For all intents and purposes, one could argue that there was no ethnic Chinese politics in the New Order period.

After the collapse of Suharto's New Order in 1998, Indonesians were free to establish political parties. Chinese Indonesians formed two parties: Partai Reformasi Tionghoa Indonesia (PARTI), led by Lieus Sungkharisma (Li Xuexiong 李学雄), an activist in the Buddhist Youth Association, and Partai Bhinneka Tunggal Ika Indonesia (PBI or PBTI), led by Nurdin Purwono (Wu Nengbing 吴能彬), a travel agency owner. As there were no Chinese political parties in the thirty-two years of the Suharto era, these young, self-proclaimed party leaders were unknown. PARTI was disqualified as it did not fulfil the requirements for general elections and only the PBI, along with the forty-seven indigenous-dominated parties, was able to contest in the first post-New Order election of 1999. The PBI won only one parliamentary seat in West Kalimantan. But at least seven more Chinese were elected, representing indigenous-dominated parties such as the Partai Demokrasi Indonesia Perjuangan (Indonesian Democratic Party of Struggle or PDI-P, for short), Golkar and Partai Amanat Nasional (National Mandate Party or PAN, for short) (see Table 9.1). It should also be pointed out that after the 1999 elections, no more "Chinese-Indonesian party" contested elections.

TABLE 9.1
DPR: 1999–2004 (8 MPs of Chinese Descent)

Name	Party	Year of Birth	Occupation	Religion
Drs Kwik Kian Gie 郭建义	PDI-P	1935	Consultant	Buddhist
Tjandra Widjaja 黄松长	PDI-P	1957	Hotel owner	Catholic
Ir Daniel Budi Setiawan 何明良	PDI-P	1958	President-Director	Christian
Dr Rekso Ageng Herman (Chinese name unknown)	PDI-P		President-Director	Christian
Johannes Lukman* (Chinese name unknown)	PDI-P	1946	Teacher/Businessman	Catholic
Drs Enggartiarto Lukito 卢尤英	Golkar	1951	Businessman	Christian
Alvin Lie Ling Piao 李宁彪	PAN	1961	Businessman	Catholic
Drs Susanto, T.L. 林冠玉	PBTI	1942	Businessman	Catholic

*Johannes Lukman died in 2000.

Sources: *Wajah Dewan Perwakilan Rakyat Republik Indonesia, Pemilihan Umum 1999* (Jakarta: Penerbit Harian Kompas, 2000), and others.

Why did Chinese-based parties fail? Four reasons can be identified. First, the number of Chinese in Indonesia is small. Before World War II, the Chinese constituted 2.03 per cent of the total population, according to the 1930 census. According to the 2010 census, the number of Chinese Indonesians fell to only 1.2 per cent. It would seem that many Chinese Indonesians refused to identify themselves as Chinese. Even if they did, the number would have not gone beyond 2 per cent as birth rates among the Chinese are exceptionally low.[5] The Chinese, like most urban dwellers in other countries, tend to have small families. Indigenous Indonesians, on the other hand, have much higher birth rates and larger families.

Second, during the New Order period, many Chinese migrated overseas. At the same time, potential Chinese migrants were prohibited from entering Indonesia.

Third, Chinese Indonesians are spread throughout Indonesia, and they are politically and ideologically divided. As a result, in areas where the number of Chinese was small, a Chinese who wanted to enter the national or local parliament would need to gain the support of both Chinese and indigenous Indonesian voters. This reality was reflected in the case of some Chinese contestants in the 2014 and 2019 elections who successfully managed to garner votes from indigenous voters.[6]

Fourth, there is a higher chance of election into parliament if Chinese candidates join mainstream political parties, as shown in the results of the five general elections beginning 1999. This pattern of political participation, i.e., Chinese Indonesians joining parties dominated by indigenous Indonesians, can be called "Assimilated Politics". The above reasons explain the decline and demise of ethnic Chinese political parties in Indonesia and the prevalence of "Assimilated Politics" for the Chinese.

In discussing Chinese-Indonesian participation in politics during the post-Suharto era, it is imperative to point out that it is no longer easy to identify Chinese MPs as the Chinese had changed their names after 1966. In that year, President Suharto issued a presidential regulation that "encouraged" Chinese Indonesians to change their Chinese names to "Indonesian names". Changing names was not compulsory, but there was pressure for the Chinese to change their names as "Chineseness" was often identified with "disloyalty" to Indonesia. Even after the fall of Suharto, when President Abdurrahman Wahid stated that Chinese Indonesians were allowed to re-use their Chinese names, many Chinese who had adopted Indonesian names refrained from reverting to their previous names.[7] As for those born after the name-changing regulation, many did not have Chinese names at all. This has made it difficult to discern their Chinese ethnicity.

Even those who had Chinese names were not always willing to reveal them for various reasons. Strong prejudice still prevails—i.e., the assumption that the Chinese are not "genuine Indonesians" unless they abandon their Chinese names. For a brief period, when Zhong Wanxue (钟万学), officially known as Basuki Tjahaja Purnama ("Ahok") became the deputy governor (2012) and later governor (2014) of Jakarta, many indigenous Indonesians in Jakarta and other urban areas began to change their perceptions of Chinese Indonesians. Nevertheless, the surfacing of identity politics in the run-up to the 2017 Jakarta gubernatorial election, which led to the fall of Purnama, and the prevalence of identity politics in the 2019 presidential election, marks the re-emergence of strong prejudice against the Chinese and non-Muslim community among indigenous Muslims. It is likely to take some time for many indigenous Indonesians to change their perceptions of the Chinese. It is worth noting that after he was released from prison Purnama stated publicly that he prefers to be called "BTP" rather than Ahok (*Metro Tempo.co* 2019). One can see the strength of ethno-nationalism in Indonesian politics.

In this study of Chinese MPs, I have employed various methods to obtain the Chinese names, or determine the Chinese identity, of the persons concerned. I have relied heavily on Chinese newspapers in Jakarta and Surabaya, publications by a Chinese association known as Forum Demokrasi Kebangsaan (Fordeka), and information provided by some researchers in Jakarta.[8] Therefore, I cannot claim that the listing of Chinese-Indonesian MPs in this chapter is comprehensive.

PARLIAMENTARY ELECTIONS

In the 2004 election, about 16 Chinese Indonesians were elected into parliament, all representing indigenous-based parties (see Table 9.2). In the 2009 election, about nine Chinese Indonesians were elected, each representing one of three major indigenous-based parties (see Table 9.3).

In the April 2014 election, 58 Chinese Indonesians ran for parliamentary seats, representing at least seven indigenous Indonesian parties.[9] However, only 14 Chinese-Indonesian candidates[10] were elected,

TABLE 9.2
DPR: 2004–9 (16 MPs of Chinese Descent)

Name	Party	Year of Birth	Occupation	Religion
Tjiandra Widjaja 黄松长	PDI-P	1951	Hotel owner	Catholic
Murdaya W. Poo 傅志宽	PDI-P	1941	Pres-Director	Buddhist
Herman Herry, SH	PDI-P	1962	Pres-Director	Christian
Ir Daniel Budi Setiawan 何明良	PDI-P	1956	Pres-Director	Christian
Philip Widjaja 黄菲力	PDI-P	1959	Company commissioner	Christian
Rudianto Tjen 曾昭真	PDI-P	1958	Businessman	Christian
Prof Dr Wila Chandrawila 陈福美	PDI-P	1955?	Law professor	Christian
Drs Enggartiarto Lukito 卢尤英	Golkar	1951	Pres-Director	Christian
Budiarsa Sastrawinata, MBA	Golkar	1955	Company commissioner	Catholic
Yorrys Raweiya (Thung) 董	Golkar	1951	Pres-Director	Christian
Dr Frans Tsai 蔡华喜	Partai Demokrat (PD)	1941	Pharmacist/ entre	Christian
Albert Yaputra 叶锦标	PD	1951	Company director	Buddhist
Surya Supeno	PD	1962	Businessman	Christian
Tony Wardoyo	PKB	1958	Pres-Director	Christian
Alvin Lie Ling Piao, MA 李宁彪	PAN	1961	Pres-Director	Catholic
Constant M Ponggawa 彭	PDS	1959	Consultant	Christian

Sources: *Wajah DPR & DPD 2004–2009* (Jakarta: Buku Pustakan Kompas, 2005), and others.

TABLE 9.3
DPR: 2009–14 (9 MPs of Chinese Descent)

Name	Party	Year of Birth	Occupation	Religion
Murdaya W. Poo 傅志宽	PDI-P	1941	Pres-Director	Buddhist
Rudianto Tjen 曾昭真	PDI-P	1958	Businessman	Christian
Sudin 蔡瑞龙	PDI-P	1964	Businessman	Buddhist
Ir Basuki Tjahaja Purnama ("Ahok") 钟万学	Golkar	1966	Geologist/ Businessman	Christian
Drs Enggartiarto Lukito 卢尤英	Golkar	1951	Pres-Director	Christian
Yorrys Raweyai (Thung) 汤	Golkar	1951	Pres-Director	Christian
Dr Ratnawati Wijana 陈娘志	PD	1962?	Consultant	Catholic?
Drs Eddy Sadeli, SH 李胜祥	PD	1940	Lawyer	Buddhist
Lim Sui Kiang 林瑞强	PD	1960	Businessman	Catholic

Sources: *Wajah DPR & DPD, 2009-2014: Latar Belakang Pendidikan dan Karier* (Jakarta: Penerbit Buku Kompas, 2010) and others.

of whom 11 were from the PDI-P, while Partai Demokrat (PD), PAN and Partai Kebangkitan Bangsa (National Awakening Party or PKB, for short) had one Chinese-Indonesian MP each (see Table 9.4).

In 2019, at least 47 Chinese contested the parliamentary election representing nine parties. However, only 11 Chinese candidates were elected, that is, nine from PDI-P and one each from Golkar and PKB.

The PDI-P has been popular among Chinese Indonesians as its founder, Megawati Sukarnoputri, is Sukarno's daughter and has a pro-Chinese image, or at least is not perceived to be against the Chinese.

TABLE 9.4
DPR: 2014–19 (14 MPs of Chinese Descent)

Name	Party	Year of Birth	Occupation	Religion
Dr Sofyan Tan 陈金扬	PDI-P	1959	Physician/ Consultant	Buddhist
Sudin 蔡瑞龙	PDI-P	1964	Businessman	Buddhist
Ir Rudianto Tjen 曾昭真	PDI-P	1958	Businessman	Christian
Eko Wijaya 刘顺严	PD	1981	Businessman	Christian
Daniel Johan 张育浩	PKB	1972	Priest	Catholic
Hang Ali Saputra Syah Pahan, SH	PAN	1961	lawyer	Buddhist
Ichsan Sulistio	PDI-P	1954	Businessman	Muslim
Darmadi Durianto, PhD 林德俊	PDI-P	1967	University staff	Christian
Charles Honoris 何震康	PDI-P	1984	Businessman	Christian
Toni Wardoyo	PDI-P	1958	Pres-Director	Christian
Prof Dr Hendrawan Supratikno 黄正德	PDI-P	1960	University staff	Christian
Indah Kurniawati	PDI-P	1962	Banker	Christian
Henky Kurniadi, SE 游经善	PDI-P	1963	Businessman	Christian
Herman Hery	PDI-P	1962	Businessman	Christian

Sources: *Buku Acuan Pemilihan Legislatif Bagi Caleg-Caleg DPR RI, DPD RI, DPRD Provinsi, DPRD Kabupaten/Kota Periode 2014-2019 Keluarga Suku Tionghoa Indonesia* (Jakarta: Pengurus Pusat Fordeka, December 2013); Komisi Pemilihan Umum (KPU), "Daftar Calon Terpilih Anggota Dewan Perwakilan Rakyat Pemilihan Umum Tahun 2014"; and others.

TABLE 9.5
DPR: 2019–24 (11 MPs of Chinese Descent)

Name	Party	Year of Birth	Occupation	Religion
Dr Sofyan Tan 陈金扬	PDI-P	1959	Physician/Consultant	Buddhist
Bambang Patijaya	Golkar	1970s	Businessman	Buddhist
Sudin 蔡瑞龙	PDI-P	1964	Businessman	Buddhist
Ir Rudianto Tjen 曾昭真	PDI-P	1958	Businessman	Christian
Daniel Johan 张育浩	PKB	1972	Priest	Catholic
Ichsan Sulistio	PDI-P	1954	Businessman	Muslim
Darmadi Durianto, PhD 林德俊	PDI-P	1967	University staff member	Christian
Charles Honoris 何震康	PDI-P	1984	Businessman	Christian
Prof Dr Hendrawan Supratikno 黄正德	PDI-P	1960	University staff member	Christian
Indah Kurniawati	PDI-P	1962	Banker	Christian
Herman Hery	PDI-P	1962	Businessman	Christian

Sources: Compiled from KPU and Chinese newspaper reports. I would like to record my appreciation of Mr Lu Ikun, a journalist with a Chinese newspaper in Jakarta who provided additional information.

If we examine the five general elections, it is clear that the PDI-P has constantly had the largest number of Chinese-Indonesian MPs while the number of Chinese-Indonesian MPs in the other major parties such as Golkar and Partai Demokrat has been declining. The newly founded Gerindra did not have any Chinese-Indonesian MP (see Table 9.6).

It should be pointed out that two new so-called Chinese parties participated in the 2019 parliamentary election: Partai Solidaritas Indonesia (PSI), led by Grace Natalie alias Wu Xiaohui, an ex-TV personality who is a third-generation Chinese; and Partai Persatuan Indonesia (Perindo), led by a Chinese media tycoon, Hary Tanoesoedibjo alias Chen Mingli (陈明立). Hary supported Prabowo Subianto's bid for

TABLE 9.6
Chinese Indonesians in DPR, 1999–2019

Year/Party	1999	2004	2009	2014	2019	Total
PDI-P	5	7	7	11	9	39
Golkar	1	3	3		1	8
PD		3	4	1		8
Gerindra						0
PAN	1	1	1	1		4
PKB		1	1	1	1	4
PBI	1					1
PDS		1				1
Total	8	16	15	14	11	64

Source: Compiled from Tables 9.1–9.5.

election as president in 2014 but shifted his support to the incumbent, President Joko Widodo (Jokowi) in the 2019 election.[11] Although led by Chinese Indonesians, both these parties are not Chinese-based. Instead, they are pro-minorities and favour pluralism, which appeals to those who share their ideologies. If PSI, which is supported by young intellectuals and the urban youth, was perceived as a Chinese-based party by some Jakarta Chinese, Perindo was not perceived as such because Hary was not close to the Chinese community. These two parties contested the election but failed to pass the threshold of 4 per cent, as a result of which neither party managed to get its candidates into parliament.

A total of 49 rather than 64 Chinese Indonesians have served in parliament between 1999 and the current term since some members have served more one term (see Tables 9.1–9.5). In terms of occupation, 44 of the 49 are either business people or company managers, two are university staff members, one is a priest, one a lawyer and one a non-practising doctor. In terms of religion, 40 are Christians (including Catholics), eight are Buddhists and one a Muslim.

Chinese Political Participation Since Independence

TABLE 9.7
Votes Obtained by Chinese MPs against Number of Chinese Residents, 2014

Name	Constituency	Number of Chinese Residents (not voters)	Votes Obtained
Dr Sofyan Tan 陈金扬	Sumut	340,320	**113,716**
Sudin 蔡瑞龙	Lampung	39,979	**64,008**
Ir Rudianto Tjen 曾昭真	Babel	99,624	72,400
Eko Wijaya 刘顺严	Babel	See above	35,570
Daniel Johan 张育浩	Kalbar	358,451	28,608
Hang Ali Saputra Syah Pahan, SH	Kalteng	5,135	22,561
Ichsan Sulistio	Banten 2	183,689	17,994
Darmadi Durianto, PhD 林德俊	Jakarta	632,372	52,861
Charles Honoris 何震康	Jakarta	See above	96,842
Toni Wardoyo	Papua	3,405	**130,642**
Prof Dr Hendrawan Supratikno 黄正德	Jateng	139,878	68,380
Indah Kurniawati	Jatim	244,393	68,497
Henky Kurniadi, SE 游经善	Jatim	See above	43,434
Herman Hery	Nusa Tenggara Timur (NTT)	8,039	**109,405**

Note: The numbers in bold show that the votes obtained exceeded two-thirds of the number of Chinese residents in the constituency. See endnotes 6 and 7.

Source: KPU and others.

TABLE 9.8
Votes Obtained by Chinese MPs against Number of Chinese Residents, 2019

Name	Constituency	Number of Chinese Residents (not voters)	Votes Obtained
Dr Sofyan Tan 陈金扬	Sumut 1	340,320 (whole Sumut)	84,395
Sudin 蔡瑞龙	Lampung 1	39,979	?
Bambang Patijaya	Babel	99,624	48,289
Ir Rudianto Tjen 曾昭真	Babel	99,624	90,150
Daniel Johan 张育浩	Kalbar	358,451	56,335
Ichsan Sulistio	Banten 2	183,689 (whole of Banten)	25,651
Darmadi Durianto 林德俊	Jakarta 3	632,372 (whole of Jakarta)	105,238
Charles Honoris 何震康	Jakarta 3	632,372 (whole of Jakarta)	102,408
Prof Dr Hendrawan Supratikno 黄正德	Jateng 10	139,878 (whole of Jateng)	86,749
Indah Kurniawati	Jatim 10	244,393 (whole of Jatim)	139,714
Herman Hery	Nusa Tenggara Timur (NTT) 2	8,039 (whole of NTT)	98,987

Source: Compiled from KPU and Chinese newspaper reports; additional information was provided by Mr Lu Ikun (see Table 9.5).

The prevalence of Christians among the Chinese-Indonesian MPs can be explained in terms of Suharto-era policy. As soon as Suharto came to power, he promoted religious identity to cripple the communist and left-wing movement; those who did not have any religious affiliation were considered to be communists or communist sympathizers. Not surprisingly, many Chinese Indonesians converted to Christianity (both Protestantism and Catholicism), which has a sizeable following among indigenous Indonesians. Confucianism and other Chinese religions were discouraged during the New Order period.

It is also worthwhile to examine the role of Chinese Indonesians, especially Chinese-Indonesian MPs, in their respective parties. With a few exceptions (e.g., Kwik Kian Gie and Basuki Tjahaja Purnama), the majority of these Chinese-Indonesian MPs served in economic or financial positions within their respective parties. This is because they themselves come from the business or financial sectors, and indigenous-dominated parties need people with such expertise. Consequently, some critics consider Chinese-Indonesian MPs to be the "ATMs" (automated teller machines, i.e., cash cows) of indigenous Indonesian politicians.[12]

ACHIEVEMENTS OF SELECTED CHINESE-INDONESIAN MPs

What can these Chinese-Indonesian MPs do in parliament? In the past, a couple of active Chinese-Indonesian MPs, together with non-Chinese MPs, were able to introduce laws that may or may not have benefitted Chinese communities. One example was Alvin Lie Ling Piao (李宁彪), who initiated the proposal to impeach President Abdurrahman Wahid. The second example involved Murdaya W. Poo (alias Poo Tjie Guan 傅志宽), who played a role in the amendment of the Indonesian citizenship law.

In the first example, Alvin Lie, an MP from PAN and a member of the budget committee in the DPR, charged President Wahid in 2000 with misusing funds from the Indonesian Bureau of Logistics, Bulog. When Wahid replied that he did not need money from Bulog as he had already received a donation from the Sultan of Brunei, the then president encountered a bigger problem. Alvin argued that it was against the law for the president to receive a donation from a foreign government without the knowledge of parliament. Initially Alvin's argument was ignored, but later he succeeded in collecting the necessary information, which resulted in the formation of a special committee (Pansus) to impeach Wahid. The impeachment resulted in Wahid's resignation as president in 2001 (Sudrajat 2001, pp. 40–58). Consequently, Alvin Lie was awarded the title of "one of the best DPR members of 2001" by the journalists who covered parliament.

In the second example, Murdaya Poo, then an MP representing the PDI-P, was made the first deputy chairman of the parliamentary special committee on the Indonesian citizenship law (2005–6) (*GoAceh.co* 2019). The committee succeeded in drafting a new Indonesian citizenship law, which reflected the new spirit of using both *jus soli* and *jus sanguinis* as the principles guiding citizenship. Its draft was endorsed in 2006, when it became a law. According to the law, Indonesia-born Chinese who are Indonesian citizens will be regarded as "indigenous Indonesians" (*Indonesia asli*), similar to other "indigenous Indonesians".

The third example of achievements by Chinese-Indonesian MPs was that of Purnama, who was elected to parliament in 2009 representing Golkar. He was well known as a good speaker and one who strongly advocated clean and efficient governance. However, before the end of his term he resigned from parliament and successfully contested the Jakarta gubernatorial election of 2012 as deputy to Jokowi. He later succeeded Jokowi as governor when the latter became president in October 2014.

The issues that the MPs dealt with in parliament are not directly relevant to Chinese Indonesians, with the exception of the citizenship law. One could argue that informal political participation by Chinese Indonesians has brought more tangible results for the Chinese community.

INFORMAL POLITICAL PARTICIPATION

Ethnic Chinese organizations were either banned or suppressed during the Suharto era but re-emerged after the fall of Suharto. The largest ones today are: Paguyuban Sosial Marga Tionghoa Indonesia (PSMTI), established in 1998 and known in the Chinese language as the Hundred Surnames Associations (Yinhua baijiaxing xiehui, 印华百

家姓协会), and the Perhimpunan Keturunan Tionghoa Indonesia (印尼华裔总会), established in 1999 and later re-named as Perhimpunan Indonesia-Tionghoa (INTI). The founding president of PSMTI was a retired general, Teddy Jusuf (Him Tek Ie 熊德怡), while INTI was led by an entrepreneur cum public intellectual, Eddie Lembong (Ong Joe San 汪友山). The latter left INTI subsequently and established his own foundation known as Yayasan Nabil (Nation-building Foundation). Besides these, there are several clan associations, such as the Hakka clan associations, the Hokkien clan associations and Chinese school alumni associations, all of them established by Chinese-speaking Chinese businessmen. It is also worth noting that the Supreme Confucian Council (Majelis Tertinggi Agama Khonghucu or Matakin), which was suppressed during the Suharto period, became active again after his fall and played quite an important role in promoting the religious identity of the ethnic Chinese.

In fact, many new laws and regulations that benefitted Chinese Indonesians as a group did not arise through the parliamentary route but in the form of presidential instructions or ministerial decisions. In other words, Chinese-Indonesian MPs did not play any direct role in the promulgation of these new laws and regulations. They were the result of informal politics, i.e., the political efforts of the above-mentioned Chinese associations outside parliament. Three examples can be singled out.

The first example was the annulment in 2001 of Presidential Instruction (PI) No. 14/1967, which had prohibited the public celebration of Chinese festivals, and the revocation in the same year of a circular from the Home Affairs minister, SE Menteri Dalam Negeri No. 477/74054 dated 18 November 1978, which had de-recognized Confucianism (Agama Khonghucu) as one of the six official religions of Indonesia. It was reported that many Chinese Indonesians, especially those in Matakin, had succeeded in appealing to President Wahid to replace PI No. 14/1967 with a new presidential instruction permitting the public celebration of Chinese festivals (INPRES No. 6/2001) and to replace the de-recognition of Confucianism with Keputusan Menteri Agama RI No. 13/2001, which restored Confucianism as one of the country's six officially recognized religions (Suryadinata 2014, p. 34). In fact, Wahid was well known for his espousal of pluralism and was sympathetic to the Chinese-Indonesian community.

The second example was the call to make the Lunar New Year (Chinese New Year) a national holiday. Wahid made the Lunar New Year an "optional holiday". Although it was not a national holiday, Chinese Indonesians were allowed to take a day off work. Wahid was the first Indonesian president to attend a Lunar New Year celebration organized by Chinese associations, particularly Matakin. Subsequently, Megawati who succeeded Wahid as president, issued a presidential instruction (Keppres No. 19/2002) to declare the Lunar New Year an Indonesian national holiday.[13] It is public knowledge that Megawati is friendly with the Chinese community.

The third example was the abolition in 2014 of the derogatory term *"Cina"* during the last days of Susilo Bambang Yudhoyono's presidency. Why did President Yudhoyono issue Presidential Decree No. 12 (2014)? The decree stated that Cabinet Presidium Circular No. 6 (1967), which changed the terms *"Tiongkok/Tionghoa* to *Tjina (Cina)"* had "created a psychological and discriminative impact on social relations which are experienced by members of the Indonesian nation who are of Chinese descent". It also noted that the term "is discriminatory and is against existing Indonesian anti-racist laws" and therefore had to be withdrawn. In addition, the decree noted that "the relations between Indonesia and the PRC [People's Republic of China] have been very close and it is proper to revert the name of the country to the Republik Rakyat Tiongkok."[14]

President Yudhoyono appeared to have two objectives in issuing Presidential Decree No. 12 (2014). Domestically, he wanted to improve ethnic relations as he realized that the term *"Cina/Tjina"* was derogatory. Internationally, by restoring the original Indonesian name for the PRC, he wanted to send a signal to Beijing that Jakarta was willing to further improve their relationship.

Nevertheless, these reasons do not answer the question of why the decree was issued only on 12 March 2014. In fact, debates on *"Cina"* and *"Tionghoa/Tiongkok"* had been taking place intermittently over the years. Many leading Chinese Indonesians, including lawyer Eddie Sadeli (Lin Xiangsheng 李祥胜),[15] sent petitions to successive presidents and the High Court, requesting the nullification of the 1967 cabinet circular. Nevertheless, all these efforts encountered failure. In early 2014, heated debates on the term *"Cina"* took place again in Jakarta. Many leading Chinese Indonesians were resentful of the use of the term. The aforementioned Eddie Lembong, the founding president of Perhimpunan INTI and founder of Yayasan Nabil (Nation-Building Foundation), was particularly critical of the existence of the 1967 cabinet circular. According to one report, at a dinner reception on 12 February 2014, Eddie Lembong met Murdaya Poo,[16] who was close to President Yudhoyono. The two men discussed the matter, and the following day, Eddie provided Murdaya with all the necessary information regarding the cabinet circular and the history of the use of the term "*Cina*".[17]

On 26 February, Murdaya mobilized his Hakka Federation (Keshu Lianyi Hui 客属联谊会) to form a delegation to visit Yudhoyono at his Bogor Palace and submit a petition.[18] On the same day, Eddie Sadeli, representing the PSMTI, drafted a petition to be sent to the president.[19] In less than two weeks, the president made up his mind and decided to issue Presidential Decree No. 12 (2014). On 11 March 2014, one day before Yudhoyono signed the decree, Minister of Tourism and Creative Economy Mari Pangestu (alias Feng Huilan 冯慧兰), speaking at the New Council Ceremony of Huian Huiguan (惠安会馆), a Chinese clan association in Jakarta, revealed that the president was about to sign a decree to nullify the cabinet circular on the usage of terminology offensive to Chinese Indonesians.[20]

THE 2014 PRESIDENTIAL ELECTION AND CHINESE INDONESIANS

Chinese political participation was also seen in two direct presidential elections in Indonesia: the 2014 election and the 2019 election. Direct presidential elections had, in fact, already begun in 2004. However, identity politics was not evident in the elections of 2004 and 2009. Therefore, this chapter will focus on the two most recent presidential elections.

In 2014, the presidential election was held on 9 July, three months after parliamentary elections. Initially there were three presidential candidates, namely Prabowo Subianto, a retired general and former son-in-law of President Suharto; Jokowi, the popular Jakarta governor at that time, and Aburizal Bakrie, the chairman of Golkar. Aburizal Bakrie gained little support and eventually withdrew from the competition, leaving Prabowo and Jokowi to contest the election.

Both candidates announced their vice-presidential candidates only much later. Prabowo selected Hatta Rajasa of PAN, while Jokowi selected Jusuf Kalla, the former general chairman of Golkar and vice-president during the first Yudhoyono presidency.

It is important to discuss Chinese-Indonesian attitudes towards the two presidential candidates. As in the case of the parliamentary elections, Chinese-Indonesian voters were not united in their views. Their preferences were linked to the backgrounds of the candidates. Prabowo, as the former head of the Special Forces Command (Kopassus), had a long record of human rights violations. He was allegedly responsible for kidnapping students and young activists who opposed the Suharto regime during the last days of the New Order (*Jakarta Post* 2014a). But more importantly for the Chinese, he was believed to have been the mastermind behind the May 1998 anti-Chinese riots, especially in Jakarta, during which Chinese women were systematically raped. Prabowo denied this allegation and instead pinned the blame on General Wiranto, who was then the commander-in-chief of the Indonesian armed forces. Some Chinese Indonesians bought Prabowo's explanation, some also forgot about the 1998 anti-Chinese riots, but the majority appeared to remember the events and refused to vote for Prabowo as president or for his party, Gerindra, in the parliamentary elections.

Many Chinese favoured Jokowi (who was nominated by the PDI-P at a late stage) as he was considered to be a good man who had no record of violence or corruption. His good record first as mayor of Solo (Surakarta) and then as a capable and pro-people governor of Jakarta made him a symbol of new hope. The fact that he got along with his deputy governor, Purnama, an ethnic Chinese, and his tolerance of other religions made him acceptable to many non-Muslim voters, especially Chinese voters. Nevertheless, the Chinese in Makassar expressed their reservations about voting for the Jokowi team as they did not like Jusuf Kalla, whom they perceived as anti-Chinese.[21] They believed that Jusuf Kalla was behind the 1998 anti-Chinese riots in Makassar.

These varied responses show that the Chinese community in Indonesia was not united, although the majority were sympathetic to Jokowi. Nevertheless, Chinese-Indonesian associations were careful during the presidential election. PSMTI and INTI invited both Prabowo and Jokowi to address their organizations separately in a show of neutrality.[22]

As Chinese Indonesians are small in number, their votes become important only when the margin between two candidates is close; otherwise, the presidential vote is determined by indigenous voters, who form the absolute majority in the country. The most important function of Chinese Indonesians in the presidential election was perhaps in terms of finance. As presidential election campaigns require massive funding, many candidates sought out Chinese tycoons for financial help.

According to the limited information available, Chinese tycoons were divided on whom to support; some clearly backed the Prabowo team while others supported the Jokowi team. Those who tended to side with the Prabowo team were tycoons who were closely connected with the New Order regime. They were so used to the old system that they refused to countenance any change; however, those who were initially associated with the Suharto regime but later lost favour tended to support the Jokowi team. This was the general orientation, but, to play safe, many tycoons provided funding support to both candidates.

Most of the Chinese tycoons refrained from openly supporting their preferred presidential candidates; only a few openly displayed their support during the campaign period. The aforementioned Hary Tanoe, Surabaya's media king, was one such person who openly showed his support. Hary Tanoe was associated with Suharto's son and Anthony of the Salim Group, one of Indonesia's largest conglomerates.[23] He joined the NasDem party of Surya Paloh, another media baron, but in the 2014 parliamentary election, he joined the Hanura Party, led by retired General Wiranto, and accepted the latter's offer to become his running mate in the presidential race. However, after Hanura Party failed to meet the threshold at the parliamentary election that would allow it to field a candidate in the presidential election, Wiranto decided to join the Jokowi coalition. Hary Tanoe, on the other hand, supported Prabowo, resulting in a split between Wiranto and Hary Tanoe.

Another tycoon, the owner of Lion Air, Rusdi Kirana alias A Tjiong, joined PKB and supported the party during the parliamentary election. After the election, when PKB joined Jokowi's coalition government, Kirana, too, rendered his support to Jokowi.

Yet another tycoon, James Riady of the Lippo Group, was seen as supporting Jokowi. It was reported that when Suharto stepped down, the Lippo Group supported his successor, B.J. Habibie. James Riady became the spokesman of the new regime and enjoyed various privileges, while the Salim Group fell out of favour.

Another open supporter of Jokowi was Sofjan Wanandi alias Liem Bian Khoen, who is with the CSIS. His brother, Jusuf Wanandi alias Liem Bian Kie, supported Jusuf Kalla during the 2009 presidential election and later became an ardent supporter of the Jokowi team during the 2014 presidential election.

CHINESENESS IN THE PRESIDENTIAL ELECTION OF 2014

It is interesting that in the 2014 presidential election, Chineseness became an issue again. Initially, pre-election opinion polls favoured Jokowi. As the election drew nearer, Jokowi continued to lead in the polls; there was still a wide gap between the two candidates. According to the Indo Barometer survey research institute, between 28 May and 4 June, Jokowi–Kalla still scored 49.9 per cent while the Prabowo–Hatta team's popularity stood at only 36.5 per cent (*Jakarta Post* 2014b). However, the situation changed about three weeks before election day, with the gap between the two candidates becoming narrower. An Indo Barometer survey conducted between 16 and 22 June showed the margin between the two teams to be a mere 3 per cent. One of the major reasons for this change was the smear offensive against Jokowi amid intensified campaigning as election day drew nearer.

The Prabowo team systematically spread the rumour that Jokowi was, in fact, a Chinese and the son of a tycoon, Oey Hong Liong, who now lives in Singapore. Jokowi was said to be a Christian, named Herbertus Joko Widodo, not a Muslim. The disinformation was widely peddled towards the end of the campaign period. It was published in a tabloid called *Obor Rakyat*, which was distributed free to *pesantrens* (Islamic boarding schools) across Java. The message was that Jokowi was not fit to be elected as president.

Prior to the distribution of the tabloid, on 2 May, a fake obituary of Jokowi was released in social media (see Figure 9.1). The obituary claimed that "Ir. Herbertus Joko Widodo", aged 53 years, had died, that his body was lying in state at the office of PDI-P at Lenteng Agung and that it would be cremated on 6 May 2014. The "obituary" was purportedly put up by Jokowi's wife, Iriana Widodo. It carried in

Chinese characters the name Huang Jinlai (黄金莱), implying that it was the Chinese name of Jokowi. Absurdly, however, immediately below the name "Ir. Herbertus Joko Widodo", another Chinese name, rendered in the Latin script, appeared in parenthesis, i.e., Oey Hong Liong, the name of Jokowi's putative father. This "obituary", or "fake news" in today's parlance, which was widely publicized on social media, was aimed at discrediting Jokowi among indigenous Indonesian Muslims.

FIGURE 9.1
Fake Obituary for Jokowi

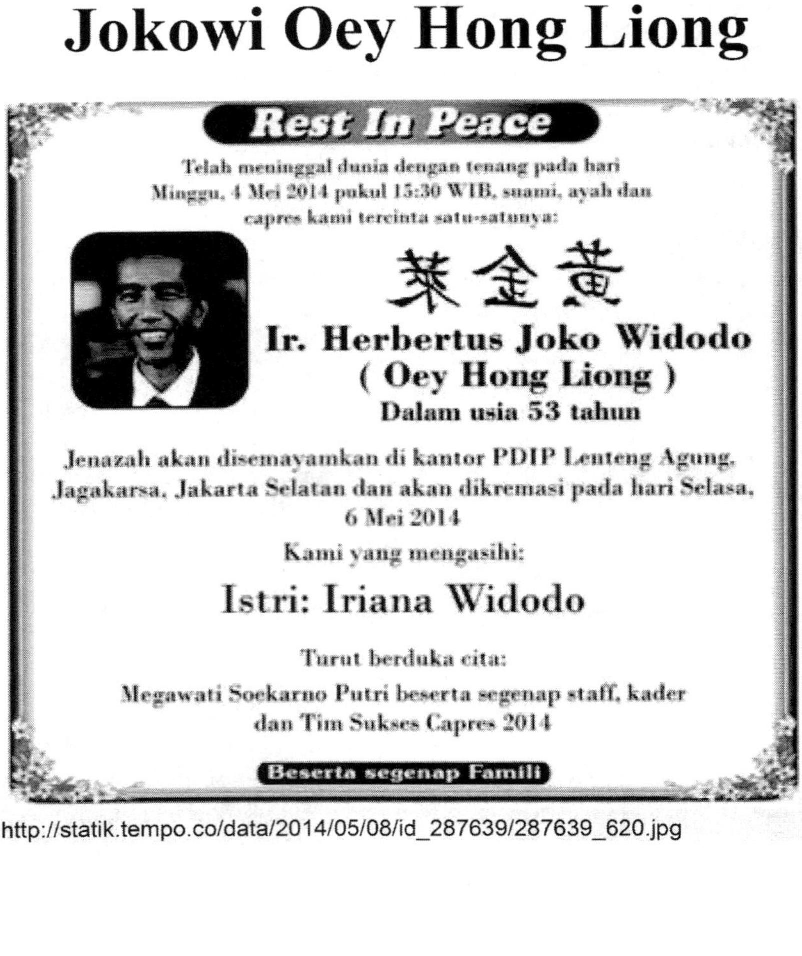

Jokowi Oey Hong Liong

Rest In Peace

Telah meninggal dunia dengan tenang pada hari Minggu, 4 Mei 2014 pukul 15:30 WIB, suami, ayah dan capres kami tercinta satu-satunya:

莱金黄

Ir. Herbertus Joko Widodo
(Oey Hong Liong)
Dalam usia 53 tahun

Jenazah akan disemayamkan di kantor PDIP Lenteng Agung, Jagakarsa, Jakarta Selatan dan akan dikremasi pada hari Selasa, 6 Mei 2014

Kami yang mengasihi:

Istri: Iriana Widodo

Turut berduka cita:

Megawati Soekarno Putri beserta segenap staff, kader dan Tim Sukses Capres 2014

Beserta segenap Famili

http://statik.tempo.co/data/2014/05/08/id_287639/287639_620.jpg

Initially, the fake obituary did not affect Jokowi–Kalla in the opinion polls, presumably because it had not reached many people. But a few weeks later, especially after the distribution of the story in *Obor Rakyat*, the smear campaign became quite effective. In rural areas, including in the *pesantrens*, which are the main educational institutions in the villages in Java, many believed that Jokowi was indeed a Chinese Christian (*Tempo* 2014, pp. 35–36).[0] Jokowi denied the allegation and was prepared to take the slanderers to court but the damage had already been done. *Majalah Tempo* published a special report on 29 June in which it argued that the smear campaign had really hurt Jokowi but that young volunteers had started campaigning for him (*Tempo* 2014b, pp. 38–39).[1] In addition, on 6 July, four days before voting day, Jokowi decided to perform a minor haj (*umrah*), which was widely publicized. This strategy contributed to the eventual victory of Jokowi–Kalla, who obtained 53 per cent of the votes, narrowly defeating their rivals, who obtained 47 per cent.

THE 2019 PRESIDENTIAL ELECTION

Identity politics, involving both Chinese and Muslim identity, was again used during the 2019 election. At this juncture, the issue of the Jakarta gubernatorial election of 2016–17 must be addressed. As mentioned earlier, Basuki Tjahaja Purnama alias Ahok decided to seek re-election as governor. However, Prabowo and his conservative and radical Muslim supporters organized rallies and demonstrations using race and religion to attack Purnama, who is a Chinese Indonesian and a Christian. The so-called 212 Movement (the name signalling the date of the movement's crystallization, i.e., 2 December 2016) successfully pushed identity politics to its peak. Although popular and competent as a governor, Purnama was eventually voted out. Anies Baswedan, an Indonesian of Arab descent, and indigenous business tycoon Sandiaga Uno were elected as governor and deputy governor of Jakarta, respectively.

The same tactic was used by the conservative and radical Muslim opposition during the 2019 presidential election in the hopes that it would succeed again. However, the difference was that Jokowi was not Purnama. Nevertheless, the opposition still used the hoax of Jokowi being Chinese to smear him. The "Chinese background" of Jokowi was not as extensively used as in the 2014 presidential election but he was portrayed as a PKI member and anti-Islam by his opponents. Many of the voters were still captive to identity politics, and, towards the end, Jokowi himself also resorted to identity politics to win the election. At the eleventh hour, he selected Ma'ruf Amin, a conservative cleric and chairman of the Majelis Ulama Indonesia (the council of Indonesian Islamic scholars or MUI for short), to be his running mate. This decision led to dissatisfaction within the Jokowi camp, and many civil society groups that had previously supported him urged voters to boycott the election or cast blank votes, known as *golput* (*golongan putih*). Jokowi's supporters, for their part, feared the blank vote campaign would harm the president's re-election chances as Prabowo supporters would not heed the call. Therefore, Jokowi had to go out of his way to urge people not to cast blank votes.

The Chinese community seemed split on the issue of which team to support. Among the Chinese businessmen who openly supported Prabowo was Lieus Sungkharisma (Li Xuexiong). He had formed Partai Reformasi Tionghoa Indonesia (Parti), but his party was unable to develop and failed to participate in any national parliamentary election. Lieus later set up a group called Komunitas Tionghoa Anti-Korupsi (Chinese Community Against Corruption) and attacked Governor Purnama for his "misbehaviour".

Jusuf Hamka (A Bun), another Chinese businessman, collaborated with Lieus in his campaign against both Purnama and Jokowi. Jusuf Hamka converted to Islam during the Suharto era. He established the Muslim Tionghoa Indonesia (Indonesian Chinese Muslims) group as his base. When Prabowo supported the anti-Purnama demonstrations led by the Islamist Front Pembela Islam (FPI) in 2016, both Lieus and Jusuf Hamka openly sided with the FPI. In the name of the Chinese-Indonesian community, they jointly nominated the leader of the FPI, Habib Rizieq Shihab, as "Man of the Year, 2016". They praised Rizieq for his leadership of the 212 Movement, claiming it led a peaceful demonstration that did not spark off racial or religious conflict (Mei Amelia 2016).

Apart from these two personalities, those who openly supported Prabowo appeared to be few in number. Those opposed to the pro-Prabowo group reacted against Lieus and Yusuf Hamka. Anton Medan (Tan Kok Liong 陈国隆), chairman of Persatuan Islam Tionghoa

Indonesia (PITI), the largest Chinese Muslim organization and one with a long history, commented that "only two of them [Lieus and Hamka] were present at the honouring [Rizieq] occasion and they did not represent the Chinese community but themselves" (Manafe 2016). Anton, an ardent supporter of Purnama, further argued that Hamka did not represent Chinese-Indonesian Muslims either (ibid.).

On the other hand, some Chinese-Indonesian businessmen were dissatisfied with Jokowi, complaining in private discussions with me that his fight against corruption in government was not "conducive" to business as bureaucrats tended to be exceptionally slow in issuing permits whenever kickbacks were not forthcoming. Many businessmen were not happy either with Jokowi's heavy taxes to finance various infrastructure projects. Others who had not been able to enjoy benefits under the Jokowi administration were hoping that a different government would make life easier for them.

On 7 December 2018, a group of Chinese businessmen organized a gala dinner at Sun City Jakarta, located in the Chinese business district. They invited Prabowo to grace the event as guest-of-honour and to give a talk on the topic "Chinese and business in the eyes of Prabowo Subianto". They also planned to solicit donations for the Prabowo presidential campaign fund. The Chinese businessmen who attended the function appeared to be from small and medium-sized enterprises (SMEs); no one from the Forbes list of Indonesian tycoons was present. As published the very next day, donations raised at the event from fifteen donors amounted to a paltry sum of Rp435 million (approximately S$43,500) (Natalyn and Sada 2018).

Wealthy Chinese tycoons in general refrained from openly expressing their support for Jokowi or Prabowo because doing so would not serve their interests. But Chinese businessmen from the SME sector did not have such qualms as they are not so well known and hence not at significant risk. However, one Chinese-Indonesian tycoon did publicly express support for Jokowi, namely, the aforementioned Hary Tanoe, who leads Perindo. Additionally, a party led by a Chinese Indonesian that strongly supported Jokowi as president was PSI. This is a party comprised of younger generation Chinese and it was actively urging the urban youth not to cast blank votes. The high turnout to vote for Jokowi in the urban areas may have been partially the result of PSI's campaign. The Jokowi–Ma'ruf Amin team eventually gained 55.5 per cent of the votes while Prabowo–Sandiaga managed to obtain only 44.5 per cent.

CONCLUSION

Chinese-Indonesian participation in politics has a long history. Political participation takes place at two levels, i.e., the formal level, involving participation in the electoral process and elected positions, and the informal level, where participation takes place outside the electoral system. Participation has existed at both levels, but it has become more prominent only since the fall of Suharto, with the freedom to form sociocultural and ethnic organizations. As the Chinese in Indonesia constitute a minority, their ability to achieve their goals through formal politics appears to be less effective than their use of informal politics. This can be seen from their pressure through informal channels for presidential instructions/decisions to annul various discriminatory laws and regulations against the Chinese minority and promulgate new laws and regulations in their place.

Participation patterns can also be divided into national (non-ethnic) and ethnic approaches. After the fall of Suharto, especially since the 2004 election, Chinese formal politics can be categorized as national (non-ethnic) in nature as there were no more ethnic Chinese political parties running in parliamentary elections. The ethnic Chinese who entered the national parliament did so by joining parties dominated by indigenous Indonesians. However, at the informal politics level, there are still many sociopolitical organizations that are ethnic-based. Therefore, one can argue that Chinese politics, even after 2004, is a combination of national politics and ethnic politics.

What is the function of Chinese Indonesians in politics? Some critics argue that Chinese Indonesians only serve as ATMs for indigenous Indonesians. Their role in the parties is mainly in finance and economic-related positions/activities. However, this assertion is not entirely true. Economist Kwik Kian Gie (an MP and cabinet minister) was the head of the research section in PDI-P. In Purnama's case, he was picked as a candidate for the position of deputy governor of Jakarta when he joined Gerindra. Since the fall of Suharto, some Chinese-Indonesian politicians have established themselves as role models for the community. Kwik Kian Gie was known as someone who dared to speak up against rampant corruption while Purnama, who was deputy governor and later, governor of Jakarta, set an example by running a clean, efficient and no-nonsense municipal government. However, with the rise of identity politics, it would be more difficult for ethnic Chinese to occupy elected high positions.

Participation in both parliamentary and presidential elections has been significant for the Chinese-Indonesian political identity. It has made the Chinese-Indonesian identity clear, and Chinese Indonesians have become part of the Indonesian political system. They are Indonesians of Chinese descent but they do not represent only the Chinese minority. Some have even denied that they represent the Chinese; as they have been elected by both indigenous Indonesians and the Chinese, they insist that they serve all Indonesians regardless of ethnicity.

NOTES

1. There is no clear indication that these eleven members of parliament (MPs) are indeed of Chinese descent as they do not self-identify as such. I managed to discern their ethnic backgrounds from various sources. This point will be explained later in this chapter.
2. Owing to the lack of information, this chapter will not look at Chinese participation in local legislative elections.
3. For information on the various Chinese parties and their political ideologies, see Suryadinata (1979).
4. Perhaps the most important factor that hindered the development of the new PTI revolved around Liem Koen Hian himself. In 1951 he was arrested by the Sukiman government on suspicion of being a communist. Upon his release he repudiated his Indonesian citizenship and left politics. See Suryadinata (2015), p. 152.
5. For the number of Chinese Indonesians, see Suryadinata (2004), pp. 63–74.
6. See Tables 9.7 and 9.8. Note that the number of Chinese voters is not available. However, the number of Chinese residents in each province (not constituency) is available. It shows that most Chinese candidates contested in provinces where there were significant numbers of Chinese residents. However, at least two contested in provinces with few Chinese residents. Their successful election shows that they were voted in largely by non-Chinese voters.
7. The reasons for this are complex. First, they are already known by their Indonesian names. Second, it is difficult to have one's name changed. Third,

Chinese Political Participation Since Independence

there is still the pressure of ethno-nationalism. For a brief discussion of this issue, see Liao (2001).

8. Chinese newspapers such as *Guoji Ribao* (国际日报) in Jakarta and *Qiandai Ribao* (千岛日报) in Surabaya often publish the Chinese names of Chinese Indonesians, sometimes together with their Indonesian names and at other times with no Indonesian names at all. Fordeka used to issue lists of Chinese leaders in government and various political institutions as well as lists of candidates for the DPR and DPRD prior to general elections. The list often included Chinese names, although many were listed without their Chinese names. Occasionally, Fordeka wrongly identified indigenous Indonesians as Chinese Indonesians. Since the death of Drs Hartono (Li Boqiao), who was behind the project, Fordeka has ceased to publish its lists.
9. See the list provided by Fordeka (2013), pp. 5–7. Bondan Winarno was on the list but he is Javanese.
10. One source says 16 were elected, but the ethnic identities of two candidates it listed (Dr Verna Gladies Merry Inkiriwang and Robert Joppy Kardinal, SAB) have not been verified.
11. For a discussion of these parties, see Suryadinata (2019).
12. Christine Susanna Tjhin from the CSIS commented that "In some cases the parties also do not engage these ethnic Chinese politicians and are just content to see them as party's ATMs. ... but they should really invest more time to build their base of constituents." Quoted in Lee (2009).
13. "Keputusan Presiden Republik Indonesia No.19 Tahun 2002 Tentang Tahun Baru Imlek", issued on 9 April 2002.
14. For a detailed discussion of this issue, see Suryadinata (2014b).
15. For the various attempts made by Eddie Sadeli, see an interview with him published in *Guoji Ribao*, 15 March 2014.
16. Murdaya Poo was elected as an MP representing PDI-P. He was expelled from the party after the 2009 presidential election because he had supported Yudhoyono's candidacy, not that of Megawati, who was the leader of PDI-P.
17. "Angpao besar di Perayaan Cap Go Mei 2014" (statement provided by the Secretariat of Yayasan Nabil, 18 March 2014), *Yinni Xingzhou Ribao* (印尼星洲日报), 22 March 2014.
18. "Zongtong chexiao Zhinaqishixing chenghu" 总统撤销支那歧视性称呼, *Yinni Xingzhou Ribao* (印尼星洲日报), 22 March 2014; *Guoji Ribao* (国际日报), 22 March 2014.
19. "Huazu yiyuan houxuanren fangtanlu" 华族议员候选人访谈录, *Guoji Ribao* (国际日报), 22 March 2014.
20. "Youduoyuenuo jijiang qianshu zongtong minglingshu" 尤多约诺即将签署总统命令书, *Qiandao Ribao* (千岛日报), 13 March 2014.

21. Interview in Jakarta with several Chinese from Makassar, May 2014.
22. Information provided by members of both associations, July 2014.
23. For a discussion of the connection between Harry and Anthony Salim, see Borsuk and Chng (2014), pp. 438–41.

REFERENCES

Borsuk, Richard and Nancy Chng. 2014. *Liem Sioe Liong's Salim Group: The Business Pillar of Suharto's Indonesia*. Singapore: Institute of Southeast Asian Affairs.

Fordeka. 2013. *Buku Acuan Pemilihan Legislatif bagi Caleg-Caleg DPR RI, DPD RI, DPRD Provinsi, DPRD Kabupaten/Kota Periode 2014-2019: Keluarga Suku Tionghoa Indonesia*, December 2013.

GoAceh.co. 2019. "Ma'ruf Cahyono: Kewarganegaraan Menjadi Fokus Kajian MPR", 17 December 2019. https://www.m.goaceh.co/berita/baca/2019/12/17/maruf-cahyono-kewarganegaraan-menjadi-fokus-kajian-mpr.

Huntington, Samuel and Joan N. Nelson. 1976. *No Easy Choice: Political Participation in Developing Countries*. Cambridge, MA: Harvard University Press.

Jakarta Post, The. 2014a. "Prabowo 'ordered by Soeharto to kidnap activists'", 11 June 2014. https://www.thejakartapost.com/news/2014/06/11/prabowo-ordered-soeharto-kidnap-activists.html (accessed 25/10/2020).

———. 2014b. "Jokowi Leading against Prabowo: Survey", 18 June 2014. https://www.thejakartapost.com/news/2014/06/18/jokowi-leading-against-prabowo-survey.html.

Lee, Lynn. 2009. "More Chinese in Indonesian politics". *The Straits Times*, 10 June 2009.

Liao Jianyu. 2001. "Yinni huaren xingming yu rentong wenti" (印尼华人姓名与认同问题). *Lianhe Zaobao* (联合早报), 28 July 2001.

Manafe, Adiel. 2016. "Lieus dan Jusuf Mengatasnamakan Tionghoa, Ini Kata Anton Medan". *Netralnews.com*, 26 December 2016. https://archive.netralnews.com/news/megapolitan/read/44025/lieus.dan.jusuf.mengatasnamakan.tionghoa..ini.kata.anton.medan.

Mei Amelia R. 2016. "Komunitas Tionghoa Nobatkan Habib Rizieq Sebagai Man of The Year". detikNews, 20 December 2016. https://news.detik.com/berita/d-3375755/komunitas-tionghoa-nobatkan-habib-rizieq-sebagaiman-of-the-year (accessed 16 December 2018).

Metro Tempo.co. 2019. "Surat Ahok ke Pendukungnya: Minta Dipanggil dengan Nama BTP", 18 January 2019. https://metro.tempo.co/read/1166129/surat-ahok-ke-pendukungnya-minta-dipanggil-dengan-nama-btp.

Natalyn, Ezra and Anwar Sada. 2018. "Ahok Donatur Terbesar Gala Dinner Pengusaha Tionghoa Dukung Prabowo". Viva.co.id, 8 December 2018. https://www.viva.co.id/berita/politik/1101543-ahok-donatur-terbesar-gala-dinner-pengusahationghoa-dukung-prabowo.

RSIS. 2014. "The Indonesian Presidential Election: How Will the Balance Tip?" *RSIS Policy Report*, 8 July 2014.

Somers, Mary A. 1965. "Peranakan Chinese Politics in Indonesia". PhD thesis, Cornell University.

Sudrajat. 2001. "Alvin Lie Ling Piao: Politisi Penjaja Jamu". In *Anggota DPR Terbaik Pilihan Wartawan*. Jakarta: Koordinatoriat Wartawan DPR/MPR RI.

Suryadinata, Leo. 1979. *Political Thinking of Indonesian Chinese 1900–1977*. Singapore: Singapore University Press.

_____. 2004. "How many ethnic Chinese are there in Indonesia?" *Asian Culture* 28 (June): 63–74.

_____. 2014a. "State and 'Chinese Religions' in Indonesia: Confucianism, Tridharma and Buddhism during the Suharto rule and After". In *Chinese Overseas: Religions, Identity and Traditional Networks*, edited by Tan Chee Beng. Singapore: World Scientific Publishing.

_____. 2014b. "An End to Discrimination for China and the Chinese in Indonesia". *ISEAS Perspective*, no. 2014/26, 25 April 2014.

_____. 2015. *Prominent Indonesian Chinese: Biographical Sketches*, 4th ed. Singapore: ISEAS – Yusof Ishak Institute.

_____. 2019. "Chinese Participation in the 2019 Indonesian Election". *ISEAS Perspective*, no. 2019/58, 25 July 2019.

Tempo. 2014a. "Propaganda Kelam Obor Hitam", 29 June 2014.

_____. 2014b. "Juru Tangkal Serangan Gelap", 29 June 2014.

PART III:

Regional Dynamics

10

"AWAKENING THE SLEEPING BULL": CENTRAL JAVA IN THE 2019 INDONESIAN ELECTIONS

Budi Irawanto

> *Biar gepeng, tetap banteng.*
> (Even if we are flattened, we'll remain a bull!)
> **Slogan of Partai Demokrasi Indonesia Perjuangan**

One of the key provinces contributing to the victory of Joko Widodo (Jokowi) in the 2019 presidential election was Central Java. By achieving a landslide in the province—77.2 per cent of the total votes—Jokowi was able to offset his loss in three major provinces outside Java. Furthermore, Jokowi improved his performance in Central Java by 10.55 percentage points, compared with his performance in the 2014 presidential election. He won all 29 districts and six cities in the province, replicating his victory in 2014. In contrast, his challenger, Prabowo Subianto, not only failed to steal votes from Jokowi's stronghold, but his vote share shrank by 10.6 percentage points, compared with 2014. Prabowo failed to capitalize on the increase in registered voters in Central Java from 27,385,217 in 2014 to 27,896,902 in 2019.

This chapter aims to examine local dynamics in the 2019 elections. The case study is Central Java Province, home to ethnic Javanese and a province with the third largest electorate in the country. Aside from the presidential election, this chapter will look at the fierce competition between political parties in the legislative elections, where 1,046 legislative positions were up for grabs in Central Java. The legislative positions were for national, regional and local parliamentary seats. Because the elections were held simultaneously, this chapter will also examine the coat-tail effects of the presidential election.

The chapter poses three principal questions. First, why did Jokowi win with such a big margin in Central Java despite aggressive attempts by Prabowo's camp to infiltrate the province? Second, why did the Prabowo camp's efforts to mobilize voters through identity politics involving religion seem to be futile in Central Java, compared with its efforts in other parts of Indonesia? Third, why did the Partai Demokrasi Indonesia Perjuangan (Indonesian Democratic Party of Struggle or PDI-P, for short) still garner a significant number of votes amid the ferocious competition between political parties in Central Java?

To answer those questions, I conducted fieldwork in several major cities and districts in Central Java (Semarang, Solo, Boyolali, Tegal and Brebes) from February to April 2019. I argue that while the election results seem to reflect the revival of what is known as *aliran* politics in contemporary Indonesia,[1] they also reflect the peculiar dynamics of electoral politics at the local level. These dynamics cannot be understood simply as a derivative of national politics. The political cliché that all politics is local was probably true in the 2019 election in Central Java.

THE LOCAL CONTEXT

Central Java is the third largest province, after West Java and East Java, in terms of population size and number of registered voters. With 29 districts, six cities, 568 sub-districts and 8,568 villages, the province had established 115,390 polling stations that served 27,896,902 registered voters or 14.5 per cent of total voters in Indonesia. Seven districts and one city in Central Java have more than one million registered voters: the districts of Kebumen, Grobogan, Pemalang, Brebes, Tegal, Banyumas and Cilacap and the city of Semarang.

The presidential election aside, 1,046 candidates ran for election to 77 seats representing Central Java in the national parliament (*Kumparan* 2019). Unlike the 2014 presidential election, voter turnout rose significantly, from 69.58 per cent in 2014 to 80 per cent in 2019, perhaps due to the appeal of the presidential candidates, the tight competition among political parties in the province and the simultaneous presidential and legislative elections. This high voter turnout contributed to Central Java becoming one of the key provinces to winning the presidential election.

Since free and fair elections were called for post-1998 *Reformasi*, Central Java has become a stronghold for the PDI-P. This province is famously known as *kandang banteng* (literally, the bull pen) because of its propensity to vote for PDI-P. *Banteng* (a bull) is the logo of PDI-P, symbolizing the people's high spirit to fight for truth and justice.

PDI-P was established on 14 February 1999 in Jakarta. It was formed as a result of infighting over leadership within the Partai Demokrasi Indonesia (Indonesian Democratic Party or PDI, for short) of the New Order era. PDI itself was a political party created by the Suharto government as a forced fusion of five political parties representing two different ideologies: Nationalists and Christians.

The infighting started at the PDI's congress of 1996 to elect a new chairman. The New Order government handpicked Suryadi for the position, but his challenger, Megawati Sukarnoputri, had the backing of the PDI's base. Suryadi lost the election but he had the backing of the government, which acknowledged him as leader. This propelled Megawati into forming a splinter party out of PDI in 1999, adding the modifier *perjuangan* (struggle) to the party's name, hence Partai Demokrasi Indonesia Perjuangan (PDI-P).

In the 2014 election, PDI-P occupied the majority of seats (31 out of a total of 100 seats) in the Central Java provincial parliament. Gerindra, Prabowo's political party, held only 11 seats. In 2019, the total number of seats in the provincial parliament was expanded to 120. PDI-P managed to increase its number of seats to 42 or 35 per cent of the total. This is an increase of four percentage points from the previous term. PDI-P also set a record since this is the biggest number of parliamentary seats held by a party in Indonesia. Gerindra, on the other hand, retained almost a similar share of seats as in 2014 (10.8 per cent or 13 seats).

PDI-P has also held the office of the governor since 2013. In 2018, Ganjar Pranowo and his running mate, Taj Yasin, who were nominated by the PDI-P-led coalition of Partai Persatuan Pembangunan (PPP), Golkar, NasDem, and Partai Demokrat, won re-election, receiving 58.78 per cent of the total votes. The pair won in 31 districts and cities. Their opponents, Sudirman Said and Ida Fauziyah, who were nominated by the Gerindra-led coalition, obtained 41.22 per cent of the votes, winning only in four districts, namely, Brebes, Purbalingga, Kebumen and Tegal. Clearly, the PDI-P has strong political roots in Central Java. Its success in capturing the governorship has provided much-needed support for every PDI-P candidate running for office in the province. Soon after he was re-elected in 2018, Ganjar publicly endorsed Jokowi's candidacy for the presidency. He even asked his volunteer organizations to mobilize voters for Jokowi, particularly in districts where he himself had lost in the gubernatorial election.[2] The PDI-P's political dominance in Central Java and the mobilization efforts of Governor Ganjar constituted an important factor in Jokowi's sweeping victory in the province.

"AWAKENING THE SLEEPING BULL": MILITANCY AND VOLUNTARISM

Since Central Java has a relatively large number of registered voters and it is Jokowi's stronghold, Prabowo's campaign team intensified its efforts to peel back Jokowi's support or at least steal a significant number of voters away from him. The province had practical and symbolic meaning for Prabowo. A Jokowi defeat in his own backyard would deliver a highly symbolic success for Prabowo. If Prabowo won the election and became Indonesian president, a win in Central Java would certainly have given strong legitimacy to his presidency.

Prabowo moved his campaign resources from Jakarta to Central Java and his campaign team expected to weaken the support that Jokowi enjoyed. The Prabowo camp also relocated its headquarters to Solo, Jokowi's birthplace and a city where the president had started his political career as mayor. The vice-chairman of Gerindra in Central Java hoped that Prabowo would win 51 per cent of the total votes in Central Java[3] and erode PDI-P's hold on the region.

However, these aggressive attempts ended in failure. Instead of creating a new wave of voters to support Prabowo, the campaign faced a backlash. It lit the fire of militancy among Jokowi' supporters, with the Jokowi camp intensifying its voter outreach. In order to raise the passions of Jokowi's supporters, his Tim Kampanye Nasional (National Campaign Team or TKN, for short) encouraged PDI-P cadres and sympathizers to set up command posts (*posko*).

As Bambang Wuryanto, the chairman of PDI-P in Central Java and head of Jokowi's campaign team, said, while the relocation of Prabowo's national campaign headquarters to Central Java was a legitimate move, it was akin to awakening the "sleeping bull" (CNN Indonesia 2018). Wuryanto's statement can be interpreted as the willingness of the PDI-P to fight back fiercely to defend its perceived territory, Central Java.

Both camps were competing in erecting their respective *poskos*. In Solo, anywhere the Prabowo camp set up a *posko*, Jokowi supporters would respond by setting up their own *posko*. Jokowi's supporters even dared to set up *poskos* opposite Prabowo's own *poskos* and multiply their *posko* numbers in adjacent areas.

For instance, in Sumber which is close to downtown Solo and where the Prabowo team's national campaign headquarters was located, Jokowi supporters established five *poskos*, practically besieging Prabowo's headquarters. Indeed, Prabowo's decision to establish his campaign headquarters in Sumber was intentional and driven by its close proximity to Jokowi's private house. According to Mudrick Setiawan Sangidoe, the coordinator of "Mega Bintang", the volunteer group supporting the candidacy of Prabowo and his running mate, Sandiaga ("Sandi") Uno, the strategy was aimed at "stabbing the enemy at its heart" (*menusuk ke jantung pertahan lawan*)[4] since Central Java Province was the "fortress of the bull" (*bentengnya banteng*). Sangidoe claimed that although PDI-P was still strong in Solo, there was a crack among Jokowi's supporters, especially within Muslim quarters. According to him, some of Jokowi's supporters felt he had broken many promises, such as promises to resolve past human rights violations, fill his cabinet with professionals instead of his political supporters, lower the prices of basic necessities, stop the import of agricultural commodities and create new jobs.

But Gerindra elites seem to have over-estimated their chances in Central Java. They gauged their support from the results of the 2018 gubernatorial election.[5] Their candidates, Sudirman Said–Ida Fauziyah, had performed better than expected. They had initially thought the pair would be swept aside by a landslide victory for Ganjar Pranowo and his running mate. The pair, who got 41.22 per cent of the votes, won in only four districts but their overall performance in some of the other districts was much better than expected. Therefore, the Gerindra campaign team predicted that a nationally known figure like Prabowo would be able to garner more votes, especially in the western parts of the province.

This optimistic prediction failed to materialize. The Prabowo camp obviously neglected the crucial role of Nahdlatul Ulama (NU), the largest traditional Muslim organization in Indonesia. The candidate for vice-governor in the 2018 gubernatorial election, Ida Fauziyah, is a NU member. She managed to bring in significant numbers of NU voters, especially from NU's women's wings, Muslimat and Fatayat. However, Gerindra itself had limited support in Central Java. It gained 11 seats in the provincial parliament while PDI-P won more than double the number of seats it had won in 2014.

As has become more common since 2014, volunteers have begun to play a central role in presidential campaigns. A party may have cadres and an official campaign team but at the grassroots level the campaign relies heavily on volunteer organizations. The official campaign team, which usually comprises party functionaries, is registered with the General Elections Commission (KPU) but volunteer organizations are not. Interestingly, volunteer organizations are not tightly connected to campaign teams. One PDI-P local leader said that volunteer organizations were under the aegis of the "directorate of volunteers" in PDI-P's organizational set-up, but there was no strict top-down coordination between regional campaign teams and the volunteers.[6] Therefore, volunteers had the freedom to hold any activity as long as they were in line with support for the presidential candidate.

The campaign team may hold an event without coordinating with volunteer organizations. Jokowi's rally in Solo on 9 April 2019, just eight days before the election, for example, was organized by the PDI-P machine in Central Java with little volunteer involvement. As a result, the rally-goers were not only residents of Solo but also supporters from throughout Central Java.[7]

For the 2019 presidential election, volunteers formed community-based organizations to support Jokowi at the grassroots level. Without assistance from the PDI-P or the campaign team, they organized and worked closely with the communities on the ground. A volunteer organization called "Semut Ireng" (Black Ants), for example, was organized in the president's hometown without coordination with the local PDI-P branch. They were just supporters of the president. Even bigger volunteer organizations such as "Alap-Alap" (literally, Falcons) and "Rejo" (Relawan Jokowi or Jokowi's Volunteers) were established across cities and districts in Central Java. The volunteer organizations were informal in their structure, which gave them some flexibility to act, especially in countering Prabowo's campaign moves. They tried to campaign on Jokowi's Javanese roots and his humble beginnings before rising to become the most powerful man in the country.

Another volunteer organization worth mentioning was "Srikandi Indonesia". It was established by women from various professional backgrounds such as lawyers, paediatricians and business persons. The original purpose of this organization was empowering businesswomen. But close to the presidential election, it shifted its focus to supporting Jokowi's re-election campaign. According to Yanti Rukmana, the leader of Srikandi Indonesia, the support for the president among businesswomen was overwhelming.

Rukmana also said that businesses in Central Java were all supportive of Jokowi. In Solo, the president's hometown, almost 90 per cent of furniture entrepreneurs supported the president.[8] This is understandable since prior to entering politics in 2002 Jokowi was the first chairman of the Solo branch of Asmindo (Association of Indonesian Furniture Entrepreneurs), which has 200 members. With his background as a furniture manufacturer and businessman, Jokowi has paid serious attention to the development of the furniture industry in Indonesia.

Prabowo's campaign, on the other hand, appealed to different segments of the electorate. Prabowo relied heavily on the support of the Partai Keadilan Sejahtera (Prosperous Justice Party or PKS, for short). This party is known for its militant cadres and orderly organization and its targets are Islamic voters. Prabowo was also supported by non-traditionalist Muslim organizations, whose main argument was that the Jokowi administration's policies ran against Muslim interests. They referred to the banning of Hizbut Tahrir Indonesia (HTI), a pan-Islamist movement bent on reviving the caliphate, and the arrest of several controversial and hardline preachers (*ustadz*) who had insulted Jokowi in their sermons. These Muslim organizations tried to frame these acts as "criminalization of the *ulama*" (criminalization of Islamic scholars).

In a biography by Alberthiene Endah, Jokowi was said to have confessed that banning the HTI was a tough and difficult decision to take. It raised some objections among Jokowi's inner circle, who were afraid that the ban would create a backlash from the conservative Muslim community (Endah 2018). Political scientist Thomas Power characterized the president's move as an "authoritarian turn".[9] Ben Bland, who wrote an English-language biography of Jokowi, claimed that the move was aimed at legitimizing and co-opting certain conservative Islamic organizations and individuals but exercising state power against other organizations like HTI (Bland 2020). Consequently, some conservative Islamic organizations characterized the Jokowi administration as "anti-Islam" and campaigned on the issue.

It was quite clear that the conservative and hardline Islamic organizations supported Prabowo simply because he was not Jokowi. They were not interested in Prabowo and his party's platforms and did not believe it would genuinely serve Muslim interests. The distrust of Prabowo reverberated at the local level. The leader of the Shari'a Council of the City of Surakarta (DSKS), Mu'inudillah, stated that the support for Prabowo, who, according to him, has imperfect Islamic credentials, can best be characterized as choosing the lesser evil. Prabowo, he said, was seen as more respectful of *ulama* and followed the advice of the *ulama*. Mu'inudillah expressed the hope that the Prabowo presidency would provide more space for the application of Shari'a laws and would create an Indonesian society based on Islamic principles.[10] In other words, the support of Muslim hardline organizations like DSKS for Prabowo was instrumental rather than ideological.

While Prabowo gained a string of supporters from among Indonesia's conservative Muslim organizations, his failure to capture Central Java can be attributed to his political gaffes. The most notable gaffe occurred at the end of October 2018 when Prabowo inaugurated a *posko* for his campaign in Boyolali District. In his speech Prabowo made what was considered a derogatory statement regarding the "Boyolali look" (*tampang* Boyolali). He said people who had the "Boyolali look" were typically unlikely to be well received at fancy hotels in the big cities, implying that the Boyolali community represents lack of prosperity and backwardness.

The speech drew ire in Boyolali. It triggered condemnation on social media and later mass protests. Although it happened at the local level, it gained national attention. Jokowi's supporters capitalized on this gaffe to incite passions on the ground. Their social media machine worked at full speed to do damage to Prabowo's campaign.

Prabowo was forced to apologize for his remark but the damage had been done. Prabowo and his Gerindra party fared poorly in Boyolali and the surrounding Greater Solo regions (Sragen, Sukoharjo, Karanganyar, Wonogiri, Solo, Boyolali and Klaten districts). Jokowi garnered more than 80 per cent of the votes in these areas. According to the Boyolali General Elections Commission, Jokowi and his running mate, Ma'ruf Amin, garnered 581,477 votes (86.02 per cent), while Prabowo–Sandiaga managed to obtain only 94,464 votes (13.98 per cent).

The head of Boyolali District, Seno Samodro, said that Prabowo's political gaffe had created negative sentiments among Boyolali voters and led to his failure there.[11] Prabowo's performance also dragged down his party's performance at the local level. Gerindra failed to add more seats in the district's parliament. The results also revealed the strong impact of mass protests by PDI-P supporters in Boyolali.

Jokowi's campaign did not just rely on PDI-P. It was also supported by Partai Kebangkitan Bangsa (National Awakening Party or PKB, for short), which is often associated with NU. Jokowi's vice-presidential candidate, Ma'ruf, is the supreme leader of NU.

The hand of NU and PKB were apparent in Brebes District, a region in the northwestern part of the province. Governor Gandjar Pranowo had lost this district during his 2018 re-election campaign. Jokowi, however, captured it by a landslide, obtaining 69.92 per cent of the votes, while Prabowo received only 30.08 per cent. Ganjar Pranowo's loss in Brebes can be explained best by the NU and PKB factor. As noted earlier, Ida Fauziah, the vice-governor candidate who ran against Ganjar Pranowo, is an NU activist. The candidate for governor that she was running with, Sudirman Said, is a native son of Brebes and a former Minister of Energy and Mineral Resources in the early years of Jokowi's first term (2014–16). He shifted his allegiance to Prabowo after being sacked from the cabinet in 2016. Still, his credentials as a native son did not save Sudirman Said. After losing the 2018 gubernatorial election, he lost again in his 2019 bid for a seat in the national parliament from an electoral district that includes Brebes. A community leader who was also a volunteer for Ganjar Pranowo's gubernatorial campaign, explained that Sudirman Said's loss was due to his indifference to his fellows in Brebes. He had abandoned and neglected them when he held a ministerial position in Jakarta.[12] Jokowi's landslide results were undeniably related to organizing by NU and PKB voters. The same voters also supported Ida Fauziah during her bid to become Central Java's vice-governor.

Prabowo's loss in Central Java was shocking not only because his campaign team had poured sizeable resources into the province to cut Jokowi's edge, but also because they were, in fact, only hoping to lose by a much smaller margin, which would damage Jokowi's overall chances for re-election. Instead, Prabowo's loss in Central Java was greater compared with his performance in 2014. It is not surprising then that the Prabowo team suspected election irregularities.

Gerindra's party secretary, Ahmad Muzani, asked rhetorically: "In Central Java, [Prabowo and Sandi received] 22%. Is that so? In 2014, Prabowo and [then running mate] Hatta Rajasa received 26% [sic!] of the vote. Have the people of Central Java changed their minds so much?" (Paath 2019). Muzani apparently underestimated the many blunders that the Prabowo camp had made in Central Java. The decision to move the headquarters of Prabowo's campaign to the heart of Jokowi's base had awakened the bull, so to speak. Their aggressive strategies had boosted the fighting spirit of Jokowi's volunteers and PDI-P cadres. Moreover, the volunteer organizations that had supported Ganjar Pranowo in his 2018 re-election campaign were still intact. Organizations such as "Sedulur Ganjar" (Ganjar's Brotherhood) and "Kader Komunitas Juang" (Juang Cadre Community) were easily turned into Jokowi's volunteers.

THE USE OF IDENTITY POLITICS

Sharp religious and ethnic division in Indonesia has come to the fore since the huge protest against, and then imprisonment of, the then governor of Jakarta, Basuki Tjahaja Purnama (popularly known as Ahok), in 2016–17. The Purnama case has changed the political landscape in Indonesia. Jokowi took the cue from the case and placed more emphasis on religion-based identity politics than he did in his first presidential campaign in 2014. Haunted by the protests against Purnama, Jokowi picked as his running mate Ma'ruf Amin, a cleric who is chairman of the Indonesian Ulama Council (MUI) and, as mentioned earlier, supreme leader of NU. Ma'ruf was also the leader behind the issuance of the *fatwa* (religious edict) that led to Purnama's imprisonment.

Prabowo had also seriously considered putting up an Islamic cleric as his running mate. He approached Ustadz Abdul Somad, an immensely popular preacher who was also recommended by the congregation of the *ulama* (*ijtima' ulama*) to be his running mate. However, Abdul Somad emphatically refused the offer (*Liputan 6* 2018). Prabowo might have picked another cleric, Habib Rizieq Shihab, who organized the big rally against Purnama on 2 December 2016 that led to what is known as the so-called 212 Movement. But Rizieq had exiled himself in Saudi Arabia since 2017 following a controversial sexting leak (Nurita 2018). Rizieq is a founder of the Islamic Defenders Front (Front Pembela Islam or FPI, for short) and known to its FPI members as the grand imam. Prabowo eventually ended up with Sandiaga, a successful businessman but a novice in politics. In the campaign arena, Prabowo maintained a populist platform tailored to appeal to both conservative Muslims and nationalists.

Religion-based identity politics featured strongly in the presidential elections in Central Java, particularly in Solo, a city where nearly three-quarters of the population are Muslims. Solo is known as a "short fuse" (*sumbu pendek*) city, having experienced repeated anti-Chinese riots since colonial times. It is also home to several conservative Islamic organizations and has experienced attacks on minority houses of worship.

Prabowo tried to capitalize on the success of the 2 December 2016 protest against Governor Purnama in Jakarta to redirect the passions of its supporters to his campaign. Replicating the success of that protest, a large reunion of the Alumni of the 212 Movement (Presidium Alumni 212 or PA 212) was held at the National Monument (Monas) in Jakarta on 2 December 2018. The PA 212 also held a *tabligh akbar* (mass Qur'anic recital and sermon) on Jalan Slamet Riyadi, the main street in Solo, on 13 January 2019, which was attended by thousands of people. Prabowo and Sandiaga planned to attend the *tabligh akbar* but cancelled it at the eleventh hour, probably out of concern that the gathering would violate campaign law. One of the participants of the *tabligh akbar* said the police conducted security checks and dissuaded many people from joining the event.[13] A Jokowi volunteer later reported the *tabligh akbar* to the authorities because the preachers had used the event to talk about political issues and had explicitly endorsed Prabowo's presidential candidacy.

Prior to the elections, several developments occurred that could be perceived as the heightening of religion-based identity politics in Solo. The Shari'a Council of Surakarta City (Dewan Syariah Kota Surakarta or DSKS, for short), established in 2015 with the aim of enforcing the Shari'a in society, was actively protesting against the local government and demanding that it respect Islam. For instance, it launched a protest against the Lantern Festival during the Chinese New Year. In its view, Chinese culture should not be prominently exhibited in the Muslim-majority society. It also protested against the installation of cross-like tiles near the mayor's office. The cross is a symbol of Christianity and the mayor happened to be a Catholic. DSKS also criticized the mayor over the appointment of local officials whom they accused of sidelining the Muslims.

Many thought that Prabowo would easily ride on identity politics in Solo. His campaign was uniting local hardliners. The last round of Prabowo's campaign rallies in Solo on 10 April 2019 was attended by local Muslim hardline organizations such as FPI, the National Movement for Guarding Fatwa of the Indonesian Ulama Council (GNPF–MUI), the Islamic Defenders Militias (LPI) and Kopasandi (the Ulama Command for Prabowo–Sandi's Victory). It was choreographed as an imitation of Prabowo's large campaign rally in Senayan, Jakarta, on 7 April 2019. Like the Senayan rally, large numbers of PKS supporters and supporters of the disbanded HTI joined the rally in Solo. One of their characteristics was the flying not only of Palestinian flags but also flags depicting *tauhid* (literally, the oneness of God, referring to monotheism).

In order to show their distinct Muslim identity, Prabowo's supporters arrived at the venue of the rally early in the morning and later conducted congregational prayers (*sholat berjamaah*) at noon before listening to speeches by Prabowo and his campaign team. Women campaign-goers wore *hijab*s while men wore white *baju koko* (male Muslim attire) with white caps. The Qur'an recital was conducted before the campaign officially began while religious songs were played during the break. Indeed, despite the overwhelming presence of politicians, some Muslim preachers such as Bachtiar Nasir and Muhammad Najih Maimoen (Gus Najih) blended political messages with religious sermon by reminding voters that electing Prabowo also meant heeding the Qur'anic injunction of enjoining the good and forbidding evil (*amar bi-l ma'ruf wa nahi ani-l-munkar*).

Jokowi's campaign, in contrast, emphasized Indonesia's cultural and ethnic diversity. His campaign strategy dovetailed with PDI-P's identity that promotes pluralism and diversity. Although most of the supporters who attended his campaign events wore their respective party uniforms, some wore traditional Javanese attire. When Jokowi arrived at the rally venues, he was typically welcomed by a carnival atmosphere, whereby participants from the various ethnic groups wore their respective traditional attires. Jokowi consciously wanted to send a message of inclusiveness to appeal to voters from different ethnic and religious backgrounds. His final campaign in Senayan on 13 April 2019, which resembled a musical concert, was consistent with this inclusive approach.

In order to counter the hardliners, the Jokowi team sought the assistance of NU. On 23 February 2019, NU held an event commemorating the ninth anniversary of the death of former president Abdurrahman Wahid (affectionately known as "Gus Dur"), which was known as Haul Gus Dur and held in Solo. The commemoration featured a march themed "Millions Colours in One Indonesian Soul". The march passed the city's main roads before ending at Taman Sriwedari, a famous cultural site in Solo. Central Java Governor Ganjar Pranowo, Solo Mayor FX Rudy Rudyatmo, and Gus Dur's daughter, Yenny Wahid, joined the 3-km march. Mayor Rudyatmo, who led the parade, emphasized that the event was not a political one as there were no chants and campaign-related attributes; rather, he said, it was a commemoration of Gus Dur as a defender of humanity and the father of pluralism.

Identity politics, which featured heavily in Prabowo's campaign, did not work well in Solo. Prabowo's campaign, in fact, underperformed in Solo. Prabowo–Sandi garnered only 17.77 per cent of the total votes (or 65,272), while Jokowi–Ma'ruf captured 82.23 per cent (301,995). It should be noted that Prabowo was able to hold huge campaign rallies and religious events because his supporters mobilized people from outside Solo. This provided the misleading impression that Prabowo had wide support and was leading in Solo. The use of Islamic symbols during Prabowo's campaign in Central Java gave an exclusivist image of him, which alienated non-Muslims as well as *abangan* (non-observant) Muslims. It is clear that the use of religion-based identity politics in Central Java and Solo in particular was not effective and even created a backlash, especially from non-Muslim and nominal Muslim voters.

However, there was another identity element at play during the 2019 presidential election—Jokowi's ethnic identity. Jokowi is a Javanese and Central Java is an overwhelmingly Javanese province. Jokowi's Javanese manner was more acceptable to Javanese voters, compared with Prabowo's. Prabowo's campaign often stressed his roots in Banyumas in Central Java and the fact that he is a descendant of Raden Banyakwide, a Javanese hero during the Java War of 1820–25 and a lieutenant of the legendary Prince Diponegoro. This narrative apparently did not play well because Prabowo's comportment is more that of a cosmopolitan Jakarta personality.

Moreover, Jokowi had successfully cultivated the image of a person of humble beginnings, the son of a petty bamboo hawker who grew up in a riverside shack before his ascendancy to the pinnacle of power.[14] He maintained his close connection with ordinary people through his casual leadership style involving what is known as *blusukan* (a Javanese word for impromptu visits), which became his political stock-in-trade.

Unsurprisingly, Jokowi has been dubbed *merakyat* (close to the people). With his humble demeanour and relatable face, he is easily underestimated by his political rivals. After his election as president in 2014, Jokowi explained his campaign tactics to a foreign journalist: "My programme was: simple, polite and honest. That's it. As long as people believed me, I was sure I would win." (Bland 2020). During the 2019 presidential election, Prabowo's supporters mocked Jokowi on social media as a simple-minded person lacking competence in English. However, for the Javanese people, particularly those in the rural areas, the humility, proximity to the people and down-to-earth character of Jokowi strongly resonated. As a former economics and business journalist, Vasuki Shastry wrote, Jokowi's popularity and approachable leadership style compared with his more formal predecessors captured the imagination of Indonesia (Shastry 2018). Therefore, the black propaganda campaign portraying Jokowi as an "enemy of Islam", which was launched by some radical Muslim organizations in Central Java which militantly supported Prabowo, was apparently futile in destroying Jokowi's image of integrity.

THE UNBEATABLE *KANDANG BANTENG* IN CENTRAL JAVA

With eight dominant parties (PDI-P, Golkar, Gerindra, Demokrat, PKB, PKS, PPP and Partai Amanat Nasional or PAN, for short) competing for national and local parliamentary seats in Central Java, a discernible pattern that emerged was that the parties largely reflected Indonesia's traditional *alirans* or cultural streams based on ethno-religious orientations. Votes for the eight parties reflected voters' respective *alirans*: PDI-P gained support predominantly from *abangan* Muslims, Golkar, Demokrat and Gerindra had the *priyayi* (secularists or nationalists) as their main supporters, while PKB, PAN, PKS and PPP received support mainly from the *santri* (pious Muslim) community. A noteworthy point, however, is that the *alirans* are not static groupings; instead, they are shaped by the dynamics of sociopolitical conditions. Notably, the growing "Islamization" of the *priyayi* and the *abangan* in the urban areas has changed the *aliran* matrix (Hasyim 2019). Moreover, Indonesia has also witnessed an important transformation in its popular religious heritage, such as the wanning of heterodox and syncretic varieties of Islam, both in Java and the outer islands (Hefner 2011).

PDI-P is deeply rooted in Central Java owing to its long history as a nationalist as well as populist party dating back to its origins in the 1950s as the Indonesian Nationalist Party (PNI) before it was forced to merge with several other parties to form the PDI (Rocamora 1970). PNI outnumbered all the other parties in the 1955 general election, taking 22.3 per cent of the total votes cast, particularly in Central Java, where it obtained 35.8 per cent in the race for the national parliament, winning 21 out of 37 districts/cities in the province.

After experiencing intense internal conflicts in the 1990s engineered by the Suharto regime (Elköf 2003), PDI is now finally helmed by Megawati Sukarnoputri, the daughter of its founder, Sukarno, and its name changed to Partai Demokrasi Indonesia Perjuangan (PDI-P) or Indonesian Democratic Party of Struggle. Megawati has restored the image of PDI-P as an independent party and one with a direct lineage to its founder. Some scholars have labelled PDI-P as a party "with [a] dynastic party tradition" (Fionna and Tomsa 2017). It is centred on its leader, whose matriarchal style of leadership has given her unmitigated control of the party until today (ibid.).

It is not surprising that constantly capitalizing on Sukarno's image has been an effective tool in constructing the image of the PDI-P as a *partai wong cilik* (literally, little people's party). The phrase is a throwback to the ideology of "Marhaenism", the term Sukarno coined on 4 July 1927 to denote a dedication to the interests of the proletariat in Indonesia's societal conditions. The term, which was incorporated into the PNI logo with the words "Front Marhaenis" (Marhaenist Front), has captured the imagination of many Indonesians and PDI-P claims it as its inheritance.

PDI-P has utilized images of Sukarno in its campaigns because his name resonates with many people in Central Java, who still respect him. It is common to see Sukarno's photograph hanging in the living rooms of some people in Central Javanese despite regular changes of president. During election campaigns, the image of Sukarno wearing his grand attire emblazoned with various insignias is typically displayed on the billboards or posters of PDI-P legislative candidates to boost their standing as nationalists and the defenders of "little people". This is similar to PNI's campaign strategy in the 1955 election. That strategy identified Sukarno as a cadre of PNI and the party as inheriting his ideology of Marhaenism (Minarno 2011).

In the same vein, it is not difficult to portray Jokowi as belonging to PDI-P despite the fact that he does not officially hold a party position nor is part of the party elite. This is because Jokowi has been perceived as a true inheritor of Sukarno's teachings (*ajaran Sukarno*). Jokowi's governing programmes, known as Nawacita (Nine Ideals), were adapted from Sukarno's principles.

Interestingly, Prabowo too claims the mantle of Sukarno. His supporters often refer to him as "*Sukarno kecil*" (little Sukarno) because of his fierce nationalist stance, his opposition to foreign economic dominance and his efforts to improve Indonesia's standing abroad (Pranoto 2018). However, unlike Jokowi, Prabowo comes from an elite family and runs many businesses. As a result, ordinary people still associate him with the elite. This is evident from his aforementioned political gaffe of mocking the "Boyolali look". It became his biggest gaffe during the campaign because it showed that, despite his claims of being a Javanese and a descendant of a *priyayi* family, he did not fully understand Javanese values, in this case, the fact that for the Javanese people one's face is not merely a physical element but also a symbol of honour and respect.

Like PNI did in the 1955 general election, PDI-P utilized local elected officials as an instrument to mobilize voters in the 2019 elections. The role of local leaders cannot be underestimated. The campaign in Central Java was marked by the mobilizational force of elected officials, from district heads and mayors down to village heads. Governor Ganjar Pranowo, an ally of Jokowi and a PDI-P politician, led the efforts to effectively turn these elected officials to Jokowi's political advantage. Thirty-one heads of districts and mayors, whose election was backed by the PDI-P or who were in alliance with the party, pledged to support Jokowi. According to a coordinator of Jokowi's volunteer group, voter mobilization by elected leaders was highly effective, especially in the rural areas.[15] In a paternalistic society, the rural population tend to follow the political preferences of their leaders, especially if those leaders are capable of improving the welfare of the people.

Prabowo's camp was unperturbed by the governor's move. In their campaign rhetoric, they argued that the election was a *pesta rakyat* (people's festivity) and not a *pesta pejabat* (government officers' festivity).[16] While playing up what they claimed was deep dissatisfaction among farmers and fishermen in the northern coastal areas of the province over government policies that affected their trades, the Prabowo campaign also raised questions about the use of state resources in the election. Prabowo's stand was supported by former and retired government officials and military officers. However, these officials were no longer in power and did not have the resources at their disposal that could swing the election in Prabowo's favour.

Given that Jokowi was the PDI-P's presidential candidate, it was expected that PDI-P politicians running for legislative seats would be able to ride to success on his coat-tails. PDI-P candidates made the most of this potential by frequently displaying images of Jokowi–Ma'ruf on their posters and billboards. That PDI-P candidates won the greatest number of seats in the national parliament (26 seats) suggests the coat-tail effect may have worked. In contrast, the other parties in the Jokowi coalition for the 2019 presidential election were not able to ride on the coat-tails of Jokowi as much as the PDI-P could, with PKB gaining just 13 seats, Golkar 11, NasDem five and PPP four seats. In the 2014 legislative election, PDI-P grabbed 18 seats in the national parliament, while the other parties obtained limited numbers (PKB—10; Golkar—11; NasDem—five; PPP—six). Furthermore, Megawati's daughter, Puan Maharani, who ran in Central Java for a seat in the national parliament seat, received 404,304 votes from four electoral wards in Central Java (Boyolali, Klaten, Sukoharjo, and Kota Surakarta), the biggest win among legislative candidates in the 2019 parliamentary election. In short, Central Java is the PDI-P's stronghold and may remain so in the years to come.

CONCLUSION

The election results in Central Java Province show the peculiar political dynamics at the local level, which were at variance with politics at the national level. The incongruence was due to local conditions in Central Java, how the respective political candidates were perceived by the local people and the presence of grassroots volunteer organizations. These particular characteristics of Central Java Province begged more specific political strategies in mobilizing voters, which cannot simply be followed in a nationwide campaign strategy.

PDI-P still has strong roots in Central Java Province, as reflected in its landslide victory in the presidential and legislative elections, preceded by a similar victory in the 2018 gubernatorial election. It can be argued that the PDI-P draws its support from those who have traditionally been loyal to the party. Gerindra's attempts to defeat PDI-P in its stronghold were marred by political miscalculation and political gaffes by Prabowo. The party's decision to relocate its campaign headquarters to Solo, hometown of President Jokowi and a city that elected him twice (one by a landslide), was equal to "awakening the sleeping bull". Prabowo's political gaffe in Boyolali also tarnished his image among the Javanese voters and lowered his party's chance of winning a bigger share of parliamentary seats.

Notwithstanding strong support from the Islamic hardline organizations, Prabowo did not fare well in Central Java. His exploitation of religion-based identity politics did not appeal to moderate and *abangan* Muslims. On the other hand, Jokowi's campaign messages were inclusive in nature, attracting non-Muslims and, more importantly, moderate Muslims. The role of NU was essential in drawing moderate Muslim voters, who formed the majority at the grassroots level. Jokowi custom-tailored his campaign messages at the local level. In the northern, coastal areas of the province, which tend to be dominated by the *santri*, he tasked NU to mobilize voters. In the southern hinterland, where *abangan* Muslims predominate, he used PDI-P to appeal to voters.

NOTES

1. For a discussion of the presence of *aliran* identities and the resurgence of ideology in current Indonesian politics, see Fossati (2019).
2. Personal communication with the coordinator of one of Jokowi's grassroots volunteer organizations, 5 February 2019.
3. Personal communication with Abdul Wachid, 12 February 2019.
4. Personal communication with Mudrick Setiawan Sangidoe, 14 February 2019.
5. Personal communication with Sriyanto Saputro, 12 February 2019.
6. Personal communication with Bambang Hariyanto, 11 February 2019.
7. Personal communication with the coordinator of Jokowi's grassroots volunteer organizations in Solo, 9 April 2019.
8. Personal communication with Yanti Rukmana, 9 April 2019.
9. For a more extensive and critical discussion of the "authoritarian turn" in the Jokowi regime, see Power (2018).
10. Personal communication with Mu'inudillah, 9 April 2019.
11. Personal communication with Seno Samodro, 13 February 2019.
12. Personal communication with Haji Likun, coordinator "Sedulur Ganjar" in Brebes, 10 April 2019.
13. Personal communication with one of Prabowo's supporters in Solo, 14 February 2019.
14. See Mas'udi and Ramdhon (2018). A *Jakarta Post* journalist, Sita W. Dewi, debunked claims of Jokowi's humble beginnings. See Dewi (2013).

15. Personal communication with the coordinator of one of Jokowi's grassroots volunteer organizations, 5 February 2019.
16. Personal communication with Abdul Wachid, 12 February 2019.

REFERENCES

Bland, Ben. 2020. *Man of Contradictions: Joko Widodo and the Struggle to Remake Indonesia*. Docklands, Melbourne: Penguin Random House Australia.

CNN Indonesia. 2018. "PDIP: Tim Prabowo Bagunkan 'Banteng Tidur' di Jateng", 14 December 2018. https://www.cnnindonesia.com/nasional/20181214100557-32-353620/pdip-tim-prabowo-bangunkan-banteng-tidur-di-jateng.

Dewi, Sita W. 2013. "Man of the House, Man of the Moment". *The Jakarta Post*, 20 November 2013. https://www.thejakartapost.com/news/2013/11/20/man-house-man-moment.html.

Elköf, Stefan. 2003. *Power and Political Culture in Suharto's Indonesia: The Indonesian Democratic Party (PDI) and Decline of the New Order*. Copenhagen: NIAS Press.

Endah, Alberthiene. 2018. *Jokowi: Menuju Cahaya*. Solo: Tiga Serangkai.

Fionna, Ulla and Dirk Tomsa. 2017. "Parties and Faction in Indonesia: The Effects of Historical Legacies and Institutional Engineering". *ISEAS Working Paper Series*, no. 01.

Fossati, Diego. 2019. "The Resurgence of Ideology in Indonesia: Political Islam, *Aliran* and Political Behaviour". *Journal of Current Southeast Asian Affairs* 38, no. 2: 119–48. DOI: 10.1177/1868103419868400.

Hasyim, Syafiq. 2019. "Abangan, Santri and Priyayi: Three Streams in Indonesia Electoral's Politics". *RSIS Commentary*, no. 16, 17 April 2019.

Hefner, Robert W. 2011. "Where have all the Abangan gone? Religionization and the Decline of Non-standard Islam in Indonesia". In *The Politics of Religion in Indonesia: Syncretism, Orthodoxy and Religious Contention in Java and Bali*, edited by Michel Picard and Remy Medinier, pp. 70–91, London and New York: Routledge.

Kumparan. 2018. "Daftar Caleg DPR RI di Provinsi Jawa Tengah", 6 December 2018. https://kumparan.com/kumparannews/daftar-caleg-dpr-ri-di-provinsi-jawa-tengah-1544091306396557597/full.

Liputan 6. 2018. "Menolak Jadi Wapres, Ustaz Somad Berikan 4 Alasan", 10 August 2018. https://www.liputan6.com/citizen6/read/3615303/menolak-jadi-cawapres-ustaz-somad-berikan-4-alasan.

Mas'udi, Wawan and Akhmad Ramdhon. 2018. *Jokowi: dari bantaran Kalianyar ke istana*. Jakarta: Gramedia Pustakatama.

Minarno, Santoso. 2011. "Strategi PNI dalam Memenangkan Pemilihan Umum 1955 di Jawa Tengah". Unpublished BA thesis, Universitas Negeri Semarang, Semarang.

Nurita, Dewi. 2018. "Kisah Pelarian Pemimpin FPI Rizieq Shihab di Luar Negeri". *Tempo.co*, 17 February 2018. https://nasional.tempo.co/read/1061564/kisah-pelarian-pemimpin-fpi-rizieq-shihab-di-luar-negeri/full&view=ok.

Paath, Carlos K.Y. 2019. "Kubu Prabowo-Sandi Rasakan Kejanggalan Hasil Pilpres di Jawa dan Bali". *BeritaSatu.com*, 12 May 2019. https://www.beritasatu.com/jaja-suteja/politik/553810/kubu-prabowosandi-rasakan-kejanggalan-hasil-pilpres-di-bali-dan-jateng.

Power, Thomas P. 2018. "Jokowi's Authoritarian Turn and Indonesia's Democratic Decline". *Bulletin of Indonesian Economic Studies* 54, no. 3: 307–38. DOI: 10.1080/00074918.2018.1549918.

Pranoto, Susilo. 2018. *Prabowo: macan Asia harapan bangsa?* 2nd printing. Yogyakarta: Palapa.

Rocamora, J. Eliseo. 1970. "The Partai Nasional Indonesia 1963–1965". *Indonesia* 10 (October): 143–81.

Shastry, Vasuki. 2018. *Resurgent Indonesia: From Crisis to Confident*. Singapore: Straits Times Press.

Interviews

Abdul Wachid, Semarang, 12 February 2019
Bambang Hariyanto, Semarang, 11 February 2019
Haji Likun, Brebes, 10 April 2019
Iskandar, Solo, 14 February 2019
Mudrick Setiawan Sangidoe, Solo, 14 February 2019
Mu'inudillah, Solo, 9 April 2019
Seno Samodro, Boyolali, 13 February 2019
Sriyanto Saputro, Semarang, 12 February 2019
Yanti Rukmana, Solo, 9 April 2019

11

LESSONS FROM MADURA: NAHDLATUL ULAMA, CONSERVATISM AND THE PRESIDENTIAL ELECTION[1]

Ahmad Najib Burhani

INTRODUCTION

Unlike in previous presidential elections, the 2019 election saw the Nahdlatul Ulama (NU), Indonesia's largest Muslim organization, announcing full support for the incumbent, Joko Widodo (Jokowi). NU has about 50 million members and sympathizers, and its former *rois 'am* (supreme leader), Ma'ruf Amin, was Jokowi's running mate. As indicated by some analysts, the reasons for NU to do *cancut tali wondo* (be actively and fully involved) (al Amin 2019, p. 7) in the election are varied. According to the Institute for Policy Analysis of Conflict (IPAC), NU's involvement was "partly transactional, but its opposition to the Islamists behind Prabowo was deeply ideological" (IPAC 2019). In his ethnographic study of selected *pesantrens* (traditional Islamic boarding schools) in Java, Edward Aspinall too found that the narratives adopted by some of the *kiais* (leaders/caretakers of *pesantrens*) to support Jokowi–Ma'ruf were mostly ideological, most notably in wanting to counteract radical Islam, Salafism, Wahhabism and the Hizbut Tahrir (HTI), the pan-Islamist movement for the revival of the caliphate (Aspinall 2019). Although some subscribed to transactional narratives, the more important argument for these local *kiais* was ideological. The transactional narratives, which became common narratives within the circle of NU leaders and the elite of the NU-affiliated party, Partai Kebangkitan Bangsa (National Awakening Party or PKB, for short), revolved around the number of seats the party's representatives could secure in the cabinet and the upgraded status of NU from being the main beneficiary of government aid to becoming *ashabul qoror* (decision makers) in government.

To what extent did NU's support contribute to Jokowi's triumph? This is an important question since support for the winning candidate (in this case, Jokowi) becomes a bargaining chip to secure positions in the cabinet or a greater share of the pie in Jokowi's administration. Immediately after the announcement of Jokowi's triumph, some politicians were making claims and counter-claims as to who and which party had played the most critical role in Jokowi's victory. Fachrudin, an NU activist and academic, emphasized the significance of NU's role by outlining the swing in several big *pesantrens* in East Java (Fachrudin 2019a, 2019b). For Shofia and Pepinsky, Ma'ruf Amin "was a crucial factor in Jokowi's victory" but he "did not create an advantage for Jokowi in NU-dominant districts". Ma'ruf's main contribution was to shield Jokowi from attacks by opponents who were using the religious card; in the NU context, he "eliminated Jokowi's relative disadvantage in NU-dominant districts" (Shofia and Pepinsky 2019; Burhani 2018).

This chapter focuses on Madura, where almost 100 per cent of the population are loyal NU members. Some have even joked that the religion of the Madurese people is not Islam, but NU (Pribadi 2014, p. 11). Interestingly, despite their loyalty to NU, the people of Madura defied instructions from the central leadership to vote for Jokowi. What were the factors that made the Madurese people reject an incumbent who had chosen their *rois 'am* as his vice-presidential candidate? Bangkalan was the only district in Madura where Jokowi won a majority of the votes, that is 57 per cent; Prabowo prevailed in all the other districts. The result in Bangkalan was a tremendous swing for Jokowi from the 2014 presidential election, in which he had garnered only 18.80 per cent of the votes. What explains this vote swing to Jokowi in Bangkalan in 2019? Without excluding other possible factors, this chapter focuses on how religion, particularly loyalty to NU as a religious organization, shaped the voting pattern in Madura.

MADURA AND THE ELECTION RESULTS

Although Madura is part of East Java Province, it has a culture that is distinct from that of other areas in that province. Scholars classify East Javanese culture into sub-cultures: Mataraman, Arek, Tapal Kuda, Osing and Madura. Even the Madurese sub-culture is sometimes sub-divided based on the districts in Madura, i.e., Sumenep, Pamekasan, Sampang and Bangkalan. Madura's population of 3.9 million people constitutes 10 per cent of East Java's population of 39 million. The Madurese, however, are not limited to those who live on Madura island. A large number live in other districts in East Java, such as Pasuruan, Situbondo, Bondowoso and Jember.[2]

Madura is a dry and barren island, with a low rate of rainfall. This geographical feature has contributed to poverty on the island. According to Statistics Indonesia (BPS), in 2016, four districts in Madura were among the districts in East Java with the highest rates of poverty: Sampang (1), Bangkalan (2), Sumenep (4), and Pamekasan (6) (*Tumoutounews.com* 2017). Poverty has forced some Madurese to migrate in search of jobs to other districts in East Java, the other islands like Kalimantan, and even to foreign countries. In terms of literacy, the same statistics note that Sampang, Sumenep and Bangkalan were the three districts with the highest illiteracy rates in East Java.

Sunni Islam is the main religion in Madura; the Shi'as and non-Muslims constitute only a small minority. According to BPS, the four districts of Madura had a Muslim population of 3,735,757 in 2016 and only 21,299 non-Muslims (Protestants, Catholics, Hindu, Buddhist and Confucian) (*Tumoutounews.com* 2017). NU is the dominant religious organization in Madura although Muhammadiyah, Indonesia's other major religious organization, does have some members on the island. Being Muslim in Madura is almost synonymous with being NU, both culturally and in terms of religious affiliation.

In the context of elections, one of the cultural values in Madura is summarized in the saying *"bhuppa'-bhabhu', guru, rato"* (parents, teachers/*kiai*, state leaders or those holding formal office), which reflects the hierarchy of leaders that influence how individuals make decisions in Madurese society.[3] This patrimonial culture means that these three categories, in order, are the most respected persons and role models in Madurese society.[4] During elections, this "hierarchy of obedience" is telling and decisive; the voices and advice of these three categories of persons are important in determining the vote. This is in line with Yanwar Pribadi's observation on the fanaticism of the Madurese people to the Partai Persatuan Pembangunan (United Development Party or PPP, for short): "So long as the *kiai* of these *pesantrens* remained [sitting] as functionaries or at least supporters of the PPP and championed the party, their constituents would vote [for] the PPP" (Pribadi 2014, p. 10). The authority of the *kiai* to determine the vote of the people of Madura during elections was particularly strong during the New Order era; today, it is less evident although some *kiai* and *pesantren* still retain that sway over the people.

According to the order of obedience, *rato* or state leaders and those holding formal office were the most respected and obeyed persons on political issues in the past, but their position declined "during the concomitant emergence of *kiai* (*ghuru*) as popular leaders in the nineteenth and early twentieth century" (Pribadi 2018, p. 207). Today *kiais* seem to have become the most respected persons in Madurese society and "their word far outweighs national and regional laws" (Lucking 2016, p. 14). Sometimes, what is decided at the national level, both by the government and the NU, has little relevance in Madura; it is the local leader and *kiai* who is heard most by the people. Someone who can combine the roles of *rato* and *ghuru*, like the late Fuad Amin Imron, a great-grandson of Syaichona Cholil of Bangkalan (the most respected *kiai* in Madura), and former district head in Bangkalan, then would have been highly influential during elections.

MAP 11.1
Results of the 2019 Presidential Election in East Java

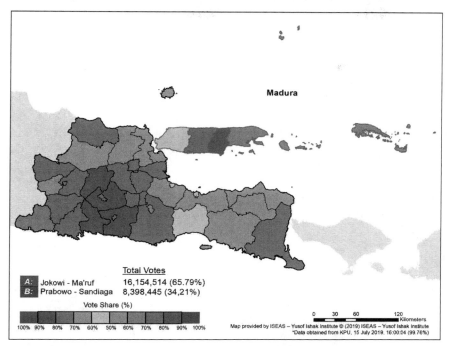

On 21 May 2019, the General Elections Commission (KPU) announced that Jokowi–Ma'ruf had won the presidential election with 55.50 per cent of the votes, or a total of 85,607,362 votes. Prabowo and his running mate, Sandiaga Uno ("Sandi"), received 68,650,239 or 44.50 per cent of the votes. In 2014 Jokowi and his then running mate, Jusuf Kalla, won 53.15 per cent of the votes, whereas Prabowo and his then running mate, Hatta Rajasa, won 46.85 per cent.

In East Java, Jokowi–Ma'ruf won with 65.7 per cent of the votes, a significant increase (12 percentage points) from the 2014 presidential election. Back then, Jokowi and Jusuf had won with 53.17 per cent. Prabowo and Hatta received 46.83 per cent or almost the same as they did at the national level. The districts in East Java where Prabowo defeated Jokowi in 2019 were Sumenep, Sampang, Pamekasan, Bondowoso, Situbondo and Pacitan. Except Pacitan, the hometown of the former president, Susilo Bambang Yudhoyono, the other five East Java districts where Prabowo won are effectively "Madurese" districts, with significant numbers of Madurese residents. It is often said that Bondowoso and Situbondo as well as Jember and Pasuruan are "Madurese districts" outside Madura Island.

As noted earlier, in Madura, Jokowi lost the vote in three of the province's four districts in the 2019 election. His vote share, in fact, declined compared to the 2014 presidential election. He won only in Bangkalan, with a huge vote swing. I call it a "magic swing" (*keajaiban*) because of the size of the swing—one cannot find a similar swing in any other district in the 2019 presidential election. In the 2014 presidential election, Prabowo–Hatta won in Bangkalan with 81.20 per cent of the votes while Jokowi–Jusuf managed to win only 18.80 per cent. In 2019, however, Jokowi–Ma'ruf won with 57.83 per cent of the votes while support for Prabowo decreased tremendously to 42.1 per cent.

MAP 11.2
Results of the 2019 Presidential Election in Madura

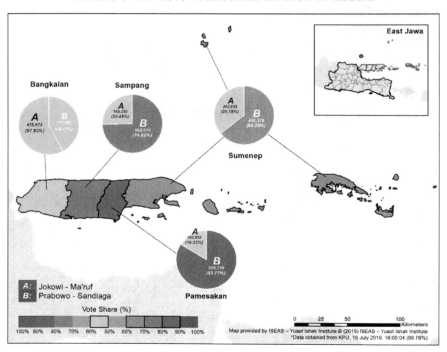

FACTORS: FPI, CONSERVATISM AND THE VENERATION OF *HABAIB*

From a religious perspective, there are several factors that contributed to Jokowi's defeat in Madura. The first was the growth of the Front Pembela Islam (Islamic Defenders Front or FPI, for short) and a long-held tradition of venerating *habaib*. *Habaib* is the plural form of *habib* and it literally means "beloved" or "most loved". The term is used to honour and address descendants of the Prophet Muhammad.

One of my interviewees, a *kiai* and the head of an NU branch in East Java, explained that instead of Banser, the paramilitary group under NU, it is the Laskar Pembela Islam (LPI), the paramilitary group under FPI, that has grown in size in Madura.[5] This statement is confirmed by a number of events where NU and FPI had collaborated, such as the *tabligh akbar* (mass religious gathering) to celebrate the Islamic New Year in Pamekasan on 2 October 2018, and the *haul akbar masyayikh dan habaib se-Madura* (mass gathering to commemorate great teachers and *habaib* in Madura) in Sampang on 26 February 2019.

In other parts of East Java, FPI often found it difficult to exist, let alone grow, because Banser persistently tried to block its establishment and activities. In Madura, however, FPI and NU have been in harmony and have often collaborated with each other. This, in effect, restricted or even curtailed the existence and growth of Banser. It is certainly a strange situation since Banser is the official paramilitary wing of the NU, whereas FPI, although culturally also affiliated with the NU, has different objectives as a paramilitary group.[6] This success and prominence of FPI in Madura was the outcome especially of the patronage of respected *kiai* on the island during the group's early stages.

The first FPI branch in Madura was officially opened during the *haflat al-imtihan* (official celebration at the end of examinations) at the *pesantren* of Syaichona Cholil I in Kademangan, Bangkalan, on 5 September 2005. FPI leader Habib Rizieq Shihab delivered a speech at the event. The first leaders of the branch were from the family of Syaichona Cholil, famously known as the Kademangan family, with the *kiai* of that pesantren, i.e., Abdullah Schal,[7] becoming the chairman of its Shura Council (consultative council) and Fahrillah Aschal the chairman of the Tanfidz (executive council) (Hamdi 2013, p. 78). Since then, the leadership of the FPI in Madura has always been held by *kiais* and leaders of NU.

Besides the patronage of Madurese *kiais*, the growth of FPI in Madura can be attributed to the role of Rizieq and other *habaib*. Quoting a statement from Muhaimin Iskandar, the chairman of PKB, the reason why NU members in Madura preferred to join FPI (rather than Banser) is simply that they can wear *sorbans* (turbans) and *jubahs* (robes). He said: "By joining FPI, they can wear *sorbans* and *jubahs*. In NU, only district-level *kiai* can wear *sorbans* and *jubahs*. Kiai at sub-district and village levels are shy about wearing *jubahs*. Wearing *sorbans* and *jubahs* is somewhat restricted in NU circles. Conversely, by joining FPI, they can immediately use the *sorban* and there is no hesitation about wearing the dress code."[8] This is a simplified explanation for something that actually has deep roots among the Madurese, i.e., the veneration of *habaib* and the love for imitating their ways of life, including the dress code. Because FPI is led by a *habib* and it has adopted white robes as its uniform, it attracts Madurese people to join its ranks.

Arabs and Arabness are still regarded as a model of religious life in Madura. As shown by Mirjam Lucking, Madurese people are very keen on, and proud of, imitating Arab traditions, particularly the dress code. For Madurese people, displaying Arabness not only symbolizes Islamic identity, but also piety, religious knowledge, spiritual skills, and even connection to the Holy Land (Mecca and Medina) (Lucking 2016, p. 15). From her fieldwork, Lucking has noticed that the use of turbans, white *jubahs*, the Arabic language and listening to Arab music are prevalent in Madura during *khaol* (commemoration of death) and various celebrations (*haflah*), including the celebration of the return from the *hajj*. Thus, the seemingly odd statement by Muhaimin Iskandar reveals a unique attitude and tradition in Madurese society.

The respect of Madurese people for the Arabs is probably in part an extension of their veneration for KH Muhammad Kholil bin Abdul Latif of Bangkalan (1820–1923) or Syaichona Cholil, believed to be of *hadhrami* origin (denoting people from the Hadramaut region in today's Yemen)—particularly from the Basyaiban family. However, it mostly relates to their traditional understanding of the "Arabs", which is synonymous with "Islamic".[9] This traditional understanding is different from the "anti-Arabness" of the NU, which mostly refers to the organization's opposition to Wahhabism and radicalism. In short, there are contrasting images when it comes to how the "Madurese NU" and the "mainstream NU" perceive Arabness. Whereas the Madurese NU venerate Arabs and associate them with Islam, the NU mainstream focuses on Arabs as the source of extremism and Wahhabism. As a counterweight to what is commonly perceived as "misguided Arabism" (*SuaraMuhammadiyah.id* 2017; *Tempo.co* 2017), NU, since its thirty-third congress in Jombang, East Java, in 2015, has intensively promoted "Islam Nusantara".

Putting aside the controversy over Arabization and Arabness, the respect of the Madurese people for Arabs provides a platform for Habib Riziq Shihab and FPI to grow in Madura. Riziq was an influential figure, if not the most important one, in the so-called 212 Movement of 2 December 2016 calling for the then governor of Jakarta, Basuki Tjahaja Purnama ("Ahok"), to be charged for blaspheming Islam. Although Riziq was living in self-exile in Saudi Arabia from 2017 to November 2020, his influence could be felt during the series of *ijtima ulama* (congregations of Islamic scholars) that endorsed the candidacy of Prabowo–Sandi. His photograph, placed above those of Prabowo and Sandi, illustrated his role as spiritual protector for Prabowo–Sandi, and was widely found in various places during the campaign. His choice of candidates in the election was followed by members of FPI, including in Madura and, according to a respondent, the majority of *habaib* in East Java.[10] This was one of the reasons why the Madurese people defied instructions from the leaders of NU to vote for Jokowi. The number of votes for Prabowo in Sampang, Pamekasan and Sumenep actually increased in 2019 compared with the numbers received in the election of 2014. Although the Madurese are loyal and fanatical members of the NU, they are closer to its "conservative faction" or the "FPI faction" than NU members in Java are.

The second factor in Jokowi's defeat in Madura is the growth of conservatism. Madura has seen growing exclusivism and sectarianism since 29 December 2011, when the Shi'a community was attacked in Sampang district. The Shi'as were not only declared infidels, they were also displaced from their homes and villages. Since their displacement from their temporary shelter at the Sampang Sport Stadium on 20 June

2013, hundreds of them have been living in a semi-permanent shelter in Sidoarjo named Puspa Agro (Afdillah 2016, p. 1). The Madura branches of the Majelis Ulama Indonesia (MUI), Indonesia's peak Islamic clerical body, were among the first to issue *fatwas* (religious rulings) declaring the Shi'a a heretical group in Islam. MUI members in Madura have also lobbied the central board of MUI and NU leaders to follow suit or to endorse their *fatwas* (Afdillah 2016, p. 70). To make the opposition to the Shi'as in Madura even more solid, the Anti-Heresy Front (Front Anti Aliran Sesat or FAAS, for short) was established in Sampang on 29 September 2013.

The case of the Shi'a in Sampang has not been fully resolved until today, and some *ulama* in Madura still reject the return of the displaced Shi'a community to their villages (*Tempo.co* 2018). This discrimination against the Shi'a community in Sampang is the most important indicator of conservatism in Madura. Another is the initiative to implement Shari'a bylaws in Madura. Pamekasan, for instance, has implemented three Shari'a-based bylaws, i.e., Perda No. 18 (2001) on the Prohibition of Alcoholic Beverages, Perda No. 18 (2004) on the Prohibition of Prostitution and Perda No. 05 (2014) on Controlling Activities during the Month of Ramadan. Furthermore, a large number of Madurese participated in the 212 rally on 2 December 2016 calling for Purnama's removal (*Beritatrans.com* 2017). In this respect, despite being dominated by NU, Madura has the same religious characteristics as Aceh, West Sumatra and West Java. Thus, it is not surprising that in the 2019 presidential election a large number of Madurese joined other conservative Muslim groups in supporting Prabowo. It would seem that the more conservative an area, the more the tendency to vote for Prabowo in the 2019 presidential election.

The growth of FPI and discrimination against the Shi'a community seem to be two parallel developments related to rising conservatism. However, that is not the case in Madura and in Indonesia, in general. Rizieq and FPI, for instance, tend to be tolerant of the Shi'a community and there do not seem to have been any reports of FPI attacking or discriminating against the Shi'as (*Satuislamwordpress.com*, N.d). During the election, however, FPI worked with Islamists and anti-Shi'a and anti-minority groups to defeat Jokowi. The voting result in Madura is the story of this combination.

The third factor behind Jokowi's defeat was the influence of big *pesantrens*, most notably Pesantren Sidogiri of Pasuruan and Pesantren Asembagus of Situbondo, which have large numbers of Madurese teachers and have produced large numbers of Madurese alumni. It is common in the tradition of *pesantren* for students and alumni to follow and obey their teachers and *kiais* (*Duta.co* 2019). The *kiais* of these pesantrens, especially Lora Kholil As'ad of Situbondo and Abdulloh Syaukat Siroj of Sidogiri, both decided to support Prabowo (ibid.).

The support for Prabowo in Sidogiri is rooted in the conservative tendency of the *pesantren*, highlighted by its opposition to "deviant" or heretical groups such as the Shi'a and the Ahmadiyya movement. They claim that their position of opposing the Shi'as and Ahmadiyya characterizes the "correct" NU and have even named it NU Garis Lurus (straight or correct path of NU. Or NUGL, for short). This position is in opposition to that taken by NU leaders, particularly Said Aqil Siradj (SAS). One of Pesantren Sidogiri's publications on this issue is *Sidogiri menolak pemikiran KH. Said Aqil Siroj* [Sidogiri rejects the thoughts of KH Said Aqil Siroj] (Tim penulis Pondok Pesantren Sidogiri 2016). Alex Arifianto (2017, pp. 241–64; 2018) finds that besides being involved in promoting NUGL, Pesantren Sidogiri has been criticizing SAS' views and opposing him since the NU congress in Jombang in 2015.[11]

According to the accounts of a number of individuals, personal factors also contributed to Jokowi's defeat and Prabowo's victory in Madura, such as the issue of Mahfud MD and La Nyalla Mahmud Mattalitti. The disappointment of the Madurese people with Jokowi found additional justification in the way the president had treated Mahfud MD, a native of Madura and former head of the Constitutional Court. Jokowi's eleventh-hour decision to drop Mahfud as running mate in the 2019 presidential election was a blow to the Madurese people. Although Mahfud himself accepted Jokowi's decision, some Madurese people considered the president to have deceived him and they used the issue as a reason for not voting for Jokowi. In the case of La Nyalla, the businessman and elected senator from East Java, had said during the presidential campaign, perhaps jokingly, that he would kill himself by slitting his throat if Prabowo were to win in Madura. This statement infuriated some Madurese into voting for Prabowo in order to see La Nyalla dead or at least shame him into "licking his own spit" (taking back his words).

MAGICAL SWING IN BANGKALAN

As briefly mentioned at the beginning of this chapter, there was a huge swing of votes in Bangkalan in favour of Jokowi that deserves special attention. In the 2014 presidential election, Prabowo won in this district with 81.2 per cent of the votes while Jokowi obtained only 18.8 per cent. While the number of votes that Jokowi obtained in the three other districts of Madura fell in the 2019 election, he won in Bangkalan with 57 per cent of the votes, a hefty 39-point increase from the 18 per cent of 2014. It can be called a "magical swing" because no other district in the 2019 election experienced such a tremendous swing. There are two possible explanations for this swing: the construction of Suramadu bridge and the *kiai* factor.

The construction of Suramadu (Surabaya–Madura) bridge, completed in 2009, had been expected to help the social and economic development of Madura. Bangkalan, a district adjacent to Suramadu, was predicted to reap most of the benefits. The bridge, no doubt, has facilitated travel to Surabaya for the Madurese people for education or social and economic activities. Yet, the construction of the bridge has not fulfilled expectations in terms of industrialization, modernization and socio-economic enhancement in Madura (Lucking 2016, p. 14; Nooteboom 2015). Therefore, the swing from Prabowo to Jokowi in the 2019 presidential election in Bangkalan cannot be associated with the development of the bridge. Ethnicity and religion seem to have played more significant roles in the election.[12]

Discussing the magical swing, one of my interviewees explained: "Do you want to have a good answer or a true answer?" The good answer, according to her, is that Bangkalan people are now more educated and economically better off than before; they are also becoming more "*melek politik*" (aware of political contestation). This transformation began after the Suramadu bridge had opened in 2009. However, she said, this was not true. She rejects the claim that the transformation began after the opening of Suramadu bridge.

The main factor for the swing, in her observation, is not the construction of Suramadu bridge and economic improvement and educational advances in Bangkalan, but patron-client politics. Patron-client politics plays a significant role in Indonesian democracy. In the Bangkalan context, Fuad Amin, the former head of Bangkalan District, who was in jail for corruption during the election, is a powerful figure and a great-grandson of the aforesaid Syaichona Cholil. During the election, many from Madura visited him in jail for his blessings and probably heard his views on the election. Some politicians believe Fuad Amin was the key player in Bangkalan, and that his call to vote for Jokowi through a video message recorded from jail unleashed the magical swing in Bangkalan (YouTube 2019).

For some, the high reliance on patron-client theory in understanding Indonesian democracy does not really make any sense, particularly in contemporary times. Madura, however, is an exception. Explaining the phenomenon, a news report in *Kompas*, a Jakarta-based national newspaper, carried an interesting title: "Madura, Ya, Begitu Itulah..." (That is Madura!) (*Kompas.com* 2014). Another report on Madura from *Mojok.co*, a satirical website, used a no less interesting title, i.e., "Selamat Datang di Madura, Daerah Di Mana Pemilihan Caleg Nggak Ada Gunanya" (Welcome to Madura, an Island Where Legislative Election Has No Meaning) (*Mojok.co* 2019). It has become a common saying that people in Bangkalan mostly did not vote or, if they did vote, simply followed a *kiai* or other important figures there. The pervasiveness of the view that the people of Bangkalan can be swayed by important leaders lends to the conclusion that the underlying factor behind the magical swing in Bangkalan is patron-client politics, which sometimes involves manipulating the people's choices in elections. The votes of the people in Bangkalan depend on *kiais*. If a *kiai* like Fuad Amin expresses a preference for a particular candidate, then the results of the voting would reflect his choice.

CONCLUSION

Madura is a microcosm of the tensions within NU, between local and national leadership, and between conservatism and pluralism. The result of the 2019 presidential election in Madura shows that the presumed binary situation—"NU versus the rest of Islam" or "traditionalist Muslims versus Islamists"—has no basis in reality. Islam in Indonesia is more complex and complicated, as is its relationship with politics. As with the conservative groups, moderate Islamic groups are not a monolithic entity. Although NU in general has been perceived as the champion of pluralism and moderation, it has another face—the "Madura faction of NU"—which can be more easily considered the "conservative faction of NU". In the 2019 election, the Madura faction refused to follow the instruction of NU leaders to vote for Jokowi–Ma'ruf. Outside the election, although the Madurese people are loyal and fanatical members of NU, their religious character makes them different from the general membership of NU. They tend to be more conservative and exclusivist. The well-documented discrimination against the Shi'a community in Sampang is the most distinct example of this tendency. Thus, the challenge for the NU brand, with its moderate and tolerant nature, does not only come from outside, but from within the movement as well.

Besides the religious issue, Bangkalan District provides a good example of how patron-client relations still play a role in Indonesian democracy. It has become a common saying that people in Bangkalan mostly did not vote or, if they voted, simply followed a *kiai* or other important figures there. There is deep deference towards eminent religious teachers (*ghuru*) and a tendency to follow their political preferences. Whichever candidate controls prominent local leaders or *kiais* will be able to use the latter's influence to get the votes of the Madurese people. Such is Indonesian democracy.

NOTES

1. I would like to thank Made Supriatma for his meticulous reading of this chapter and his comments and suggestions, some of which were taken into account in the writing of this chapter. However, any errors and omissions in this chapter are entirely mine.
2. Kalimantan is another traditional migration destination for the Madurese. There are also sizeable numbers of Madurese in West, Central, and East Kalimantan.
3. Among other cultural values in Madura are *taretan dibi* (brotherhood) and the value embodied in the saying *"ango'an pote tolang etembheng pote matah"* ("it is better to have white bones", i.e., self-esteem and honour, than white eyes, i.e., disgrace; simply put, it is better to die than to live in shame). Sometimes, this second value leads the Madurese people to do *carok* (fighting until death, usually using sharp weapons, as the last resort to defend one's honour).

4. Some analysts even say that this is not only considered a cultural value, but the worldview of the Madurese people. See Wiyata (2013), p. 217.
5. Interview with the head of an NU branch in East Java on 9 April 2019. For further information on the growth of FPI, see Hamdi (2013), pp. 71–95.
6. The motives and activities of these two paramilitary groups are different. Banser is more concerned with protecting NU's *kiais* and activities, whereas the FPI is focused more on eradicating what it considers vices. Ritually and culturally, however, these two groups follow traditional Islam.
7. Schal is an abbreviation of Syaichona Cholil.
8. See *Kumparan.com* (2018); *Detik.com* (2018). *Sorban* and *jubah*, in NU tradition, are seen as part of the dress code for *kiais* of high level or religious authority or *kiais* who have performed the *hajj*, the fifth pillar of Islam. Those who have not performed this religious duty would traditionally wear only *sarongs* and *pecis* (caps).
9. For the family tree of Cholil of Bangkalan, see Rifai (2009), pp. 15–20; Imron (2012), pp. 55–58.
10. Interview with a *kiai* and leader of NU in Kediri, East Java, on 8 June 2019.
11. Pesantren Sidogiri's support for Prabowo has a somewhat superficial ethnic connection—the founder of Pesantren Sidogiri is a *hadhrami*. However, it must be emphasized that some *hadhrami* are opposed to Rizieq Shihab and voted for Jokowi.
12. A more detailed explanation of the role of ethnicity and religion in the election can be found in Pepinsky (2019). Here, he explains that religious sentiments were more important in determining voting behaviour in the 2019 presidential election than economic circumstances and educational background.

REFERENCES

Afdillah, M. 2016. *Dari Masjid ke Panggung Politik: Melacak Akar-akar Kekerasan Agama antara Komunitas Sunni dan Syiah di Sampang, Jawa Timur*. Yogyakarta: Center for Religious and Cross-cultural Studies.

al Amin, Ainur Rofiq. 2019. "NU di Pusaran Pilpres 2019". *Kompas*, 13 February 2019.

Arifianto, Alexander. 2017. "Practicing What It Preaches? Understanding the Contradictions between Pluralist Theology and Religious Intolerance within Indonesia's Nahdlatul Ulama". *Al-Jāmi'ah: Journal of Islamic Studies* 55, no. 2: 241–64.

_____. 2018. "Nahdlatul Ulama is Home to Its Own Hardliners". *New Mandala*, 8 August 2018. https://www.newmandala.org/nadhlatul-ulama-home-hardliners/.

Aspinall, Edward. 2019. "Indonesia's Election and the Return of Ideological Competition". *New Mandala*, 22 April 2019. https://www.newmandala.org/indonesias-election-and-the-return-of-ideological-competition/ (accessed 28 November 2020).

Beritatrans.com. 2017. "40 Bus Angkut Massa Demo 212 dari Surabaya & Madura Sudah Tiba di Jakarta", 20 February 2017. http://beritatrans.com/2017/02/20/40-bus-angkut-massa-demo-212-dari-surabaya-madura-sudah-tiba-di-jakarta/ (accessed 28 November 2020).

Burhani, Ahmad Najib. 2018. "Ma'ruf Amin: A Shield from Identity Politics, but not a Vote-getter?" *ISEAS Commentary*, no. 108, 21 December 2018. https://www.iseas.edu.sg/medias/commentaries/item/8752-maruf-amin-a-shield-from-identity-politics-but-not-a-votegetter-by-ahmad-najib-burhani.

Detik.com. 2018. "Cak Imin Bandingkan Tradisi Berserban di NU dengan FPI", 23 July 2018. https://news.detik.com/berita/d-4127979/cak-imin-bandingkan-tradisi-berserban-di-nu-dengan-fpi (accessed 6 August 2019).

Duta.co. 2019. "Hari Ini Para Habaib, Kiai, dan Ulama Jatim Deklarasi Dukung Prabowo-Sandi di Sidogiri", 12 January 2019. https://duta.co/hari-ini-para-habaib-kiai-dan-ulama-jatim-deklarasi-dukung-prabowo-sandi-di-sidogiri/ (accessed 28 November 2020).

Fachrudin, Azis Anwar. 2019a. "Jokowi and NU: The View from the Pesantren". *New Mandala*, 11 April 2019. https://www.newmandala.org/jokowi-and-nu-the-view-from-the-pesantren/ (accessed 28 November 2020).

_____. 2019b. "Ma'ruf and NU Factor". *The Jakarta Post*, 18 May 2019. https://www.thejakartapost.com/academia/2019/05/18/maruf-and-nu-factor.html (accessed 28 November 2020).

Hamdi, Ahmad Zainul. 2013. "Radicalizing Indonesian Moderate Islam from Within: The NU-FPI Relationship in Bangkalan, Madura". *Journal of Indonesian Islam* 7, no. 1 (June): 71–95.

Imron, Fuad Amin. 2012. *Syaikhona Kholil Bangkalan penentu berdirinya Nahdlatul Ulama*. Surabaya: Khalista.

IPAC (Institute for Policy Analysis of Conflict). 2019. "Anti-Ahok to Anti-Jokowi: Islamist Influence on Indonesia's 2019 Election Campaign". IPAC Report, no. 55, 15 March 2019. http://file.understandingconflict.org/file/2019/03/Report_55.pdf (accessed 28 November 2020).

Kompas.com. 2014. "Madura, Ya, Begitu Itulah...", 16 July 2014. https://regional.kompas.com/read/2014/07/16/19021241/.Madura.Ya.Begitu.Itulah.?page=all (accessed 7 August 2019).

Kumparan.com. 2018. "Cerita Cak Imin soal Warga NU di Madura yang Bergabung dengan FPI", 23 July 2018. https://kumparan.com/@kumparannews/cerita-cak-imin-soal-warga-nu-di-madura-yang-bergabung-dengan-fpi-27431110790551276.

Lucking, Mirjam. 2016. "Beyond Islam Nusantara and 'Arabization'—Capitalizing 'Arabness' in Madura, East Java". *Asien* 139: 14.

Mojok.co. 2019. "Selamat Datang di Madura, Daerah di mana Pemilihan Caleg itu Nggak Ada Gunanya", 4 February 2019. https://mojok.co/kho/esai/selamat-datang-di-madura-daerah-di-mana-pemilihan-caleg-itu-nggak-ada-gunanya/ (accessed 28 November 2020).

Nooteboom, Gerben. 2015. *Forgotten People: Poverty, Risk and Social Security in Indonesia: The Case of Madurese*. Leiden: KITLV Press.

Pepinsky, Tom. 2019. "Religion, Ethnicity, and Indonesia's 2019 Presidential Election". *New Mandala*, 28 May 2019. https://www.newmandala.org/religion-ethnicity-and-indonesias-2019-presidential-election/ (accessed 22 August 2019).

Pribadi, Yanwar. 2014. "Religious Networks in Madura Pesantren, Nahdlatul Ulama and Kiai as the Core of Santri Culture". *Al-Jami'ah* 51, no. 1: 11.

⎯⎯⎯. 2018. *Islam, State and Society in Indonesia: Local Politics in Madura*. London: Routledge.

Rifai, Muhamad. 2009. *K.H.M. Kholil Bangkalan: biografi singkat, 1820–1923*. Jogjakarta: Garasi.

Satuislamwordpress.com. N.d. "Habib Rizieq Shihab: "Mengkafirkan Syi'ah Berarti Menyerang dan Menghancurkan Ahlussunnah", n.d. https://satuislam.wordpress.com/2013/12/02/habib-rizieq-shihab-mengkafirkan-syiah-berarti-menyerang-dan-menghancurkan-ahlussunnah/ (accessed 28 November 2020)

Shofia, Naila and Tom Pepinsky. 2019. "Measuring the 'NU Effect' in Indonesia's Election". *New Mandala*, 1 July 2019. https://www.newmandala.org/measuring-the-nu-effect-in-indonesias-election/.

SuaraMuhammadiyah.id. 2017. "Syafii Maarif: Hindari Misguided Arabism, Umat Islam Harus Keluar dari Kotak", 18 January 2017. http://www.suaramuhammadiyah.id/2017/01/18/syafii-maarif-hindari-misguided-arabism-umat-islam-harus-keluar-dari-kotak/.

Tempo.co. 2017. "Di Depan Uskup, Buya Syafii Beberkan Bahaya Arabisme Sesat", 3 August 2017. https://nasional.tempo.co/read/896939/di-depan-uskup-buya-syafii-beberkan-bahaya-arabisme-sesat (accessed 8 August 2019).

⎯⎯⎯. 2018. "Jenazah Pengungsi Syiah dari Sampang Ditolak Penduduk Kampungnya", 14 June 2018. https://nasional.tempo.co/read/1098059/jenazah-pengungsi-syiah-dari-sampang-ditolak-penduduk-kampungnya (accessed 28 November 2020).

Tim penulis Pondok Pesantren Sidogiri. 2016. *Sidogiri Menolak Pemikiran KH Said Aqil Siroj*. Penerbit Sidogiri.

Tumoutounews.com. 2017a. "Jumlah Pemeluk Agama di Jawa Timur Tahun 2016", 13 November 2017. https://tumoutounews.com/2017/11/13/jumlah-pemeluk-agama-di-jawa-timur-tahun-2016/ (accessed 28 November 2020).

———. 2017b. "Jumlah Penduduk Miskin di Jawa Timur Tahun 2016", 23 November 2017. https://tumoutounews.com/2017/11/23/jumlah-penduduk-miskin-di-jawa-timur-tahun-2016/ (accessed 28 November 2020).

Wiyata, A. Latief. 2013. *Mencari Madura*. Jakarta: Bidik-Phronesis Publishing.

YouTube. 2019. "Viral Video Dukungan Fuad Amin untuk Jokowi-Amin", 16 April 2019. https://www.youtube.com/watch?v=IG7tdYAkEtg (accessed 22 August 2019).

12

RELIGIOUS BINARISM AND "GEOPOLITICAL" CLEAVAGE: NORTH SUMATRA IN THE 2019 PRESIDENTIAL ELECTION

Deasy Simandjuntak

INTRODUCTION

On 21 May 2019, the Indonesian General Elections Commission announced the long-awaited electoral results: the incumbent President Joko Widodo (Jokowi) and his running mate, the Islamic scholar Ma'ruf Amin, had won, garnering 55.50 per cent of the total votes, against former general Prabowo Subianto and his vice-presidential candidate, Sandiaga Uno, who obtained 44.50 per cent. The incumbent was backed by a coalition of nationalist and Islamic parties led by the Partai Demokrasi Indonesia Perjuangan (Indonesian Democratic Party of Struggle or PDI-P, for short) whereas Prabowo was endorsed by his own party, Gerindra, and the Islamist-oriented Partai Keadilan Sejahtera (Prosperous Justice Party or PKS, for short). This was the second presidential contest for Jokowi and Prabowo as they were also contenders in the 2014 election.

The election campaign was also one of the most divisive in Indonesia's electoral history. Most notably, it showcased the culmination of Indonesia's religious–pluralist binary electoral politics, with Prabowo's camp relying on the mobilization of Islamist sentiments and Jokowi's camp generally seen as championing pluralism despite having a vice-presidential candidate who is considered by many as religiously conservative. The key term here is *electoral politics* as religious polarization is aggravated mainly during elections.

Despite the comfortable margin of 11 per cent that he had achieved, Jokowi won in fewer provinces than he did in 2014. Notably, he lost in six of the ten provinces in Sumatra, which, with its 37.8 million voters, is the island with the second largest number of voters after Java. Like the rest of the Indonesian archipelago, Sumatra is predominantly Muslim (87 per cent), while Christians make up 10.7 per cent of the population, and Buddhists (1.4 per cent), Hindus (0.4 per cent) and Confucians (0.1 per cent) are present in smaller numbers. Yet, the island is ethnically heterogeneous,[1] with Javanese (30.2 per cent), Batak (14.4 per cent),[2] Malay (13.2 per cent) and Minang (11.4 per cent) forming the main ethnicities, while smaller groups include the Chinese (1.5 per cent).

Of Indonesia's thirty-four provinces, none has more strongly shown religious binarism than North Sumatra, one of the most religiously and ethnically heterogeneous provinces in the archipelago. Here, Jokowi won by a negligible margin of 4 per cent. This chapter aims at highlighting the role of the religiously charged binarism in the presidential election in North Sumatra, where Christians comprise 31 per cent of the total population—the highest concentration of Christians in the ten provinces in Sumatra. Despite the predominance of Muslims, at 67 per cent, North Sumatra is ethnically heterogeneous, with Bataks comprising 45 per cent of the population, followed by Javanese (25 per cent), Nias (7 per cent) and Malays (6 per cent).

One of North Sumatra's unique identity-markers is its east–west geographical divide, which is consistent with its districts' religious demography. Predominantly Muslim districts are located on the east coast while Christian districts are on the west coast. During the presidential election, the religious binarism that inflamed the presidential campaign in the capital city, Jakarta, also had the effect of exacerbating North Sumatra's religious-geographical divide, leading to a political cleavage between districts supporting Prabowo (east coast) and those supporting Jokowi (west coast).

Although at the time of writing, such religious polarization has been somewhat subdued owing to President Jokowi's decision to appoint Prabowo as his defence minister—thereby accommodating him and his party in the government—the chapter argues that the divisive 2019 election has made religious sentiments an important political tool for mobilizing voters in the future. More importantly, the fact that Jokowi decided to place Prabowo in such a strategic ministerial position shows that Indonesia's religious binarism is transitory and functional—it mainly exists during, and for, electoral contestations. The chapter, therefore, also aims at shedding light on the impact of the 2019 election on the state of democracy in Indonesia.

THE 2019 PRESIDENTIAL ELECTION AND INDONESIA'S POLITICAL BINARISM[3]

Binarism, or polarization, refers to the divergence of political attitudes into two ideological extremes (Baldassarri and Gelman 2008, pp. 408–46; DiMaggio, Evans, and Bryson 1996, pp. 690–755). In binary politics, there is hardly any room for "third" alternatives. American politics, for example, often only allows two parties to participate substantially in governance, leading to binary ideological stances of "Conservative vs. Liberal" or "Left vs. Right" or even binary positions on contentious issues such as a woman's right to abortion ("pro-Life vs. pro-Choice").

Indonesia's politics, however, showcases a different type of binarism: that which is transitory and not founded on a rigid ideological cleavage as political parties are mainly catch-all parties, generally devoid of clear ideological platforms. In this aspect, Indonesia's binarism is different from the *affective polarization* that exemplifies politics in the US, because although in the US emotional reactions that underlie such polarization are similarly incited by social identities more than rigid ideologies, the political polarization in the US is still party-based while Indonesia's binarism is not.[4] Having said this however, the 2019 presidential election still marked the culmination of the polarization between the Islamists and the pluralists (consisting of mainly moderate Muslim and non-Muslim voters),[5] which was triggered by the movement in 2016–17 calling for the Chinese-Christian governor of Jakarta, Basuki Tjahaja Purnama (Ahok) to be charged with blasphemy against Islam (Simandjuntak 2017a). In the 2019 election, Indonesia's voters generally flocked into these two camps.

Owing to his nationalist–Islamist party coalition, Prabowo's campaign relied more on the mobilization of Islamic sentiments, which reinforced the image that he was accommodative to Islamic interests. In contrast, Jokowi was considered a pluralist, partly owing to PDI-P, his main supportive party, which has a nationalist platform. In fact, Jokowi was still considered a pluralist even after he appointed Ma'ruf Amin as his running mate. Ma'ruf Amin is a conservative cleric who is also the chairman of the Majelis Ulama Indonesia (MUI), Indonesia's council of Islamic scholars (ulama) (Simandjuntak 2019b). The appointment is surprising for Jokowi's pluralist supporters, as Ma'ruf was the figure behind many MUI *fatwas* (religious edicts) that were widely considered to be religiously intolerant. In fact, the *fatwa* on blasphemy, in whose formulation Ma'ruf was largely involved, was the *raison d'être* of hardline groups such as the National Movement of Fatwa Defenders (GNPF), which spearheaded massive anti-Purnama demonstrations in 2016–17 (Burhani and Simandjuntak 2018). Moreover, Ma'ruf himself became the key expert witness in the trial that sent Purnama to jail for blasphemy. The anti-Purnama groups have now formed a semi-consolidated force against the government, dubbed the "212 alumni" in reference to the date of their largest demonstration in December 2016. The movement regularly mobilizes street protests against policies that it deems detrimental to its interests.

As it turned out, the religious binarism that began in 2016 informed voter preferences in the 2019 presidential election. An exit poll showed that 51 per cent of Muslim voters voted for Prabowo, while 97 per cent of non-Muslim voters voted for Jokowi (BBC Indonesia 2019). Most notably, Jokowi lost in West Java, a province deemed the most religiously intolerant in 2017 (*Jakarta Post* 2017) and which, with its 33 million voters, was the province with the largest number of voters in 2019. Jokowi's loss in some Muslim provinces indicated that, despite having a conservative running mate, for many Muslim voters Jokowi was not Muslim enough compared to Prabowo. Some social media rumors, such as those claiming that the president would ban the call to prayer (*azan*) and erase Islamic education from the school curriculum and that he was sympathetic to the long-disbanded communist party, aggravated Jokowi's unpopularity among conservative Muslims (*Straits Times* 2017). This was however not the first time that issues questioning the president's religiosity had been used to discredit him. In 2014, the rumours that he was not a devout Muslim, and that he was in fact a Chinese, contributed to a temporary decline in his popularity (*Deutsche Welle* 2014).

As retaliation against the Islamist groups, Jokowi in 2017 issued a law prohibiting organizations deemed opposed to the country's ideology, Pancasila. While this policy garnered praises from the president's supporters, it nevertheless harked back to the Suharto regime's repressive policies and thus elicited protests from groups advocating liberal democracy (Simandjuntak 2017b). Meanwhile, although Prabowo's camp also accommodated other groups such as the ex-military elite (*Tempo.co* 2018), the Islamists were generally seen to define and front the camp. Interestingly, the Islamists did not have their own leadership figure who could be Jokowi's match, and so, despite Prabowo's lack of Islamic credentials, to which he himself had confessed (*Detik.com* 2018), they still found an ally in him. This led to a political bond that was consolidated by Prabowo's pledge to prioritize Islamic interests if he became president (*Jakarta Post* 2018).

Unlike in the US politics, Indonesia's political binarism is therefore lacking in ideological substance and is merely transitory and functional. The 2019 election showed that Indonesia's binarism, in contrast to the American variant, only surfaced during elections and mostly functioned as the basis to mobilize voters. The current political constellation is testimony to this argument. In October 2019, President Jokowi made Prabowo, his former electoral rival, the new minister of defence. Some Western observers scorned this decision and likened it to witnessing the implausible situation where US President Donald Trump would make ex-rival Hillary Clinton one of his ministers (Gammon 2019). What these observers failed to understand was that Indonesian "democracy" does not follow any Western model. Comparing it with that of American democracy is to take the matter out of context—not to mention that there is in fact no "formula" on what democracy really is.[6] Still, taking US democracy as the gauge for the success of Indonesia's democracy seems to be inevitable, not only for some Western observers, but also, ironically, those they deem to be advocates of authoritarianism. Before his official appointment as minister of defence, Prabowo was said to have likened himself to William Seward, President Abraham Lincoln's former rival, whom the latter later appointed as secretary of state (*Tempo* 2019a). Clearly, both Western observers—who consider themselves experts on democracy—and those they consider as authoritarian archetypal figures have both used US democracy to prove very different points.

In order to identify the role of Indonesia's variant of binary politics in the presidential election, the next section highlights the voting pattern in North Sumatra, which was congruent to its districts' religious demography. Interestingly, it also closely resembled the pattern during the province's gubernatorial election in 2018, indicating the predominance of religion-based voting in North Sumatra's electoral democracy.

CORRUPTION AND IDENTITY POLITICS PRIOR TO RELIGIOUS BINARISM

Prior to the intensification of religious binarism that was influenced by national politics, two electoral strategies were known to be popular in North Sumatra, namely money politics and identity politics based on ethnicity. As in many places in Indonesia, there are at least two stages where money is important during elections (Simandjuntak 2015): first, when there is a need to cajole or remunerate parties for endorsement and, second, when there is a need to entice potential voters during an election campaign. In mayoral or district-head and gubernatorial elections (dubbed *pilkada* and *pilgub*), some parties required aspiring candidates seeking their endorsement to pay a "financial contribution" or *mahar*, amounting in many cases to substantially large sums.[7] The congruence of ideologies between the aspiring candidate and the political party generally mattered less than the material benefits that the former could provide. Because parties lack financing channels, this process encouraged corruption.[8]

Although the regional election law forbids the receiving of *mahar*, media reports indicate that such patronage for cash is prevalent among almost all parties, regardless of whether they are in power or in the opposition and regardless of ideology (*Harian Terbit* 2015; *Republika.co.id* 2015). Interestingly, such patronage was generally centralized, which means that while the local branch of a political party was the official endorser of a candidate, the central leadership had the authority to approve the said candidate and, thus, collect the fee. In an interview during North Sumatra's first-ever mayoral and district-head elections in 2005, a party branch member in Karo district lamented the arrangement: "The central leadership takes the money; we're just signing formalities here." (Simandjuntak 2009, p. 89).

Money is also used to buy votes. According to Nichter, vote-buying, or electoral clientelism, is "the distribution of rewards to individuals or small groups during elections in contingent exchange for vote choices. Rewards are defined as cash, goods (including food and drink), and services" (Muhtadi 2019). Burhanuddin Muhtadi's research estimated that in the 2014 legislative election, 25–33 per cent of Indonesia's 187 million registered voters were targets of vote-buying, i.e., they were offered cash or other material benefits in return for their votes (Muhtadi 2019).

As a campaign strategy, money is not simply used to "buy" votes, because rarely could a candidate be sure that the amount distributed would be enough to secure votes. Rather, the distribution of gifts to their potential voters during campaigns functions as a mechanism to develop loyalty. Thus, the distribution of banknotes does not only pertain to their monetary worth but is also a symbolic gesture. In this sense, money plays the kind of role that gift-giving in exchange for political loyalty has had in patrimonial societies such as North Sumatra; gift-giving from patron to clients is aimed at assuring the latter that the former will attend to their needs. In such patrimonial societies, followers tend to prefer powerful leaders who are not only wealthy but also generous enough to "share" their wealth.

My past observation of North Sumatra's first local elections revealed that cash was distributed both to "brokers" (those who claim they could get votes for a candidate), as well as campaign attendees. In June 2005, forty civil servants from a district office secretly attended a campaign meeting held on behalf of an opposition candidate in the district head election. They were then given around Rp300,000 (US$22) each, a considerable sum at that time, to pay for the "operational costs" to entice more voters for the said candidate (Simandjuntak 2012, pp. 99–126).

Observers tend to agree that the rampancy of money politics during elections is likely to lead to post-election political corruption and rent-seeking practices as elected leaders struggle to offset their campaign "costs" (Rose-Ackerman 1999, pp. 363–78). The same can be said about North Sumatra, a province with the most graft cases involving elected officials. High-profile cases in the past decade involved at least six elected leaders: two North Sumatra governors, mayors of North Sumatra's capital city, Medan, and one deputy mayor of Medan. Syamsul Arifin, who in 2008 became the first directly elected governor of North Sumatra, was convicted of corruption in 2012 involving the embezzlement of Rp98.7 billion (US$7 million).[9] He was replaced by his deputy, Gatot Pujo Nugroho. However, the latter himself was convicted of corruption on four different counts, involving a total of more than US$46,000.[10]

Three consecutive mayors of Medan serving from 2005 to 2009 were also apprehended for corruption, the latest one being Dzulmi Eldin, who won election in 2015 but was charged in October 2019 with graft in a case that was ongoing at the time of writing (Prireza 2019). His predecessor, Rahudman Harahap, who became mayor in 2010, was convicted in 2014 of embezzling Rp2 billion (US$142,000) from a village civil service fund. Rahudman himself was the successor to Abdillah, the first ever directly elected mayor of Medan, who took office in 2005. Abdillah had a lavish campaign supported by nine political parties and won by a landslide of 62 per cent. Yet, in 2008 he and his deputy were convicted of two graft offences involving Rp50.58 billion (US$3.6 million).[11]

Looking at the corruption cases involving elected leaders, North Sumatra's politics seemed to be more prone to electoral clientelism than religious politics. In the Batak areas especially, money politics also influenced the early district-head election campaigns, with gift-giving assuming traditional significance when the elites of different Batak clans vied to become the leader of each district (Simandjuntak 2009).

However, since 2010, ethno-religious politics has grown to become more prominent. In the first round of the 2010 mayoral election in Medan, there were ten electoral tickets and each pair represented a particular ethnic and/or religious group (single identity ticket) or two ethnic/religious groups (mixed identity ticket). Of the ten pairs, Sofyan Tan and Nelly Armayanti attracted attention because Sofyan is a Chinese Buddhist, an ethnic minority in Medan, while Nelly is a Muslim. At the end of the first round, the two pairs that managed to get through to the second round were the Sofyan–Nelly pair and an all-Muslim ticket, the aforesaid Rahudman Harahap and Dzulmi Eldin. Despite Sofyan's minority identity, Sofyan–Nelly managed to secure considerable votes in the first round because the Muslim votes had been divided among the nine other pairs while the Chinese votes were concentrated on the Sofyan–Nelly team by virtue of the ethnic affinity with Sofyan (Nasution 2014, pp. 496–505). However, this also meant that the campaign in the second round became very religiously charged, with the North Sumatra branch of MUI calling on Muslims to vote for the all-Muslim ticket. Eventually, the Rahudman–Eldin team won, although, as mentioned earlier, Rahudman was convicted of corruption in 2014 while Eldin, who later succeeded him as mayor, was apprehended in 2019 and is the subject of an ongoing graft case.

Seeing that religious campaigning was successful where there were two pairs of candidates representing two different religions, the campaign teams in the 2018 gubernatorial election used a similar strategy (Simandjuntak 2018b). The two pairs in this election, were former general Edy Rahmayadi (Malay-Muslim) and Musa Rajeckshah (Muslim, and according to some, with Afghan blood), who formed the all-Muslim ticket and were endorsed by the coalition that included Gerindra and the Islamist-oriented PKS; and Djarot Saiful Hidayat (Javanese-Muslim) and Sihar Sitorus (Toba Batak-Christian), who formed the mixed ticket and were endorsed by the coalition led by PDI-P. Despite the mixed ethnicity of both tickets, the campaign was mainly religiously charged, with the Edy–Musa ticket benefitting to a greater degree from the mobilization of Islamic sentiments. Banners were put up during campaigns calling on voters to vote for Muslim leaders (*Kompas.com* 2018). Similarly, in its parade, the GNPF called on Muslims to vote for Muslim, and not *kafir* (infidel) leaders, clearly referring to the Christian Sihar. The religious divide also accentuated the discrepancy in the political affiliation between the districts in the eastern and the western coasts. Owing to its being predominantly Muslim, the east coast and the southern region mainly supported the all-Muslim ticket of Edy–Musa. Similarly, the Christian district in the west coast mainly supported the mixed-religion ticket of Djarot–Sihar (see Maps 12.1 and 12.2). Other issues were at play too. For example, Edy–Musa underlined the fact that they were "sons of the soil" because Musa's politically notable family was widely known in Medan and Edy had a military career as the former Bukit Barisan military district commander, based in Medan. Yet, the religious cleavage was the most influential aspect of the 2018 gubernatorial election.

Interestingly, the competition between Djarot–Sihar and Edy–Musa resembled the 2017 Jakarta gubernatorial election as well as the 2019 presidential election in three aspects (Simandjuntak 2018a). First, the North Sumatra election showcased the rivalry between PDI-P and Gerindra–PKS, just as in the 2017 Jakarta election, where the candidate supported by PDI-P, Purnama, battled Anies Baswedan, supported by Gerindra–PKS. It was also reflected in the 2019 presidential contest between the incumbent, supported by PDI-P, and Prabowo, supported by Gerindra–PKS. Second, in terms of the backgrounds of the candidates, the presidential election resembled the North Sumatra election as Edy Rahmayadi and Prabowo are both former military generals and accordingly campaigned for "stronger" governance. Third, North Sumatra, like Jakarta, is an ethnically heterogeneous region, yet largely religiously homogeneous, with Islam being the predominant religion. The gubernatorial campaigns in both regions were thus unsurprisingly similar, with the mobilization of religious sentiments influencing the political preference of voters. Learning from their success in 2018, Gerindra–PKS used similar religiously charged campaigns in North Sumatra for the 2019 presidential election. The next section shows that the mobilization of religious sentiments did influence the presidential election and aggravated the difference in political preferences between the east and west coasts.

BINARISM AND RELIGIOUS-GEOPOLITICAL BIFURCATION

North Sumatra's overall voting pattern was consistent with its districts' religious demography, with Muslim districts overwhelmingly voting for Prabowo and Christian districts voting for Jokowi. The similarity to the 2018 gubernatorial election is also striking. Back then, Muslim districts voted for Edy Rahmayadi and Musa Rajeckshah, the all-Muslim ticket supported by PKS–Gerindra, while Christian districts voted for Djarot Saiful Hidayat and Sihar Sitorus, the mixed-religion ticket supported by PDI-P. In Table 12.1, the first seven rows show the areas where the PKS–Gerindra gubernatorial candidate won in 2018, which were where Prabowo also won in 2019. The next four show where the PDI-P gubernatorial candidate had won in 2018, which corresponded to where Jokowi also won in 2019.

TABLE 12.1
North Sumatra's 2018 Gubernatorial and 2019 Presidential Elections Compared

No	Areas	Edy-Musa %	Djarot-Sihar %	Prabowo %	Jokowi %	Religions %	Ethnicities %
1	Medan North	61.28	38.72	54.4	45.6	Islam 59.68 Christian 28.26 Buddha 9.9	**Batak 35.2** **Javanese 33** Chinese 9.7 Malay 6.9
2	Medan South	51.88	48.12				
3	Deli Serdang.	61.15	38.85	54.33	45.67	Islam 78.24 Christian 19.5	**Javanese 51.9** Batak 30.64 Malay 6.39 Chinese 2.32
4	Serdang Bedagai, Tebing Tinggi city.	65.64	34.36	53.8	46.2	Islam 89 Christian 18.64	**Javanese 48** Batak 30 Malay 6.73 Chinese 4.7
5	Asahan, Tanjung Balai, Batu Bara	81.40	18.60	63.2	36.8	Islam 87.2 Christian 37.3	**Javanese 38.6** **Batak 33.2** Malay 21.13 Chinese 2.7
6	Labuhan Batu, South Labuhan Batu, North Labuhan Batu.	81.77	18.23	60.7	39.3	Islam 82 Christian 17.6	**Batak 46.5** **Javanese 45.5** Malay 4.3 Chinese 1

TABLE 12.1 (con't)

7	South Tapanuli, Mandailing Natal, Padang Lawas, Padang Sidempuan city.	86.21	13.79	74.6	25.4	**Islam 89.1** Christian 10.7	**Batak 82.8** Javanese 9.4 Malay 0.62
8	Langkat, Binjai city.	70.41	29.59	61.1	38.9	**Islam 86.55** Christian 10	**Javanese 54.35** Batak 21 Malay 10.1 Chinese 3.55
9	Nias, South Nias, North Nias, West Nias, Gunungsitoli.	29.18	70.82	8	92	**Christian 96** Islam 4	**Nias 99**
10	North Tapanuli, Central Tapanuli, Tobasa, Humbahas, Sibolga city.	13.8	86.82	13.7	86.3	**Christian 75** Islam 23	**Batak 85.65** Javanese 3.2 Malay 1 Chinese 0.87
11	Simalungun, Siantar city.	40.40	59.60	29	71	**Islam 49.6** **Christian 48.3**	**Batak 58** Javanese 35.38 Chinese 2.5
12	Dairi, West Pakpak, Karo.	13.55	86.45	16.6	**83.4**	**Christian 74.23** Islam 25.4	**Batak 93.23** Javanese 4.32

Source: Data for the 2018 North Sumatra gubernatorial election was derived from Simandjuntak (2018a).

In 2019 North Sumatra's thirty-three administrative districts were divided into three large electoral districts. However, for the purpose of comparison, Table 12.1 groups these administrative districts into twelve smaller clusters according to the electoral districts in the 2018 gubernatorial election.

Maps 12.1 and 12.2 indicate that the east coast, the predominantly Muslim districts that had voted for the all-Muslim ticket (Edy–Musa) in 2018, also voted for Prabowo in 2019. Similarly, the west coast, the largely Christian districts that had voted for the mixed ticket (Djarot–Sihar) in 2018, also voted for Jokowi in 2019. In addition, Table 12.1 shows the failure of ethnicity to curb religious voting, both in 2018 and 2019. Batak-Muslim districts, for example, voted for the all-Muslim pair, rather than the mixed pair with a Christian-Batak vice-governor candidate. Voting along religious lines thus highlights the geographical divide between the Muslim east coast and the Christian west coast.[12]

MAP 12.1
Distribution of Votes in North Sumatra's 2018 Gubernatorial Election

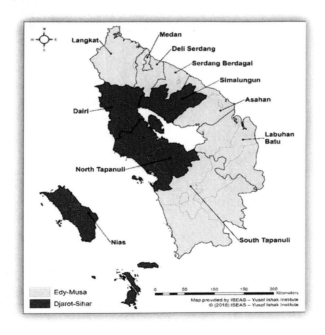

MAP 12.2
Distribution of Votes in North Sumatra's 2019 Presidential Election

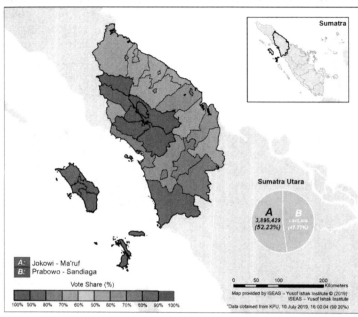

Source: Maps taken from Simandjuntak (2018b, 2019a).

In some Christian districts, however, Jokowi won by generally larger margins compared to Djarot–Sihar in 2018. This consolidation of Christian votes may have been caused by the anxiety that Christian voters felt over the trend towards conservatism, which was exemplified by the triumph of PKS–Gerindra in 2018.[13] Nevertheless, local politicians and academics revealed that religious voting was not uncommon in North Sumatra,[14] where PKS gubernatorial candidates have won in three consecutive elections. This "geopolitical" divide along religious lines thus reflects the national-level binarism.

Among political elites, religious voting seemed to be tolerated in 2019, if not encouraged. An interview with Raden Syafii, member of the national parliament from Gerindra, revealed his view on the supremacy of Muslim leaders in Indonesia's nation-building.[15] When asked what his party would do to curb the influence of Islamism that is propagated by PKS, a member of their coalition, he asserted with slight agitation that "people should not doubt the compatibility of democracy and Islam" and that "Muslim leaders were the most prominent contributors of Indonesia's independence in 1945". Yet, he also recognized that the rigid religious polarization was caused by the fact that there were only two presidential candidates. Although Gerindra is officially a nationalist, and not an Islamic, party, the fact that it had partnered with PKS made "non-Muslim voters reluctant to vote for it", he said. Further, lamenting the simultaneity of the presidential and parliamentary elections, he claimed that the latter was not as popular as the former. The different platforms of political parties seemed not to have mattered anymore in the election, because "voters are only interested in presidential candidates".

A discussion with Aswan Jaya, vice-head of PDI-P's North Sumatra branch, a member of the local Nahdlatul Ulama (NU), Indonesia's largest moderate Muslim organization, and the coordinator of Ma'ruf Amin's provincial campaign team, revealed an interesting observation: that the contestation was not between Muslim and non-Muslim, as it seems to be on the surface, but between "moderate Islam" and "conservative Islam".[16] Concerned with the lack of government control over the quality and the teachings of religious leaders, which had resulted in the proliferation of religious preachers who propagated values that are inappropriate for the Indonesian context, he highlighted the influence of hardline values, which he considered as "foreign", in the practice of local politics in North Sumatra. These hardline values, according to him, inspired the anti-Jokowi voters in the province.

Most local political observers and practitioners agree that political parties were less influential in forming voters' preference in the presidential election, as they mostly rallied behind religious banners. Emphasizing this, Walid Sembiring, lecturer and political observer at the North Sumatra University, stated that even if the presidential candidate did not campaign, most local voters would have already formed their political preferences that were congruent with their religious affiliations.[17] Political parties, thus, would not have had mattered much. For local voters, (fake) news such as Jokowi's camp distributing banknotes in envelopes or stories about Prabowo frequently losing his temper during rallies were not significant enough to alter their political loyalties, except where there had been an extraordinary incident that incited religious sentiments, such as the speech that Purnama made in 2017 that was considered blasphemous.

In addition, Walid discerned that potential voters had come to see Prabowo's camp as religiously homogeneous, so non-Muslim voters tended not to vote for him. Several days after Prabowo's massive rally at the Jakarta sports stadium in April 2019, during which a mass Islamic prayer was conducted, former President Susilo Bambang Yudhoyono, head of the Democrat Party, which is in the Prabowo coalition, was reported to have voiced his concerns over the lack of "inclusiveness" at the rally, which he considered a "show-of-force" of religious-based identity politics (*Kumparan* 2019). This expression of concern could be considered as Yudhoyono's message to reach out to Prabowo's non-Muslim potential voters, assuring them that Muslim interests would not be prioritized over other interests, and indicating that his party, a nationalist party, stood as proof that the coalition would uphold diversity. Nevertheless, Yudhoyono's views could also denote his genuine concern that his coalition had become too Islamist.

Sofyan Tan, a Medan-based Chinese-Buddhist member of the national parliament from PDI-P, considered this trend towards religious politics a decline in the quality of Indonesia's democracy.[18] Sofyan is known to be among the few non-Muslim, Chinese-descent politicians who could somewhat rise above religious politics by focusing on his social welfare projects. For decades, he has been providing free education for thousands of children from poor families and various religious backgrounds. His good deeds are known among voters.[19] Thus in 2010, when he ran in the mayoral election in Medan, he managed to emerge as runner-up out of the ten candidates. In 2014, he managed to secure a seat in the parliament for PDI-P. In addition to Sofyan Tan, other prominent Chinese politicians, including Brilian Moktar, Hasyim and Wong Chun Sen, are popular provincial parliamentarians from PDI-P. None of the four parliamentarians has been known to be involved in vote-buying, which is rampant in North Sumatra. Their campaigns had instead focused on social welfare programmes that reached not only Chinese, but also non-Chinese, voters (Damanik 2017).

However, not all voters are accepting of Chinese or non-Muslim politicians. Notable among them is a group calling themselves Pribumi Bersatu (United Indigenous), which was established in 2018. Since the Suharto era the term *pribumi* has come to embody nativist connotations that exclude other races, especially the Chinese. Interestingly, citizens of Arab descent are increasingly seen as "indigenized" because they are generally Muslim, like the majority of Indonesians. The members of Pribumi Bersatu derive from the Association of Indonesian Indigenous Entrepreneurs (Asperindo), which is closely connected to Sandiaga Uno, Prabowo's vice-presidential candidate. At the national and local levels, therefore, the group focused its support on Sandiaga and was not even affiliated to Prabowo–Sandiaga's national campaign team. In North Sumatra, the group claims to have 400–500 members across the province, with an additional 600 female members calling themselves Muslimah Pribumi Bersatu (Muslim Women of the United Indigenous). Despite their support for Sandiaga, group members claimed they had not received any financial support from him and that their operational costs were voluntarily covered by the group's administrators.

Despite the epithet "indigenous", the leader of the North Sumatra branch of Pribumi Bersatu, who is a young entrepreneur based in Medan, claimed that the group, as well as Asperindo, is open to persons from any ethnic and racial group, as long as they are "born, raised in, do business in, and love Indonesia".[20] He pointed to some ethnic-Chinese figures who, according to him, fulfil this requirement and argued that they should therefore be recognized as "indigenous" in spirit. Among these figures was Lieus Sungkharisma, a Chinese-Indonesian activist who supported the 212 anti-Purnama movement and, naturally, Prabowo's candidacy (*Detik.com* 2019). The group thus seemed to imply that ethnic Chinese like the pro-Prabowo Lieus should be considered to have proven their "love for Indonesia" as they were willing to support Prabowo–Sandiaga. It also seems that, for this group, and most probably for Prabowo–Sandiaga's conservative Muslim supporters in general, ethnic Chinese (who are mostly non-Muslim) could be considered "indigenized" and thus "accepted" if they were willing to support Prabowo–Sandiaga.

It is noteworthy that during their declaration of support for Prabowo–Sandiaga in Jakarta, where Sandiaga was also present, the group yelled, *"Pribumi Bersatu, pribumi kaya, pribumi jaya, menjadi tuan di negeri sendiri!"* ["The indigenous are united, the indigenous get rich, the indigenous are glorious, become masters in our own land!"] (Redaksi 2018). These unnerving remarks are reminiscent of the inaugural speech of Jakarta's governor Anies Baswedan, who won his governorship by profiting from a bitter and religiously charged campaign launched by some Islamist groups against the then incumbent Purnama, who has a Chinese-Christian background. In that speech

Anies said, "In the past, we *pribumi* were oppressed and defeated. Now we have independence, now is the time to be the host in our own home." (Simandjuntak 2017c).

Indeed, the political role of ethnic Chinese, as well as that of non-Muslim native Indonesians, remains contentious in North Sumatra, as elsewhere in Indonesia. Even the North Sumatra branch of the new party Indonesian Solidarity Party (PSI), whose national leader is an ethnic Chinese, claimed that they did not have anyone in their management who was of ethnic Chinese descent and that this was a "natural" condition.[21] Nevertheless, the party claimed to enjoy support from non-Muslim districts as well as the urban areas, which were where the majority of the ethnic Chinese resided. It is noteworthy, however, that some of the statements made by the party's national leader, a female and a newcomer to politics, angered conservative Muslims, such as her announcement that her party was against polygamy and Shar'ia bylaws. PSI's North Sumatra chairman, who ran for a seat in the provincial parliament, mentioned that these statements created an "awkward" situation for PSI parliamentarian candidates who ran in Muslim districts.[22] On the one hand, the national PSI leadership, which supported Jokowi's candidacy, tried to attract "pluralist" votes nationally, yet, on the other hand, the new party still needed to garner as many local and national parliamentary seats as possible, which meant they needed to attract votes from Muslim regions as well.

Sentiments about the "awkwardness" of such campaigning, which was precipitated by the simultaneity of the parliamentary and the presidential elections, also were voiced by others. A senior politician who ran for a provincial parliament seat on a PDI-P ticket mentioned that the coat-tails effect did not happen for those who ran with PDI-P despite it being the main party supporting the president, since the parliamentary elections did not attract as much attention as the presidential election. The rigid and simplistic polarization between the two presidential candidates made voters pay more attention to the presidential election. In contrast, the absence of any real ideological platform that differentiated the parties also meant that candidates for parliamentary seats were forced to attract votes by various other methods. This contributed to the rampancy of money politics in some areas.

The gravest competition in the parliamentary election, according to the senior PDIP-P politician, was not between different parties, but between the candidates in each party. Thus, money also became the currency to secure the most votes among party cadres. The politician revealed that "brokers", or people who claimed to have access to a certain number of voters in his or her electoral district, regularly approached him asking for money in return for an assurance that he would get those votes.[23] Even during my interview with him, he received several phone calls from such "brokers", some speaking in his native Javanese, but he seemed to have rejected all their overtures. Nevertheless, he also mentioned that he would finance those who help him organize his campaign events in various areas.

Transactional politics, which involves vote-buying in its many manifestations, is undermining democracy in various other ways too, one of which is that it leads to the lack of accountability of politicians. According to the PDI-P politician, the logic is as follows: as long as a politician thinks that he has given money to secure potential voters, then when he is elected, he would be less inclined to voice the concerns of those voters as he has already "remunerated" them at the beginning.[24]

For the presidential election, however, money politics, even in a province like North Sumatra, seemed to be less influential compared to religious-identity politics. This is due to the perceived "distance" between voters and the candidates. Candidates for parliamentary, gubernatorial and mayoral races are running locally; thus, they are considered "closer" to the voters. The "closer" they are, the more likely that money politics would play a role in the election. In contrast, candidates for presidential elections are "far" from the voters. This means that other campaign methods would be more significant. In North Sumatra, during the simultaneous elections, voters' conversations about money politics were generally connected to the parliamentary elections, while those about religiosity and pluralism were mainly connected to the presidential election.

RELIGIOUS BINARISM AND ITS IMPLICATIONS FOR DEMOCRACY

Religious binarism has assumed centre stage in Indonesia's politics. Both presidential candidates sought to appeal to the Muslim majority in their campaigns, albeit in different ways and degrees of intensity: Prabowo, by a blatant reliance on Islamist rhetoric and the support of

Islamist groups; Jokowi, by appointing a conservative cleric as running mate to shield himself from "attacks" by Prabowo's Islamist supporters. Such appeals have led to a bitter polarization of society, which was exemplified by various attacks on Jokowi's presumed "lack" of Islamic credibility and Prabowo's presumed religious "intolerance". This binarism also led to the assumption that Jokowi was more "pluralist" than Prabowo and subsequently to the religious divergence in voting patterns. An exit poll showed that 51 per cent of Muslim voters voted for Prabowo, while 97 per cent of non-Muslim voters voted for Jokowi (BBC Indonesia 2019).

This national-level binarism has also affected the presidential election in North Sumatra, where Muslims comprise 67 per cent and Christians 31 per cent of the population. Although Jokowi won, he did so by only a negligible margin of 4 per cent, and religiously charged campaigning played a significant role in forming voters' political preferences. The data shows that Muslim districts in the east coast have overwhelmingly voted for Prabowo and Christian districts in the west coast for Jokowi.

In addition to polarization along religious lines, the election in North Sumatra aggravated the rivalry between PDI-P and Gerindra–PKS in the province. The 2018 gubernatorial election in the province involved a contestation between the candidates supported by PDI-P and by Gerindra–PKS, but in that election the candidate supported by the latter won. The fear of another triumph of an Islamist-supported candidate probably explained the consolidation of votes in Christian districts in the 2019 presidential election. This fear was not without cause: the gubernatorial candidates supported by the Islamist PKS won the last three elections. Jokowi's triumph in North Sumatra might also owe to the fact that the voter turnout for the presidential election in the province (79.9 per cent) was higher than that for the 2018 gubernatorial election (64.9 per cent). The provincial turnout for the 2019 presidential election also constituted a significant increase from that for the 2014 presidential election (68.3 per cent), and this was likely to have been due to the more intensive mobilization of religious sentiments.

Currently, religious binarism seems to be subdued at the national level as Jokowi has appointed Prabowo as his new defence minister, thereby accommodating him in his government. The Islamist groups have expressed their disappointment at Prabowo's acceptance of the appointment. The leader of the "212 Movement" even said they felt "betrayed" by Prabowo (Wardah 2019). Meanwhile, PKS remains in the opposition camp, together with the Democrat Party while the National Mandate Party (Partai Amanat Nasional or PAN, for short), which was in the opposition camp, is reluctant to be labelled the "opposition", preferring instead to be called a "critical partner" (Sari 2020). Jokowi's consolidative and transactional governance has led to a shrinkage of the opposition camp. This is not a good development for Indonesia's democracy in the long run as the lack of opposition voices impedes the checks-and-balances mechanism that is crucial for good governance.

The shrinking of the opposition camp does not mean a triumph for religious pluralism either, as issues of intolerance continue to plague the state-society relations in Indonesia. The discourse on *halal* tourism, for example, has attracted a lot of attention recently. There were even reports that the new Minister for Tourism and Creative Economy, Wishnutama Kusubandio,[25] planned to designate several regions, including Lake Toba and Bali, as *halal* tourism destinations—although he later denied them (*Tempo.co* 2019b). The problem is that Lake Toba is located in the Christian-Batak region of North Sumatra and Bali is the only province with a majority Hindu population (84 per cent). Unsurprisingly, the *halal* tourism issue harvested massive protests from both regions. In October 2019, Christians in the North Tapanuli district around Lake Toba held a "Pig and Pork Festival", celebrating traditional Batak culinary lifestyle in which pigs and pork are central (Malaea 2019). Likewise, the governor of Bali, I Wayan Koster, asserted that Bali had always been open to different kinds of tourists and therefore "requires no such [*halal*] labels", warning against "disturbing the tourism concept here in Bali" (*Coconuts Bali* 2019). Clearly, contentious religious issues such as these will continue exacerbating the divisions within the already polarized society.

As it has been proven "effective", religiously charged campaigning, which leads to religious binary politics, will continue to be at the centre stage of Indonesia's electoral politics. It is likely to be used again in North Sumatra's local elections, made possible by its religious demography. Likewise, the mobilization of religious sentiments will continue to be effective in religiously heterogeneous regions such as Jakarta, Sumatra, Kalimantan and Sulawesi.

During the December 2020 local elections, however, religious issues were not as heavily used as in the 2019 presidential election. This was most likely due to the fact that the elections were held amid a grave pandemic, which rendered it difficult for candidates to hold mass meetings—a necessary trait of religious mobilizations. The most prominent attribute was instead "dynastic" politics, illustrated, for example, by the victory of President's Jokowi's son in the Solo mayoral election and of his son-in-law in the Medan mayoral election. This, however, does not mean that religious issues would cease to be relevant in Indonesia's politics. In the upcoming 2024 presidential election, it is likely that religious mobilization will resurface as both Prabowo and Jakarta Governor Anies Baswedan are likely to run as candidates.

NOTES

1. According to the 2010 population census.
2. Some people belonging to Batak sub-groups such as Mandailing and Karo are at times reluctant to be categorized as Batak; for the Mandailing especially, their reluctance is because they are a predominantly Muslim group within a Batak community that is mostly Christian.
3. Parts of this section are drawn from Simandjuntak (2019a).
4. See, for example, Iyengar, Sood, and Lelkes (2012), pp. 405–31.
5. The term "pluralist" is used loosely here. Jokowi's move to appoint Ma'ruf Amin as his running mate shows that he too tried to avoid being too associated with non-Muslims. However, the fact that the president drew 97 per cent of his support from non-Muslims as well as traditional (moderate) Muslims shows that this support base was more "plural" than Prabowo's, which was fronted by conservative Muslims and Muslims who take a literalist approach to their holy texts.
6. Jamie Davidson claims that "democracy means different things to different people" and Indonesia's democracy is "an unfinished process replete with conflicts over power, resources, ideas and institutions". See Davidson (2018), p. 4.
7. In 2013, PKS allegedly demanded a "fee" (*mahar*) of Rp10 billion (US$869,000) from a candidate in the gubernatorial election for South Sulawesi. See Priatmojo (2013). In 2015, according to media reports, Gerindra allegedly received *mahar* of Rp3 billion (US$209,000) from a candidate. See *Tempo. co* (2015).

8. Parties are ideally financed through membership fees, donations and state subsidies. However, as the number of elections increased and state subsidies have been reduced, party membership has dwindled, and donations are given directly to politicians and not to parties. Parties depend for funds on their politicians and on their offer of nominations for executive and legislative office. See Mietzner (2013).
9. See details of Syamsul Arifin's case on the website of the KPK, https://acch.kpk.go.id/id/jejak-kasus/162-syamsul-arifin (accessed 26 November 2019).
10. This is an estimation as the case is still ongoing. See Gatot Pujo Nugroho's case details on KPK's website, https://acch.kpk.go.id/id/jejak-kasus/330-gatot-pujo-nugroho (accessed 26 November 2019).
11. See details of Abdillah's case on the KPK website, https://acch.kpk.go.id/id/jejak-kasus/271-abdillah (accessed 26 November 2019).
12. North Sumatra has recently experienced the increased influence of Islamic conservatism in its local politics, not only illustrated by the victory of the PKS–Gerindra governor, but also by incidents such as the attacks on Buddhist and Confucian temples in Tanjung Balai in 2016. These were triggered by resentment against a Chinese-Buddhist woman who had complained about the volume of a mosque's loudspeaker. The woman was eventually sentenced to imprisonment for blasphemy in 2018. See Hui and Simandjuntak (2016); Suryadinata (2019).
13. Conversations with potential voters and politicians in Medan and Deli Serdang, April 2019.
14. Interview with Dr Muryanto Amin, dean of the Faculty of Social and Political Science, North Sumatra University; Raden Syafii, member of DPR (national parliament) from Gerindra Party; F. Ginting, head of North Sumatra's branch of Indonesia Solidarity Party (PSI); Aswan Jaya, PDI-P candidate in North Sumatra, April 2019.
15. Interview with Raden Syafii, national parliament member from Gerindra Party, April 2019.
16. Interview with Aswan Jaya, vice-head of PDI-P North Sumatra headquarters and coordinator of Ma'ruf Amin's provincial campaign team, April 2019.
17. Interview with Walid Sembiring, lecturer at the Political Science Department, Faculty of Social and Political Sciences, North Sumatra University, April 2019.
18. Interview with Sofyan Tan, member of the national parliament from PDI-P, April 2019.
19. On the day of interview, a Muslim taxi driver who took me to Sofyan Tan's office became excited and asked whether he could shake hands with him, saying that "he [Sofyan] has done so much good" and that he and his family would vote for Sofyan in the parliamentary election.

20. Interview with A. Nasution, chairman of North Sumatra's branch of Pribumi Bersatu, February 2019.
21. Interview with F. Ginting, head of North Sumatra's provincial branch of Indonesian Solidarity Party (PSI), April 2019.
22. Ibid.
23. Interview with Djumiran Abdi, PDI-P provincial parliamentarian, April 2019.
24. Ibid.
25. Wishnutama Kusubandio was replaced by Sandiaga Uno as minister for Tourism and Creative Economy in December 2020.

REFERENCES

Baldassarri, Delia and Andrew Gelman. 2008. "Partisans without Constraint: Political Polarization and Trends in American Public Opinion". *American Journal of Sociology* 114, no. 2: 408–46.

BBC Indonesia. 2019. "Siapa saja yang memilih Jokowi dan Prabowo berdasarkan exit poll dan quick count?" [Who Voted for Jokowi and Prabowo according to Exit Poll and Quick Count?], 24 April 2019. https://www.bbc.com/indonesia/indonesia-48019930 (accessed 29 October 2019).

Burhani, Ahmad Najib and Deasy Simandjuntak. 2018. "The Ma'ruf Amin Vice-presidential Candidacy: Enticing or Splitting the Conservative Votes?" *ISEAS Perspective*, no. 2018/51, 4 September 2018. https://www.iseas.edu.sg/images/pdf/ISEAS_Perspective_2018_51@50.pdf.

Coconuts Bali. 2019. "'Bali Has Always Been Open to Everyone', Governor Weighs in on Supposed Plans to Transform Island into Muslim Friendly Destination", 12 November 2019. https://coconuts.co/bali/news/bali-has-always-been-open-to-everyone-governor-weighs-in-on-supposed-plans-to-transform-island-into-muslim-friendly-destination/ (accessed 29 November 2019).

Damanik, Ahmad Taufan. 2017. "Patronage-Clientelism and Political Identity of Chinese Candidate: A Case Study of PSMTI in Medan, North Sumatera in General Election 2014". *Proceedings of the Third International Conference on Social and Political Sciences (ICSPS 2017)*, November 2017. https://www.atlantis-press.com/proceedings/icsps-17/25891358 (accessed 1 November 2019).

Davidson, Jamie. 2018. *Indonesia: Twenty Years of Democracy*. Cambridge: Cambridge University Press.

Detik.com. 2018. "Prabowo: Ilmu Islam saya kurang, tapi..." [Prabowo: My Islamic Knowledge is Lacking, However...], 27 July 2018. https://news.

detik.com/berita/d-4137520/prabowo-ilmu-islam-saya-kurang-tapi (accessed 29 October 2019).

———. 2019. "Kisah Lieus Sungkharisma: dukung Jokowi, pro-Prabowo, ditangkap Polisi" [Lieus Sungkharisma's Story: Supported Jokowi, now pro-Prabowo, Arrested by Police], 20 May 2019. https://news.detik.com/berita/d-4556750/kisah-lieus-sungkharisma-dukung-jokowi-pro-prabowo-ditangkap-polisi (accessed 22 November 2019).

Deutsche Welle, 2014. "Jokowi digempur kampanye fitnah" [Jokowi Hit by a Slander Campaign], 4 July 2014. https://www.dw.com/id/jokowi-digempur-kampanye-fitnah/a-17758807 (accessed 29 October 2019).

DiMaggio, Paul, John Evans, and Bethany Bryson. 1996. "Have American's Social Attitudes Become More Polarized?" *American Journal of Sociology* 102, no. 3: 690–755.

Gammon, Liam. 2019. "What was that Election for Again?" *New Mandala*, 25 October 2019. https://www.newmandala.org/what-was-that-election-for-again/.

Harian Terbit. 2015. "PDIP: Sah-sah saja parpol minta mahar dari balonkada" [PDIP: It is Legitimate for Political Parties to Demand Fee from Aspiring Candidates in Local Elections]. http://www.harianterbit.com/hanterpolitik/read/2015/08/01/36832/41/41/PDIP-Sah-Sah-Saja-Parpol-Minta-Mahar-dari-Balonkada (accessed 28 September 2015).

Hui Yew-Foong and Deasy Simandjuntak. 2016. "Indonesia's Sectarian Violence Assumes Religious Guise". *Today*, 21 August 2016. https://www.todayonline.com/commentary/indonesias-sectarian-violence-assumes-religious-guise.

Iyengar, Shanto, Gaurav Sood, and Yphtach Lelkes. 2012. "Affect, not Ideology: A Social Identity Perspective on Polarization". *Public Opinion Quarterly* 76, no. 3: 405–31.

Jakarta Post, The. 2017. "West Java Fails to Improve Tolerance", 11 January 2017. https://www.thejakartapost.com/news/2017/01/11/w-java-fails-to-improve-tolerance.html (accessed 29 October 2019).

———. 2018. "Prabowo–Sandiaga Signs Pact with GNPF, Promises to Uphold Religious Values", 17 September 2018. https://www.thejakartapost.com/news/2018/09/16/prabowo-sandiaga-signs-pact-with-gnpf-promises-to-uphold-religious-values.html (accessed 29 October 2019).

Kompas.com. 2018. "Soal baliho, Yayasan masjid Al Jihad sebut aneh jika ada yang tersinggung" [About the Banner, the Foundation of Al Jihad Mosque Thinks It Strange If People Become Offended], 8 June 2018. https://regional.kompas.com/read/2018/06/08/21392391/soal-baliho-yayasan-masjid-al-jihad-sebut-aneh-jika-ada-yang-tersinggung (accessed 26 November 2019).

Kumparan. 2019. "SBY protes konsep kampanye Prabowo di GBK tak lazim dan exclusive" [SBY Protests That Prabowo's Campaign at the GBK was Not Normal and Exclusive], 7 April 2019. https://kumparan.com/kumparannews/sby-protes-konsep-kampanye-prabowo-di-gbk-tak-lazim-dan-eksklusif-1qq4M6XwQtL (accessed 31 October 2019).

Malaea, Marika. 2019. "Pork-loving Christian Area in Indonesia Fights Halal Tourism with Pig Festival". *Newsweek*, 10 October 2019. https://www.newsweek.com/pork-loving-christian-area-indonesia-fights-halal-tourism-pig-festival-1464301 (accessed 29 November 2019).

Mietzner, Marcus. 2013. "Political Party Financing in Indonesia is a Recipe for Corruption". *Strategic Review* (October–December). http://www.sr-indonesia.com/in_the_journal/view/political-party-financing-in-indonesia-is-a-recipe-for-corruption?pg=all (accessed 8 September 2015).

Muhtadi, Burhanuddin. 2019. *Vote Buying in Indonesia: The Mechanics of Electoral Bribery*. London: Palgrave Macmillan.

Nasution, Indra Kesuma. 2014. "Ethnicity, Democracy and Decentralization: Explaining the Ethnic Political Participation of Direct Election in Medan 2010". *Procedia Environmental Sciences* 20: 496–505.

Priatmojo, Dedy. 2013. "Ilham: PKS minta mahar Rp 10m di pilgub sulsel" [Ilham: PKS Asked for an IDR 10 Million Fee During South Sulawesi Gubernatorial Election]. *Viva.co.id*, 19 September 2013. https://www.viva.co.id/arsip/445314-ilham-pks-minta-mahar-rp10-m-di-pilgub-sulsel?page=1&utm_medium=page-1 (accessed 8 September 2015).

Prireza, Adam. 2019. "KPK resmi menahan walikota Medan Tengku Dzulmi Eldin" [KPK officially arrested Medan Mayor Tengku Dzulmi Eldin]. *Tempo.co*, 17 October 2019. https://nasional.tempo.co/read/1260687/kpk-resmi-menahan-wali-kota-medan-tengku-dzulmi-eldin/full&view=ok (accessed 26 November 2019).

Redaksi. 2018. "Pribumi Bersatu deklarasikan pemenangan Prabowo–Sandiaga" [United Indigenous Declared Prabowo–Sandiaga Victory]. *Media Purna Polri*, 16 September 2018. http://mediapurnapolri.net/2018/09/16/pribumi-bersatu-deklarasikan-pemenangan-prabowo-sandiaga/.

Republika.co.id. 2015. "Pasangan ANDI bantah beri mahar politik untuk 3 parpol pendukungnya" [The ANDI Electoral Ticket Denied Giving Political Fees to Their Three Supporting Parties], 30 July 2015. http://www.republika.co.id/berita/nasional/pilkada/15/07/30/nsas1c354-pasangan-andi-bantah-beri-mahar-politik-untuk-3-parpol-pendukungnya (accessed 28 September 2015).

Rose-Ackerman, Susan. 1999. "Political Corruption and Democracy". *Connecticut Journal of International Law* 14, no. 2: 363–78.

Sari, Haryanti Puspa. 2020. "Zukifly: PAN bukan oposisi melainkan mitra kritis pemerintah" [Zulkifli: PAN is Not Opposition, but the Government's Critical Partner]. *Kompas.com*, 12 February 2020. https://nasional.kompas.

com/read/2020/02/12/18533871/zulkifli-pan-bukan-oposisi-melainkan-mitra-kritis-pemerintah (accessed 29 November 2020).

Simandjuntak, Deasy. 2009. "Milk-coffee at 10AM: Encountering the State Through Pilkada in Indonesia". In *State of Authority: The State in Society in Indonesia*, edited by Gerry van Klinken and Joshua Barker. Ithaca: Cornell University Southeast Asia Program Publications.

⸺. 2012. "Gifts and Promises: Patronage Democracy in a Decentralised Indonesia". *European Journal of East Asian Studies* 11, no. 1: 99–126.

⸺. 2015. "Persistent Patronage: Explaining the Popularity of Former Corruption Convicts as Candidates in Indonesia's Regional Elections". *ISEAS Perspective*, no. 2015/55, 6 October 2015. https://www.iseas.edu.sg/images/pdf/ISEAS_Perspective_2015_55.pdf.

⸺. 2017a. "Faced with a Troubling Blasphemy Verdict, Ahok at least left Jakarta a Legacy of Reform". *Channel NewsAsia* commentary, 11 May 2017. https://www.channelnewsasia.com/news/asia/commentary-ahok-left-jakarta-legacy-of-reform-8836708 (accessed 29 October 2019).

⸺. 2017b. "Jokowi's Ban on Radical Groups and Pancasila's Uncomfortable Past". *Channel NewsAsia* commentary, 22 July 2017. https://www.channelnewsasia.com/news/asia/commentary-jokowi-s-ban-on-radical-groups-and-pancasila-s-9047670 (accessed 29 October 2019).

⸺. 2017c. "Why Anies Baswedan, a Governor with Big Shoes to Fill, is Echoing Hardline Sentiments?" *Channel NewsAsia* commentary, 19 October 2017. https://www.channelnewsasia.com/news/commentary/commentary-why-anies-baswedan-a-new-governor-with-big-shoes-to-9322756.

⸺. 2018a. "North Sumatra's 2018 Gubernatorial Election, the Key Battleground which Reflects National Politics". *ISEAS Commentary* 36, 6 April 2018. https://www.iseas.edu.sg/medias/commentaries/item/7259-north-sumatras-2018-gubernatorial-election-the-key-battleground-which-reflects-national-politics-by-deasy-simandjuntak.

⸺. 2018b. "North Sumatra's 2018 Election: Identity-Politics Ruled the Day". *ISEAS Perspective*, no. 2018/60, 1 October 2018. https://www.iseas.edu.sg/images/pdf/ISEAS_Perspective_2018_60@50.pdf.

⸺. 2019a. "Jokowi's Defeat in Sumatra and the Future of Religiously Charged Binary Politics". *ISEAS Perspective*, no. 2019/70, 5 September 2019. https://www.iseas.edu.sg/images/pdf/ISEAS_Perspective_2019_70.pdf.

⸺. 2019b. "Identity Politics Looms Over Indonesia's Presidential Election". *East Asia Forum*, 10 November 2019. https://www.eastasiaforum.org/2018/11/10/identity-politics-looms-over-indonesias-presidential-election/ (accessed 29 October 2019).

Straits Times, The. 2017. "Anti-communist Rally in Jakarta: A Washout", 30 September 2017. https://www.straitstimes.com/asia/se-asia/anti-communist-rally-in-jakarta-a-washout (accessed 29 October 2019).

Tempo.co. 2015. "Mahar politik calon bupati Sidoarjo dari Gerindra capai Rp 3 miliar" [Political Fee for Aspiring Candidates Seeking Gerindra Endorsement in Sidoarjo Mayoral Election Reached IDR 3 Billion], 6 August 2015. http://nasional.tempo.co/read/news/2015/08/06/078689576/mahar-politik-calon-bupati-sidoarjo-dari-gerindra-capai-rp-3-miliar (accessed 8 September 2015).

──────. 2018. "Daftar purnawirawan jenderal TNI di kubu Prabowo–Sandiaga" [List of Former Military Generals in Prabowo–Sandiaga's Camp], 19 October 2018. https://nasional.tempo.co/read/1138033/daftar-purnawirawan-jenderal-tni-di-kubu-prabowo-sandiaga/full&view=ok (accessed 29 October 2019).

──────. 2019a. "Prabowo cerita Abraham Lincoln yang beri jabatan ke lawan politik" [Prabowo Mentioned Abraham Lincoln Had Given Ministerial Position to Political Rival], 17 October 2019. https://nasional.tempo.co/read/1261012/prabowo-cerita-abraham-lincoln-yang-beri-jabatan-ke-lawan-politik (accessed 30 October 2019).

──────. 2019b. "Wishnutama: Saya tak bilang Bali dan Danau Toba jadi wisata halal" [Wishnutama: I Never Said that Bali and Lake Toba will be Halal Tourism Destinations], 13 November 2019. https://travel.tempo.co/read/1271934/wishnutama-saya-tak-bilang-bali-dan-danau-toba-jadi-wisata-halal (accessed 29 November 2019).

Wardah, Fathiyah. 2019. "Persaudaraan Alumni 212 kecewa dengan sikap Prabowo" [The Brotherhood of 212 Alumni Disappointed by Prabowo]. *VOA Indonesia*, 22 October 2019. https://www.voaindonesia.com/a/persaudaraan-alumni-212-kecewa-dengan-sikap-prabowo/5134433.html (accessed 29 November 2019).

13

MONEY OR IDENTITY? ELECTION INSIGHTS FROM SOUTH SUMATRA AND LAMPUNG PROVINCES

Made Supriatma

INTRODUCTION

Analysts and pundits mostly agree that Indonesia's 2019 general election was largely determined by the use of identity politics (Pepinsky 2019; Slater and Tudor 2019). Identities, especially religious and ethnic identities, were the most effective tool to mobilize voters. The results of the presidential election strongly indicate this tendency. Voters with moderate Islamic views and religious minorities leaned towards voting for President Joko Widodo (Jokowi) and his running mate, Ma'ruf Amin; those with more conservative Islamic leanings were inclined to cast their vote for the Prabowo Subianto–Sandiaga Uno team.

Other than religion, ethnic identity may also have influenced the outcome of the election. Regions with sizeable numbers of Javanese voters, the largest ethnic group in Indonesia, tended to vote for Jokowi–Ma'ruf while non-Javanese regions with Muslim majorities voted for Prabowo–Sandiaga.

This chapter aims to examine the assertion that identity politics was the determining factor in the 2019 election. The election was a complicated affair as there were, in fact, five races held simultaneously and there was a possibility that one election might affect the other. Many asserted that the presidential election may entail a "down-ballot effect" onto the other elections. However, as we will find later in this chapter, the presidential election was of a completely different order compared with the elections for the national parliament (Dewan Perwakilan Rakyat or DPR, for short). Likewise, the elections at the provincial and district/municipality levels were of an altogether different nature.

While identity politics was at play in the presidential election, the other elections (for the Regional Representative Council or DPD, for short, and legislatures at various local levels) were shaped more by clientelism and patronage,[1] mostly in the form of "contingent exchange" (Aspinall and Berenschot 2019; Hicken 2011). In these kinds of dynamics, the various electorates were guided to cast their votes by the material benefits they expected to enjoy. These could have been in the form of projects for their communities or neighbourhoods or just plain cash. Even if ideology was at play, the level of ideological attachment was different at each election.

Based on field research in South Sumatra and Lampung, both provinces in Sumatra Island, this chapter will elaborate when and how identity politics was used and when and how clientelism and patronage were at work during the elections. The main question to be answered is: when and why do people vote in accordance with their identity, and when and why do they vote based on material self-interest?

The chapter will begin with a discussion of theory. I will then discuss the two cases that exemplify how identity and patronage networks affected the election outcomes. Field research was carried out in South Sumatra and Lampung in March and April 2019. Finally, I will explain how identity politics worked in the presidential election but was less influential in the election of legislative members.

IDENTITY AND PATRONAGE/CLIENTELISM

The use of identity, especially ethnic identity, is limited in Indonesian politics especially in the post-New Order era. Even so, as Aspinall (2011) has noted, local politicians have learnt how to reach out to other ethnic groups and build coalitions in order to win elections. "Ethnic violence has declined steeply, and ethnic coalition building and cooperation, rather than conflict, are the norm at the local level", declares Aspinall.[2]

Political actors exploit ethnic politics by posing as "sons of the soil", and those who are not natives (although they may constitute the majority in the region) usually make room for the native son. This is why even though the Javanese are the majority in both North Sumatra and Lampung, they chose not to run for the post of governor, the highest office in their respective regions;[3] instead, they may stand for election as the running mate of a native politician. This situation is different from that during the New Order era. The Suharto government then placed Javanese, mostly active or retired military officers, at the highest office in the various non-Javanese regions.

Another source of identity is religion. Unlike ethnicity, religion has deeper roots in Indonesian politics. Since the early days of the republic, religion has been a source of political power. While Indonesia does not have any ethnic-based political party, it tolerates the growth of religious-based parties. In addition, some of the biggest civil society organizations, such as Nahdlatul Ulama and Muhammadiyah, are religious-based organizations. In the past, Indonesia even experienced rebellion in the name of religion. Moreover, religious violence is not an unusual occurrence in the country.

Based on this assumption, it is logical to say that ethnic and religious identities are highly influential in shaping Indonesian politics. Although, religion can appeal at the wider, national level, ethnicity is more likely to have appeal mainly at the sub-national level.

The general assumption in Indonesia is that party politics at the national level always takes the form of an ideological battle between secular–nationalist values and Islam. In reality, however, the ideological division is not as rigid as widely assumed. Even a politician who is a nationalist may campaign on a religious platform.[4] For example, Prabowo ran his campaign projecting strong Islamic credentials although he does not practise the religion as devoutly as his opponent.

The situation is significantly different where local politics is concerned. Here the platforms are centred more on bread-and-butter issues. Politicians at local levels deal directly with their constituents. Therefore, the use of patronage and clientelist networks becomes more salient at this level although there have been some exceptions where religious identity trumped material interests for the constituents.[5] Local politicians need to build coalitions in order to win elections. They have strong self-interest in cooperating with other groups. Indeed, in Indonesian local politics, cooperation, and not conflict, is the norm.[6]

Various studies have been carried out in connection with the exploitation of identity in electoral politics. Likewise with the important role of patronage and clientelist networks (Aspinall and Sukmajati 2016; Aspinall and Berenschot 2019). However, as stated above, there has been no study that carefully examines how identity works in influencing people's votes.

Chandra (2009) in her study of voting behaviour of the "Scheduled Caste" in India questions whether people from this caste vote sincerely based on their identity. She found out that although the Scheduled Caste voted according to their identity, they also voted strategically and split their tickets across elections. In other words, the Scheduled Caste voted differently in different elections and their votes were aligned with their strategic interests.

SOUTH SUMATRA AND LAMPUNG: AN OVERVIEW

For Indonesian politicians, each level of election requires a different approach and winning strategy. This is in recognition of the reality that voters have different political preferences when voting at different levels of elections. In other words, although these elections are held simultaneously, voters may have different expectations for each election. Thus, any analysis of these elections must be carried out by disaggregating voting behaviour according to different levels of election.

South Sumatra and Lampung were picked as case studies because of the demographic characteristics of their populations. Lampung is a province outside Java where the Javanese form the majority of the population. Javanese have been migrating to this province since the colonial era as part of the government's population transfer programme.[7] According to the 2010 population census, ethnic Javanese made up 64.05 per cent of Lampung Province. In some districts, such as East Lampung, Central Lampung, Pringsewu, Mesuji and Tulang Bawang, the percentage of Javanese, in fact, exceeded 70 per cent.

In contrast, the majority of South Sumatra's population are indigenous to the region. In fact, South Sumatra's population is more diverse than Lampung's and with no ethnic majority. But South Sumatra does have a sizeable number of Javanese (27.40 per cent of the total population), especially in several of its eastern districts. Most Javanese arrived in this province under the New Order's transmigration programme.[8] The number of Javanese exceeds more than a quarter of the population in several districts in the east of this province. The largest concentration of Javanese is in Ogan Komering Ulu Timur District, where they make up almost 70 per cent of the population. In Musi Rawas District, too, the Javanese population constitutes a majority, at 40.77 per cent. In short, Lampung is clearly a Javanese-majority province while South Sumatra is a diverse province with no ethnic majority but a significant Javanese population. Different demographic spreads produced different electoral results. It is interesting to compare the results of the 2014 and 2019 presidential elections. As is well known, the same two presidential candidates ran in the 2014 election albeit with different running mates.

In South Sumatra, Prabowo and his then vice-presidential candidate, Hatta Rajasa, won 51.26 per cent of the votes in 2014. In 2019, Prabowo, with his new running mate, Sandiaga, expanded his vote share to 59.7 per cent.

In Lampung, Jokowi and his then running mate, Jusuf Kalla, garnered 53.07 per cent of the votes in 2014, about 10 percentage points less than the proportion of Javanese people in the province. In 2019, Jokowi, running with Ma'ruf, widened his vote share to 59.3 per cent. But that was still about 5 percentage points less than the proportion of Javanese people in Lampung. Leaving aside the share of underage Javanese and those who did not vote, these figures do not necessarily allow us to take for granted that all Javanese voted for Jokowi.

PRESIDENTIAL ELECTION

Did ethnicity influence the way the electorate voted for either Prabowo or Jokowi? Based on the results in Lampung and South Sumatra, ethnicity apparently only had a moderate effect on the results. Like in other Javanese-majority regions, ethnic Javanese in both provinces voted overwhelmingly for Jokowi. However, in some districts that have sizeable numbers of Javanese, Jokowi lost.

Jokowi did not fare well in South Sumatra's district of Musi Rawas, where the Javanese constitute 40.8 per cent of the population. Jokowi won 41.1 per cent of the votes there, almost the same as the proportion of Javanese residents. This could also mean that Jokowi could not expand his constituency beyond his Javanese base. Jokowi pulled a slim victory in Banyuasin District, where the Javanese make up 37.5 per cent of the population. Jokowi carried this district with 50.4 per cent of the votes.

Jokowi lost in many districts where the Javanese constitute more than 25 per cent of the population. Those districts are: Ogan Komering Ulu, Ogan Komering Ulu Selatan, Ogan Komering Ilir, Musi Rawas and Musi Banyuasin as well as Lubuk Linggau municipality.

FIGURE 13.1
2019 Presidential Election Results in South Sumatra Measured Against Size of Javanese Population

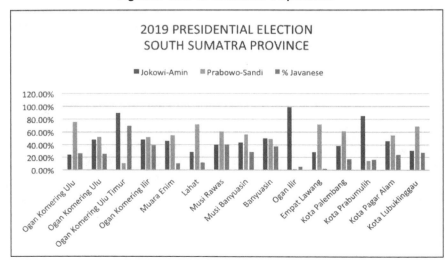

In Lampung, Jokowi also lost in Tanggamus and Lampung Utara districts and in the capital, Bandarlampung, despite these areas being home to sizeable numbers of Javanese voters: Tanggamus—44.81 per cent; Lampung Utara—50.5 per cent; and Bandarlampung—40.67 per cent.

FIGURE 13.2
Results of 2019 Presidential Election in Lampung Measured Against Size of Javanese Population

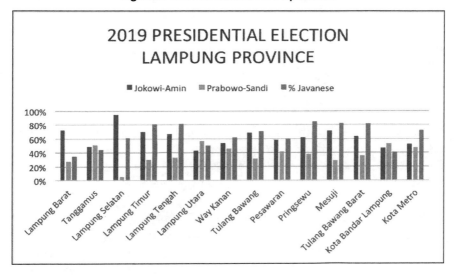

Ethnic identity may have played a limited role in the presidential elections but there were also other factors that must be taken into account. In South Sumatra, even though Javanese voters cast their votes overwhelmingly for Jokowi–Ma'ruf, the pair still lost because of their inability to attract other electorates in the province. Pundits and politicians refer to the role played by ideological voters, especially conservative Muslim voters. In South Sumatra, non-Javanese ethnic groups tend to be more religiously conservative and voted for Prabowo–Sandiaga.[9]

In Lampung, where ethnic Javanese are the majority, the religious factor proved crucial. Some quarters among the Javanese here subscribe to Islamic conservatism.[10] Various interviews conducted in both provinces revealed that religion might also have served as a determining factor in the election.

However, some interviewees[11] also acknowledged that the price of commodities (especially rubber and palm oil), which slumped during the campaign, affected the Jokowi–Ma'ruf campaign.[12] Low commodity prices prompted farmers, wholesalers and merchants to support the opposition. These constituents blamed Jokowi because they felt the national government was responsible for economic policies that affected commodity prices. In contrast, commodity prices did not become a campaign issue in legislative campaigns. Some interviewees tried to relate the economic downturn to religion by arguing that turning to religion is an expression of economic frustration.[13]

LEGISLATIVE ELECTIONS

Besides the presidential election, there were four other elections that took place simultaneously. Did these elections share similar characteristics with the presidential election? In other words, was there a "down-ballot" effect from the presidential election to the legislative elections?

The results from South Sumatra and Lampung show that the effect was limited. Voters cast their votes based on different considerations at the various levels of election: they based their votes on identity in the presidential election but voted strategically at the legislative elections. It is possible that the lower the level of election, the more likely the electorate would vote strategically.

The results in South Sumatra are telling. Comparing the results of the legislative elections at the national, provincial and district levels shows the dominance of the major parties. For the national parliament, Golkar gained the most votes (14.45 per cent), followed by Gerindra (14.29 per cent), NasDem (14.16 per cent) and the Partai Demokrasi Indonesia Perjuangan or PDI-P (13.52 per cent). They were followed by the intermediate parties such as the Democrats (9.26 per cent), Partai Kebangkitan Bangsa or PKB (7.59 per cent), Partai Keadilan Sejahtera or PKS (6.62 per cent) and Partai Amanat Nasional or PAN (5.26 per cent).

FIGURE 13.3
Legislative Elections in South Sumatra Province

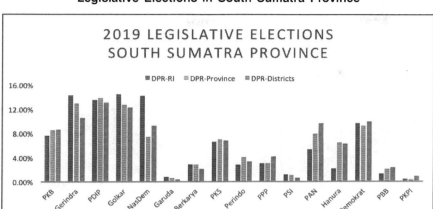

Some parties performed well at the national level but not at the local levels, while others performed consistently. In South Sumatra, PDI-P performed consistently, winning about 13 per cent at each of the three levels. Other parties that performed consistently both at the national and local levels were PKB (with its performance at the lower levels of elections marginally better than at the national level), PKS, and the Democrats. Meanwhile, Gerindra and Golkar each obtained a lower share of votes in local elections compared with their performance at the national level. The most striking results involved NasDem, which showed a sharp fall in performance at the lower electoral levels compared with the national level.[14]

Meanwhile in Lampung, the situation was slightly different. At the national level, the victorious political parties were Golkar (14.75 per cent), followed by PDI-P (13.2 per cent), Democrats (12.6 per cent), PKB (12.6 per cent) and Gerindra (11.8 per cent). The parties whose performance at the national and local elections showed significant imbalance were the Democrats, Golkar and PKB. The other parties showed consistent performance or even increased their vote share slightly in local elections, as in the case of PAN, PKS and Gerindra.

FIGURE 13.4
Results of 2019 Presidential Elections in Lampung Province

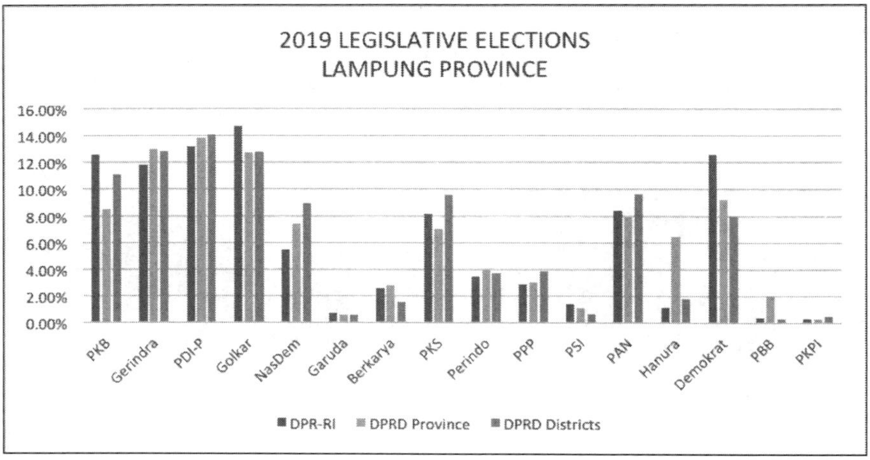

[Bar chart titled "2019 LEGISLATIVE ELECTIONS LAMPUNG PROVINCE" showing percentages from 0.00% to 16.00% across parties: PKB, Gerindra, PDI-P, Golkar, NasDem, Garuda, Berkarya, PKS, Perindo, PPP, PSI, PAN, Hanura, Demokrat, PBB, PKPI. Legend: DPR-RI, DPRD Province, DPRD Districts]

WHAT DOES THE MISMATCH MEAN?

The mismatch between performance in national and local elections indicates that campaigns by national candidates were not necessarily coordinated with party functionaries at the local level. In the presidential election campaign, this coordination issue arose because of the decision to give greater roles to volunteers. At the parliamentary level, however, the problem was twofold. First was the question of how legislative candidates were recruited. Second was the way of determining winning candidates. In Indonesia's proportional representation system, a legislative candidate must compete not only with candidates from other parties but with fellow candidates from his or her own party. This pattern of competition prevents cooperation and coordination within the party. During my fieldwork, I observed that coordination between campaign teams was an exception rather than the norm. Each candidate organized his or her own campaign team.[15]

The presidential campaigns did not coordinate with parties in their respective coalitions at the local levels. Jokowi–Ma'ruf organized their campaign at the national level by forming a National Campaign Team (TKN) and at the provincial and district levels by establishing Regional Campaign Teams (TKDs). The TKDs organized volunteers who were not under the control of any party. Likewise, Prabowo–Sandiaga formed a national-level Badan Pemilihan Nasional (BPN) with regional branches, known as BPDs. It appears that the BPN had a greater level of coordination with the parties within its coalition.[16] However, the Prabowo–Sandiaga campaign also mobilized an army of volunteers who were not controlled by any of the political parties. In South Sumatra and Lampung, most of Prabowo's volunteers come from Islamic organizations such as activists of the so-called 212 Movement, the Gerakan Nasional Pembela Fatwa—Majelis Ulama Indonesia (GNPF—MUI) and the Front Pembela Islam.[17]

Volunteers were crucial to both presidential campaigns. They tended to be more ideological and identified themselves with causes dear to their respective candidates. Their militancy was also higher compared with members of the parties in coalition with each of the presidential candidates.

In addition to ideological issues, both presidential campaigns exploited ethnic and religious identities. The Prabowo–Sandiaga camp appealed to conservative Islamic sentiments. Therefore, their campaign was more attractive to ethnic groups that are culturally close to conservative Islam. On the other hand, the Jokowi–Ma'ruf campaign appealed more to the nationalists, moderate Muslims and minorities. Jokowi's ideological position made his campaign culturally closer to the Javanese. Even though the campaign did not directly target Javanese people, its approach was tailored to reflect Javanese culture.[18]

However, appeals to ideology and ethnic/religious identities did not work strongly in the legislative elections. This is the biggest contrast between the legislative and the presidential elections. The legislative elections were strongly influenced by two factors. The first factor was the way legislative candidates were selected. Political parties nominated legislative candidates both from within and outside the party. There were two types of candidates selected from outside the party. The first kind were the vote getters, usually celebrities or artists, religious leaders, local leaders and other influential people. The second were the party "financiers". These become candidates for the legislature because of their ability to contribute funds to the party or to its functionaries.[19]

Because of this system, many national candidates did not originate from the regions they chose to represent. Also, many of them did not even join the party before the election. The party only served as a vehicle to give them a ride to parliament.

The second factor was the way candidates competed in the legislative elections. As noted earlier, Indonesia's proportional representation system requires candidates to fight on two fronts. First, they must compete with other candidates from within their party. Second, they have to fight with candidates from other parties. This system makes competition for a parliamentary seat highly intense and costly.

As a consequence, in legislative elections, the candidates' appeal is based on their personal capabilities rather than their party affiliation. A party ideology is not the determining factor in the election. Nor is ethnic/religious identity. Therefore, in legislative elections, it is more difficult to mobilize voters through identity or ideology than through material benefits. During my fieldwork, I found that candidates adopted pragmatic rather than ideological approaches in their campaigning.[20] Even if a candidate was a leader in his constituency, he would not be automatically elected if he did not have enough resources to share with his voters. It is not too surprising then that money politics is rampant in legislative elections. This is also where the patronage network to distribute material benefits plays a role (Kurniawan, Rahmatunissa, and Agustino 2017).

The Indonesian party system lacks the mechanism that connects politicians with their constituents. However, politicians who fight for parliamentary seats at the local level usually pay more attention to everyday issues and try to connect as closely as possible with their constituents;[21] the role of the political party is minimal. Candidates may not rely on the party organization to run their campaigns. Some candidates use non-party organizations to mobilize support.[22]

CONCLUSION

The presidential and legislative elections both in South Sumatra and Lampung showed fundamental differences The main difference revolved around the use of ideology and identity to mobilize voters. Presidential candidates exploited identity and ideology and the election results showed the split of support based on ideology and identity. Thus, the presidential election involved deeper appeals to emotion than the legislative elections.

The legislative elections, on the other hand, showed that ideology and identity were not significantly important factors in mobilizing voters. What mattered most was the candidates' personal appeal and the resources at their disposal. In many ways, material benefits were more important than ideology or identity. Therefore, money politics was rampant in the legislative elections.

NOTES

1. Patronage and clientelism can also work through ethnic networks. Ethnic identity provides a greater guarantee of trust in patron-client relations. However, in this case, as will be shown later in this chapter, voters can switch from ethnic patronage networks when candidates of a different ethnicity offer more "bargains" to meet their material interests. See Chandra (2009).
2. My research in regions that previously experienced communal violence showed that politicians always try to build a winning coalition with the group they once considered their opponents or competitors.
3. Javanese make up 33.49 per cent of the total population of North Sumatra Province. This ethnic group is the largest in the province. Indonesia's statistical bureau, Badan Pusat Statistik, consistently reports that the largest ethnic group are the Bataks (41.93 per cent). However, the Bataks are divided into six sub-tribes that have different languages, customs, and in some cases also religion. The first Javanese governor in North Sumatra was Gatot Pujo Nugroho (2013–15). But he was not born and raised in the province. He comes from Magelang, Central Java. He was elected as a cadre of the Partai Keadilan Sejahtera (Prosperous Justice Party or PKS, for short), an Islamist party.
4. Slater and Tudor (2019) assert that this is because the root of Indonesian nationalism is pluralism, so a nationalist politician can at the same time be seen as a pious person.
5. The most popular example was the Jakarta gubernatorial election in 2017. During the campaign, the incumbent governor, Basuki Tjahaja Purnama ("Ahok"), was accused of blasphemy against Islam. The accusation became the basis for organized protests. On 2 December 2016, hundreds of thousands of Muslims attended the protest against Purnama. Eventually, Purnama lost the election and was jailed for alleged blasphemy. Another example was the election for mayor of Medan, the biggest city in North Sumatra, in 2010. One candidate was a Chinese Indonesian, who won the most votes in the first round of elections. In the second round, he had to face a Malay-Muslim. The election became an identity contest: Muslim vs

non-Muslim and native vs Chinese Indonesian. Tan lost the election (see Aspinall, Dettman, and Warburton 2011).
6. Cooperation is the norm in inter-ethnic relations. See Fearon and Laitin (1996).
7. Another province outside Java where the Javanese form the largest ethnic group is North Sumatra. However, the migration of Javanese to North Sumatra was driven more by the need for indentured labour by plantations in the province. In Lampung, migration occurred more spontaneously even though there was also a push to work on plantations, which were far fewer in number than in North Sumatra. See Kusworo (2014).
8. Upon taking over power in early 1966, the New Order government launched a programme to move a portion of the Indonesian population from the so-called "inner islands", namely Java, Madura and Bali, to the outer islands. These inner regions were inhabited by two thirds of the population of Indonesia although they constituted only 7 per cent of Indonesia's total land area. Between 1969 and 1974, the government moved 182,000 people to the sparsely populated outer islands. This number increased to 544,000 in the period 1974–79. Between 1979 and 1984, this number exploded to 2.5 million because of the oil boom. After this period, the number of people moved under the transmigration programme declined. But during the last decades before the collapse of the New Order, the government managed to move around two million more people. See Barter and Côté (2015); Potter (2012).
9. In the western regions of South Sumatra Province, Prabowo–Sandiaga Uno won a landslide victory. These are areas that have small Javanese populations. They are also bastions of conservative Islam. In the past, these regions were the bases of Masjumi and Persis, two Islamic parties. In contrast, in the eastern part of South Sumatra Province, the number of Javanese migrants is significant; in some cases, they comprise the majority. These are regions where nationalist parties triumphed—the Partai Demokrasi Indonesia Perjuangan (PDI-P) recently and its predecessor, the Partai Nasional Indonesia (PNI), in the past. In this region, Jokowi–Ma'ruf won or narrowly lost to their opponent.
10. This is nothing new. Lampung has long been a sanctuary for hardline Islamic groups that moved from Java to avoid repression. In what is known as the Talangsari incident in East Lampung District, military officers in 1989 stormed a camp belonging to a hardline Islamic group, the Warsidi Group, which left 246 civilians dead.
11. My research involved 11 interviews in South Sumatra and 18 in Lampung. The interviewees come from different backgrounds: journalists, academics, activists and local bureaucrats. But the majority of them were politicians running for office.

12. Interview with Giri Kiemas in Palembang, 8 March 2019.
13. Interview with Budi, a local businessman in Lampung, 16 April 2019. Budi owns a gas station and is the publisher of an online magazine in Lampung.
14. NasDem is a new party founded in 2011 by the Indonesian media tycoon Surya Paloh. The party accommodates many disappointed politicians who had previously been with Golkar, the Democratic Party or PDI-P. Switching parties has become an increasingly common occurrence in Indonesia.
15. A candidate in Lampung told me that the "SDM rule" applied in campaigns. In Indonesia, SDM is the common initialism for *Sumber Daya Manusia* (human resources). But in campaign parlance, the initialism stands for *selamatkan diri masing-masing* (save yourself). Interview with a PKB candidate in Lampung, 14 March 2019.
16. In my observation, Gerindra's local secretariat often (though not always) functioned as the BPD office. This secretariat also became a gathering place for volunteers. For Jokowi–Ma'ruf's campaign, the TKDs had their own headquarters, which were centrally organized by the TKN.
17. These organizations were involved in the massive rally on 2 December 2016 that called for Jakarta's then governor, Basuki Tjahaja Purnama ("Ahok"), to be jailed for insulting Islam. See note 5.
18. For example, in Lampung, Jokowi's campaign consistently used symbols that were easily associated with the Javanese such as clothing and arts. The campaign also explicitly emphasized the secular aspects of Indonesia although this emphasis did not mean the campaign team did not use religion as a form of appeal. Jokowi's campaign was really targeted at the more moderate Muslim voters who supported pluralism.
19. *Mahar* (dowry) is the popular term in Indonesia for contributions to a party or to its functionaries. Legislative candidates or candidates for elected regional executive positions who wish to run in elections must choose a political party as their vehicle. The amount of *"mahar"* depends on the level of election. At the national level it can be several billion rupiahs; for province-level elections hundreds of millions of rupiahs and for the district level tens of millions of rupiahs. Interview with Yuriansah in Palembang, 8 March 2019.
20. A candidate from the Islamist party PKS who ran for a provincial parliamentary seat told me that his signature campaign programme involved organizing traders at a traditional market into a credit union. Impressed by his initiative, I reminded him that the notion of credit unions goes against the Islamic law that prohibits interest (*riba*). He replied that he did not really care about the notion of interest. What was more important was that a credit union would be "beneficial to my constituents". His pragmatism defied his ideology. Interview with Ade in Lampung, 15 April 2019.

21. A candidate for the Indonesian Solidarity Party (PSI) in Palembang told me that he approached his constituents by offering to repair their broken shoes or patch their leaking woks and pans. He said that this was his way of making close contact with his constituents. He lost the election.
22. I came across a candidate who mobilized voters by using Banser, a militia associated with the traditionalist Muslim organization Nahdlatul Ulama. In Lampung, I met a candidate who organized his campaign through Javanese arts organizations that performed *jathilan* or *jaran kepang*, a Javanese art form performed by buskers.

REFERENCES

Aspinall, Edward. 2019. "Indonesia's Election and the Return of Ideological Competition". *New Mandala*, 22 April 2019. https://www.newmandala.org/indonesias-election-and-the-return-of-ideological-competition/.

———. 2011. "Democratization and Ethnic Politics in Indonesia: Nine Theses". *Journal of East Asian Studies* 11, no. 2 (May–August): 289–319.

Aspinall, Edward and Mada Sukmajati. 2016. *Electoral Dynamics in Indonesia: Money Politics, Patronage and Clientelism at the Grassroots*. Singapore: NUS Press.

Aspinall, Edward, Sebastian Dettman, and Eve Warburton. 2011. "When Religion Trumps Ethnicity: A Regional Election Case Study from Indonesia". *South East Asia Research* 19: 27–58.

Aspinall, Edward and Ward Berenschot. 2019. *Democracy for Sale: Elections, Clientelism, and the State in Indonesia*. Ithaca and London: Cornell University Press.

Barter, Shane and Isabelle Côté. 2015. "Strife of the Soil? Unsettling Transmigrant Conflicts in Indonesia". *Journal of Southeast Asian Studies* 46: 60–85.

Bland, Ben. 2019. "Politics in Indonesia: Resilient Elections, Defective Democracy". Lowy Institute, 10 April 2019. https://www.lowyinstitute.org/publications/politics-indonesia-resilient-elections-defective-democracy.

Chandra, Kanchan. 2009. "Why Voters in Patronage Democracies Split Their Tickets: Strategic Voting for Ethnic Parties". *Electoral Studies* 28: 21–32.

Fearon, James and David A. Laitin. 1996. "Explaining Interethnic Cooperation". *The American Political Science Review* 90, no. 4 (December): 715–35.

Hicken, Allen. 2011. "Clientelism". *Annual Review of Political Science* 14, no. 1: 289–310.

Kurniawan, Robi Cahyadi, Mudiyati Rahmatunissa and Leo Agustino. 2017. "Vote Buying in Lampung Local Election". *Mimbar* 33, no. 2 (December): 359–67.

Kusworo, Ahmad. 2014. "Pursuing Livelihoods, Imagining Development: Smallholders in Highland Lampung". *Indonesia* 9. Canberra: ANU Press.

Mietzner, Marcus. 2019. "Indonesia's Elections in the Periphery: A View from Maluku". *New Mandala*, 2 April 2019. https://www.newmandala.org/indonesias-elections-in-the-periphery-a-view-from-maluku/.

Muhtadi, Burhanuddin. 2018. "A Third of Indonesian Voters Bribed During Election – How and Why". *The Conversation*, 20 July 2018. https://theconversation.com/a-third-of-indonesian-voters-bribed-during-election-how-and-why-100166.

———. 2019. *Vote Buying in Indonesia: The Mechanics of Electoral Bribery*. Singapore: Palgrave.

Pepinsky, Thomas. 2019. "Religion, Ethnicity, and Indonesia's 2019 Presidential Election". *New Mandala*, 28 May 2019. https://www.newmandala.org/religion-ethnicity-and-indonesias-2019-presidential-election/.

Potter, Lesley. 2012. "New Transmigration 'Paradigm' in Indonesia: Examples from Kalimantan". *Asia-Pacific Viewpoint* 53, no. 3: 272–87.

Slater, Dan. 2018. "Party Cartelization, Indonesian-Style: Presidential Power-Sharing and the Contingency of Democratic Opposition". *Journal of East Asian Studies* 18, no. 1: 23–46.

Slater, Dan and Maya Tudor. 2019. "Why Religious Tolerance Won in Indonesia But Lost in India: It Turns Out Pluralistic Nationalism Isn't Enough". *Foreign Affairs*, 3 July 2019. https://www.foreignaffairs.com/articles/india/2019-07-03/why-religious-tolerance-won-indonesia-lost-india.

INDEX

A
absolutist class rule, 51
Ahok (Basuki Tjahaja Purnama), 2, 7, 57, 80, 91, 110, 118, 155, 160n2, 171, 179, 180, 188, 209, 241
 blasphemy controversy, 2–3, 57–59, 91, 110
 defeat and incarceration, 3
 defeat of, 114–15
 mass demonstrations against, 2, 119
 mass mobilizations against, 98
 mobilization against, 155
 vocal opposition to, 114
Aidit, D.N., 98
Aku Cinta Islam (I love Islam, ACI), 161n14
"Alap-Alap" (Falcons), 205
Al-Habsyi, Fachry, 100
Aliansi Cerahkan Negeri (Brightening the Nation Alliance or ACN), 155–56
Aliansi Cinta Keluarga (AILA) or Family Love Alliance, 153–54
Ali Murtopo, 168
Al-Makmur mosque attack, 99–102
Amien Rais, 101
Andi Arief, 76
Andi Widjajanto, 78
Ansor, 121
anti-Chinese riots, 184
anti-Chinese sentiment in Indonesia, 91, 110
 anti-Chinese disinformation using social media, 91, 93, 95–99
 asing dan aseng, 92, 94
 colonization conspiracy theory, 93–94, 97–98
 conspiracy narratives, 92–94
 false narratives, 95
 May Day rally, 94
 in media, 94–95
 semaphore of Amien Rais, 94
 violence, 97–99
anti-foreign capital agitation, 56
anti-mobilization authoritarianism, 48
Armayanti, Nelly, 245–46
artificial intelligence (AI), 7, 67–68, 85
 political micro-targeting using, 67–68
Aspinall, Edward, 221
authoritarianism, 22, 48, 113, 243
Automatic Identification System (AIS), 68

B
Badan Musyawarah Betawi, 122
Badan Pemilihan Nasional (BPN), 276
Badan Permusyawaratan Kewarganegaraan Indonesia

(Indonesian Consultative
    Citizenship Body or Baperki),
    167–68
Bakrie, Aburizal, 27, 183
Bambang Soesatyo, 122
Bandung Institute of Technology
    (ITB), 76
Bangkalan, swing of votes in, 231–32
Banser, 121
Baswedan, Anies, 3
Bawaslu, 36
Belt and Road Initiative (BRI), 92
Betawi organization, 122
bi-class political economy, 48
binary electoral politics, 239–43
    ideological stances, 240
    religious binarism, 239–59
    religious-geopolitical bifurcation
        and, 247–56
black campaign, 91
Boyolali look (*muka Boyolali*), 207,
    215
Bravo-5, 148, 160n3
Buruh Go Politik ("Workers Go
    Politics"), 127

C

Cakra 19, 78
campaign hashtags
    #AksiBelaQuran, 155, 160n2
    #2019GantiPresiden, 74–75, 155–56
    #Jokowi2periode, 74
    #MeToo, 157
    #MuslimvoteMuslim, 155, 160n2
    #NoHoax, 119
    #NoIntimdasi, 119
    #PEPESDatangKelar, 150
    #PEPESKepung, 150
    #PrabowoJumatanDimana, 76–77
    #UninstallFeminism, 155
Central Java
    dominant parties in, 213–16

identity politics and ideology,
    208–13
militancy and voluntarism, 202–8
number of registered voters, 200
population size, 200
2019 presidential election, 199–217
Centre for Gender Studies (CGS),
    151
Centre for Strategic and International
    Studies (CSIS), 168
Chandra, Sri Vira, 151–52, 156
Chinese Communist Party, 97
Chinese Indonesians, 10, 183–86,
    193n8. *See also* ethnic Chinese
    political participation
Cholil, Syaichona, 232
Chung Hwa Hui (CHH), 166
civil society groups, role of politics,
    34, 37, 53, 63
class absolutism, 48
clique rule, 49–50
collectivity of cliques, 46
Communication Forum of the Sons
    and Daughters of Military and
    Police Retirees (FKPPI), 119
Confucianism, 181
Corona Team, 78–79
Corruption Eradication Commission
    (KPK), 63
Council of Indonesian Muslim
    Intellectuals and Young Ulama
    (MIUMI), 151
cyber campaign, 71–77. *See also* social
    media
    anti-Chinese disinformation, 95–99
    influencers and buzzers, 74, 85n2
    influential hashtags, 73–75, 155
    Jasmev 4.0, 80–81
    popular keywords, 71, 85n7
    using Twitter, 71, 73, 76–77, 82,
        85n6

Index

WhatsApp communications, 70, 72–73, 82, 85n6, 96–97, 156, 161n13
women's political participation, 154–57

D

democratic elections, indications of successful, 26
democratic space, 55
democratic stagnation, 6, 26–30
   factors contributing to, 32–35
   in Indonesia, 32–35
Dewan Dakwah Islamiyah Indonesia (DDII), 151
Dewan Perwakilan Daerah (DPD), 30
Dewan Perwakilan Rakyat (house of representatives, DPR), 23, 25, 151, 165
Dewan Perwakilan Rakyat Daerah (DPRD) Provinsi, 165
Dhani, Ahmad, 59
Dhyta Caturani, 157, 161n16
digital feminist activism, 157–59
disinformation campaign, 5, 7–8, 67, 100, 102–3, 152, 156
   Al-Makmur mosque attack, 99–102
   anti-Chinese, 91, 93, 95–99
   influence on voters, 68
   spread of, 99
   WhatsApp communications, 70, 72–73, 82, 85n6, 96–97, 156, 161n13
Drone Emprit, 71

E

Edy Rahmayadi, 246
Eldin, Dzulmi, 245
election characteristics and campaign strategies
   artificial intelligence (AI), use of, 67–68

big data analysis, 77–83
diversion of netizens' attention, 75–76
"one package" campaign, 131–32
patterns of cyber campaigning, 71–77
social media platforms, use of, 69–71
spread and penetration of eye-catching news, 69, 73–74
trending topics, 74
using Twitter, 71, 73, 76–77, 82, 85n6
WhatsApp communications, 70, 72–73, 82, 85n6, 161n13
electoral laws, Indonesia, 131
Elimination of Sexual Violence (Rancangan Undang-Undang Penghapusan Kekerasan Seksual, or RUU-PKS), 152, 154
elite-mass conflict, 50
emak-emak (mothers), 146–50, 152
Employees Social Security System (BPJS Ketenagakerjaan), 117, 122
Endah, Alberthiene, 206
ethnic Chinese political participation, 166
   achievement of Chinese-Indonesian MPs, 179–80
   Christians among, 179
   2014 election and 2019 election, 183–91
   informal, 180–83
   and name-changing regulation, 170–71
   in parliamentary elections, 171–79
   peranakan and *totok* (*singkeh*), 166
   during post-Suharto era, 170
   reasons for demise of, 170–71

F

Fadli Zon, 76, 95

Fajar, Ustadz (Muhammad
    Fajrudluha), 119
fake news, politics-related, 30, 34,
    68–70, 77, 85n5, 92, 95, 97, 186–87
  anti-Chinese disinformation using
    social media, 95–99
  Facebook posts, 97–98
  "mosque attack" disinformation,
    99–102
Family Resilience Bill, 154
Fatayat, 9
Federasi Serikat Pekerja Metal
    Indonesia (FSPMI), 127
feminist ideas of women's
    emancipation, 147
fiction intelligence, 93
Fitriah Abdul Aziz, 151
floating mass policy, 47
Forkabi, 112
Forum Betawi Rempug (FBR), 9, 112,
    116–20, 122
Forum Demokrasi Kebangsaan
    (Fordeka), 171
Forum Umat Islam (FUI), 114
Front Pembela Islam (Islamic
    Defenders Front, FPI), 3, 61–62,
    94, 98, 101, 110–12, 114–15, 118,
    120–23, 189, 210, 226–30, 276
  discrimination against Shi'a
    community, 229
full-fledged cyber election, 7

G

Ganjar Pranowo, 11
"#2019GantiPresiden" hashtag, 74–75
Garuda, 23
Gatot Nurmantyo, General, 6, 14n7
Gatot Pujo Nugroho, 245
General Elections Commission (KPU),
    24–27, 30–32, 34, 36, 204, 224
Gerakan Masyarakat Jakarta (GMJ),
    114

Gerakan Nasional Pembela Fatwa—
    Majelis Ulama Indonesia
    (GNPF—MUI), 276
Gerakan Rabu Biru (Blue Wednesday
    Movement or GRB), 149–50
Gerakan Rakyat Indonesia Baru
    (GRIB), 113
Gerindra party, 60, 62, 136, 201,
    203–4, 207, 274
Golkar, 4, 13n1, 23–24, 168–69,
    172–73, 175, 202, 274
governance in Indonesia, 48
Great Indonesia Movement Party
    (Partai Gerakan Indonesia Raya
    or Gerindra), 1–2
G30S (Gerakan Tiga Puluh
    September) movement, 168

H

habaib, 118, 226–28
Habibie, B.J., 186
Hakka Federation (Keshu Lianyi Hui
    客属联谊会), 183
Hamka, Jusuf, 189
Hanura, 23
Hasan, Bob, 50
Hatta Rajasa, 184, 270
Hizbut Tahrir Indonesia (HTI), 3, 59,
    71, 206, 221
Huang Jinlai, 187

I

Ida Fauziyah, 202, 204, 207
identity politics and ideology, 12, 111,
    121, 146–47, 150, 266–67
  in Central Java, 208–13
  ethnic and religious identities, 268
  ethnic Chinese, 165–68
  mismatch between performance in
    national and local elections,
    275–77

patronage and clientelist networks, 268–69
in South Sumatra and Lampung, 269–70, 273–75
ideological divide among voters, 2
illiberal democracy, 55
Indonesia Adil Makmur coalition, 13n1
Indonesia Indicator, 82
Indonesia Maju, 13n1
Indonesian Chamber of Commerce and Industry (KADIN), 150
Indonesian Council of Ulama (MUI), 3
Indonesian democracy, 4, 13, 21, 232
flaws of, 22
rule of law, 22
stagnation of, 32–35
Indonesian Democratic Party of Struggle. *See* Partai Demokrasi Indonesia Perjuangan (PDIP)
Indonesian economy, 128
Indonesian elections, 2019, 1
Indonesian Nationalist Party (PNI), 47, 49, 213–15
Indonesian National Police (Polri), 97
Indonesian police, 14n8
Indonesia-oriented Partai Tionghoa Indonesia (PTI), 166
Indonesia's electoral politics, 4
comparison of 2014 and 2019 elections, 5–8
legislative candidates, 8, 15n12
mobilization of conservative Islamic forces, 7
open proportional system, 15n11
role of Indonesian elites, 7
use of instruments of government, 6
use of new technologies, 7
"Indonesia Tanpa Feminis" (Indonesia Without Feminism), 155

Indonesia Tanpa JIL (Indonesia without Liberal Islam, ITJ), 161n14
"Indonesia Tanpa Pacaran" (Indonesia Without Dating or ITP), 155, 161n13
Instagram, 70, 74, 82, 97, 101, 155, 158–59
Intelligence Media Management (IMM), 82
International Council of Women (ICW), 146
Islamic Defenders Militias (LPI), 210
Islamic feminism in Indonesia, 10
Islamic moderates-pluralists *vs* Islamic conservatives, 2
Ismail Fahmi, 71, 86n10

J

Jasmev 4.0, 80–81
Jasmev Classic, 80–81
Jasmev Glaring, 81
Jasmev Hardcore, 81
Jasmev Millennial, 81
Jasmev Parahyangan, 81
Jasmev Playground, 81
Jejak News Agency, 100
Jokowi, 46, 54, 57, 61, 67–68, 113–14, 146, 176, 183, 186, 199, 238, 275
black propaganda against, 58
campaign strategy, 211
coalition, 11
cyber campaign, 71–74
defeat in Madura, 222–25
digital campaigns, 77
election campaigns, 70
image of integrity, 212–13
Islamic credentials, 3
political setbacks, 3
popularity of, 14n4
2014 presidential election, 186–88

2019 presidential election, 188–91,
 199–217, 271–73
 rumours about, 70
 support for, 2014 and 2019, 4, 13n1
 swing of votes in Bangkalan,
 231–32
 Twitter activity, 71
 women supporters of, 148–49
Jokowi–Prabowo presidential race,
 2014, 2, 5–6
Jusuf, Teddy, 181

K
Kalla, Jusuf, 184
Kartono, Nono, 136
Kesatuan Aksi Mahasiswa Muslim
 Indonesia (National Front of
 Indonesian Muslim Students,
 KAMMI), 161n14
Khofifah Indar Parawansa, 149
kiai (religious teachers), 11
Koalisi Aksi Menyelamatkan
 Indonesia (KAMI), 64n15
Koalisi Indonesia Hebat, 13n1
Koalisi Merah Putih, 13n1
Komunitas Alumni Perguruan Tinggi
 (Community of University
 Alumni, KAPT), 81
Kopasandi, 210
Koster Rinaldi, 72
Kwik Kian Gie, 179

L
labour movement in national politics,
 51–54, 127–28. *See also* Serikat
 Pekerja Metal Indonesi (SPMI)
 disconnection between union
  members and representatives
  in parliament, 132, 140–42
 features, 140
 ngaprak strategy, 140
 role of non-union voters, 139–40

land conflict cases and related deaths,
 53
La Nyalla Mahmud Mattalitti, 230
Laskar Merah Putih, 112, 116, 119
Laskar Pembela Islam (LPI), 226
Lembong, Eddie, 183
liberal democracy, 55
Lie Ling Piao, Alvin, 179–80
Liem Koen Hien, 167
Lieus Sungkharisma (Li Xuexiong),
 169, 189
Lippo Group, 185–86
Luhut Pandjaitan, 46
Lutfi Hakim, 117

M
Madura case, 11, 222–25
Magdalene, 157
Mahfud MD, 230
Majalah Tempo, 188
Majelis Ulama Indonesia (MUI), 123,
 153, 241, 246
majlis taklim (Islamic study groups),
 10, 147, 156
Mardani Ali Sera, 74
Ma'ruf Amin, 2–3, 11, 67, 96, 119, 146,
 189–90, 212, 220, 238, 241, 272–73,
 275–76
Masyumi Party, 49
Medan, Anton, 189
Megawati Sukarnoputri, 14n6, 52, 56,
 173, 182, 214
MEKAAR, 148
militias and civilian proxies, use in
 politics, 112–14
money politics, 28, 31, 33, 37, 243–45
212 Movement, 58, 60, 62, 112, 115,
 117–21, 124n4, 150, 241
Muhammad al-Kathath, 124n4
Muhammad Kholil bin Abdul Latif,
 227
multiparty system, 36

Index

Murba Party, 49
Musa Rajeckshah, 246
Muslimah Community for Islamic Studies (KKMI), 151
Muslim feminist movement, 157–59
Muslim women's social media, 155

N

Nahdlatul Ulama (NU), 9, 62, 115, 118–19, 158, 204, 207, 220–21, 226, 230, 268
　women's wing of, 149
Nahra, Mustofa, 74
NasDem party, 185
Nasir, Bachtiar, 151, 153
National Campaign Team (TKN), 275
National Counterterrorism Agency (BNPT), 122
nationalist "replacement theory", 93
National Monument (Monas), 209
National Movement for Guarding Fatwa of the Indonesian Ulama Council (GNPF–MUI), 210
National Movement for People's Sovereignty (GNKR), 96
National Movement of Fatwa Defenders (GNPF), 241
Neneng Hasanah, 129
Neno Warisman, 156
New Order electoral practices, 7, 146, 168, 185, 201, 268, 270
New Order era (1966–98), 26, 33, 47–49, 127, 145
　clique rule, 49–50
　electoral democracy, 54–60
　elite-mass conflict, 50
　end of single-clique rule and erosion of class absolutism, 54–60
　form of governance, 51
　trade union activity, 51–54
　transition to democracy, 54–55

Ngabalin, Abdul Ghani, 123n1
Nissa Sabyan, 74
non-elite political forces, 48
Nur Azizah Tamhid, 151–52
Nurdin, 130–32, 136–38, 141
Nurfahroji, Moh, 136–37
Nyumarno, 130–32, 137, 141–42

O

Obon Tabroni, 133–38
Obor Rakyat (People's Touch), 68, 186–87
OKE-OCE (One Kecamatan (sub-district), One Centre of Entrepreneurship), 149, 156
Omnibus Job Creation Law, 2020, 63, 130
ormas (*organisasi kemasyarakatan* or mass/social organizations), 8–9, 112–14, 116, 121

P

Paguyuban Sosial Marga Tionghoa Indonesia (PSMTI), 180, 184
Paloh, Surya, 185
Pangestu, Mari, 183
Paradoks Indonesia, 93
Partai Amanat Nasional (National Mandate Party, PAN), 23–24, 60, 94, 131, 169, 173
Partai Bhinneka Tunggal Ika Indonesia (PBI, PBTI), 169
Partai Bulan Bintang (Crescent Star Party, PBB), 23, 151
Partai Demokrasi Indonesia (Indonesian Democratic Party, PDI), 168
Partai Demokrasi Indonesia Perjuangan (Indonesian Democratic Party of Struggle, PDIP), 13n1, 23–24, 61, 131, 146, 169, 173, 175, 180, 184, 201,

203–5, 207, 213–16, 238, 241, 246–47, 274
electoral stronghold, 11
Partai Demokrat (PD), 23, 173, 175
Partai Demokrat Tionghoa Indonesia (PDTI), 167
Partai Emak-Emak Pendukung Prabowo–Sandi ("Party" of Mothers Supporting Prabowo–Sandi, PEPES), 149–50
social media presence, 150
Partai Keadilan dan Persatuan Indonesia (Indonesian Justice and Unity Party, PKPI), 23, 131
Partai Keadilan Sejahtera (Prosperous Justice Party, PKS), 23, 57, 62, 71, 74, 131, 151, 205, 238, 246
Partai Kebangkitan Bangsa (National Awakening Party, PKB), 173, 221, 274
Partai Komunis Indonesia (Indonesian Communist Party, PKI), 47, 49, 145, 166, 168
Partai Patriot, 124n2
Partai Persatuan Pembangunan (United Development Party, PPP), 23–24, 114, 131, 202
Partai Reformasi Tionghoa Indonesia (PARTI), 169
Partai Solidaritas Indonesia (Indonesian Solidarity Party, PSI), 23, 49, 176
Party of Functional Groups (Partai Golongan Karya, Golkar), 3–4, 13n1, 23–24, 168–69, 172–73, 175, 202, 273–74
patron-client politics, 231–32
Pemuda Hijrah, 155, 161n13
Pemuda Pancasila (PP), 9, 109–10, 112, 114, 116–17, 119–20, 122, 124n2

Perhimpunan Indonesia-Tionghoa (INTI), 181, 184
Perindo, 23
Permadi Satria Wiwoho, 95
Persatuan Islam Tionghoa Indonesia (PITI), 189–90
Persatuan Tionghoa (PT), 167
Pimpinan Unit Kerja (PUK), 133
Pitaloka, Rieke Dyah, 131
polarization, 2, 110–11, 116–21, 240. *See also* binary electoral politics
affective, 240
FBR's strategy, 117–22
FPI's strategy, 116–23
Islamization of Pancasila, 116–21
opportunity and benefits, 121
social and identity-based, 111, 121
political arrests and imprisonment, 52–53, 60
political campaigns, 29, 31–32
political contestation, 22
political education, 36–37
political micro-targeting, 79, 84. *See also* cyber campaign; election characteristics and campaign strategies
political participation
definition, 165
formal, 166
informal, 166
political parties,
institutionalization of, 35
simplification of, 47
politicization of identity, 30
Poo, Murdaya, 180, 183
poskos [sing. *Posko* or *Pos Komando* (command post); pl. *poskos*], 203
post-election violence in Indonesia, 90–91, 95–97, 101
post-truth phenomenon, 68–70
power-sharing arrangements, 50–51, 54, 56, 60

Prabowo–Sandiaga Uno team, 57, 67, 90, 191
Prabowo Subianto, 2, 58, 113, 118, 146, 183–84, 199, 238, 276
  alignment with 212 Movement, 58
  approach to coalition building, 57
  approach to human rights, 63
  coalition, 119
  criticism against, 76, 93–94
  electoral campaign strategy, 113
  military pedigree and New Order strongman, 112
  online strategy, 70
  #PrabowoJumatanDimana, 76–77
  2014 presidential election, 186–88
  2019 presidential election, 188–91, 199–217
  rapprochement between Jokowi and, 62
  support for, 2014 and 2019, 4
  Twitter activity, 71, 76–77
  women supporters of, 148–49
pragmatism, 33
2019 presidential election, 62, 67, 84
  anti-feminist female candidates, 147
  campaign activities of candidates, 29, 34
  casualties during polling and vote-counting, 25–26
  conduct of, 22–26
  cost of fighting elections, 28–29
  dissemination of fake news, 34–35
  Eligible Voter List (DPT) problem, 25
  ideological contestation within civil society, 62–63
  Jokowi–Ma'ruf Amin performance, 3, 23
  in Lampung and South Sumatra, 271–73
  media bias or partiality, 27–28
  money politics, 28
  performance in Central Java, 199–217
  political manipulation, 34
  Prabowo's challenges, 23, 61, 90
  problems, 25
  protests and riots post result, 90–91, 95–97, 101
  religious binarism and, 240–43
  results, 23
  role of civil society groups, 34, 37
  swing of votes in Bangkalan, 231–32
  use of identity politics, 34–35
  use of state apparatus, 29
  visions or programmes of candidates, 29–30
  vote organizing committees (KPPS), 27
  voter turnout for, 24
Prosperous Justice Party (Partai Keadilan Sejahtera, PKS), 3
Purnomo, Eko, 136
Purwono, Nurdin, 169

R
Rachmawati Sukarnoputri, 59
Rahudman Harahap, 245
Ratna Sarumpaet, 76
Reformasi (Reform) Movement, 5, 7, 10, 13, 14n2, 32, 127, 146, 201
Regional Campaign Teams (TKDs), 275
regional politics, 10–12
"Rejo" (Relawan Jokowi or Jokowi's Volunteers), 205
relawan, 139
religious binarism, 11, 243–59
  ideological stances, 240
  implications for democracy, 256–59
  2019 presidential election, 240–43
  voter preferences, 241–42
Riady, James, 185–86

right-wing militia groups, 53
Rizieq Shihab, Habib, 58–59, 94, 110, 115, 120–21, 123, 189, 226, 228
Rukmana, Yanti, 205
Rumah Bersama Pelayan Rakyat (Community House to Serve the People or RBPR), 72, 81–83
Rusdi Kirana, 185

S
Sandiaga Uno, 2, 12, 22–23, 57, 60–62, 79, 146, 149–50, 160n5, 188, 191, 203, 207, 209–10, 224, 238, 254, 266–67, 270, 272, 276, 279n9
    OKE-OCE programme, 149, 156
Sasbuzz, 82
satgas, 112
Scheduled Caste voting behaviour, 269
"Semut Ireng" (Black Ants), 205
Serikat Pekerja Metal Indonesia (SPMI), 127
    deals struck with political candidates, 129
    2017 election for *bupati* of Bekasi District, 128, 133–36
    "Go Politics" merchandise, 133
    Legislative Election, 2019, 136–39
    2014 local legislative elections, 128, 130–33
    membership, 129
    "no money politics" policy, 133
    political participation, 128–39
    problem of campaign resources, 133
    reasons for political participation, 129–30
    volunteers of Jamkeswatch, 139
    wage negotiations, 130
Shari'a Council of Surakarta City (Dewan Syariah Kota Surakarta or DSKS), 210
Shi'a community, 229
Siauw Giok Tjhan, 167–68
Silitonga, Baris, 136
Sin Po, 166
Sinulingga, Arya, 77
Siradj, Said Aqil, 230
Situngkir, Hokky, 78–79
social media, 150
    anti-Chinese disinformation using, 95–99
    election campaign strategies using, 69–73, 76–77, 82, 85n6, 161n13
    women's political campaigning using, 154–57
Sofian Wanandi, 168, 186
Somad, Ustadz Abdul, 209
Srikandi Indonesia, 205
stolen election, 8
Sudirman Said, 202, 207–8
Sudjono Humardhani, 168
Suharto, President, 47, 49, 56–57, 145
    resignation and resulting changes, 50–51
    suppression of the Left, 49–50
Sukarno, 173, 214
    teachings (*ajaran Sukarno*), 214
Sukarno–Left alliance, 47
Sulaeman, 136
Supreme Confucian Council (Majelis Tertinggi Agama Khonghucu or Matakin), 181
Suramadu (Surabaya–Madura) bridge, 231
Syafei, Major General Theo, 78
Syamsul Arifin, 245

T
tabligh akbar, 209–10
Tan, Sofyan, 245–46
Tanoe, Hary, 185
Thohir, Erick, 27
tim bayangan, 77

Index

Tim Kampanye Nasional (National Campaign Team or TKN), 203
"*Tiongkok/Tionghoa* to *Tjina (Cina)*", 182
Tjan Silalahi, Harry, 168
Tjoo Tik Tjhoen, 167
trade unions, 51–54
Trans Media Social, 82
Twitter, 70–71, 73–76, 80, 82, 85n6, 97

U

Undang-undang Informasi dan Transaksi Elektronik (Law on Information and Electronic Transactions or UU ITE), 53
union nominees, 9
union politics, 9–10
Usman Kansong, 72

V

vote-buying programme, 136

W

Wahid, Abdurrahman, 51, 149, 170, 181–82, 211
Wahid, Yenny, 149
Wanandi, Jusuf, 168, 186
Wardhani, Putri K., 148

WhatsApp communications, 70, 72–73, 82, 98, 156, 161n13
women's groups, 10
Women's March movement, 157
women's political participation, 146–47
  affirmative action policies, 151
  online and offline campaigns, 154–57
  ultra-conservative female candidates, 151–54
Wuryanto, Bambang, 203

Y

Yap Thiam Hien, 168
Yapto Soerjosoemarno, 116
Yasin, Taj, 202
Yayasan Nabil (Nation-Building Foundation), 183
YouTube "rabbit hole" phenomenon, 96
Yudhoyono, Agus H., 62
Yudhoyono, Susilo Bambang, 182
Yusron, Ulin, 74

Z

zipper system, 151, 160n8
Zulkarnain, Tengku, 153